Sociological Life Course Research

Matthias Wingens

Sociological Life Course Research

 Springer

Matthias Wingens
BIGSSS – Bremen International Graduate
School of Social Sciences
Universität Bremen
Bremen, Germany

ISBN 978-3-658-37465-5   ISBN 978-3-658-37466-2   (eBook)
https://doi.org/10.1007/978-3-658-37466-2

© The Editor(s) (if applicable) and The Author(s), under exclusive licence to Springer Fachmedien Wiesbaden GmbH, part of Springer Nature 2022
This book is a translation of the original German edition „Soziologische Lebenslaufforschung" by Wingens, Matthias, published by Springer Fachmedien Wiesbaden GmbH in 2020. The translation was done with the help of artificial intelligence (machine translation by the service DeepL.com). A subsequent human revision was done primarily in terms of content, so that the book will read stylistically differently from a conventional translation. Springer Nature works continuously to further the development of tools for the production of books and on the related technologies to support the authors.
This work is subject to copyright. All rights are solely and exclusively licensed by the Publisher, whether the whole or part of the material is concerned, specifically the rights of translation, reprinting, reuse of illustrations, recitation, broadcasting, reproduction on microfilms or in any other physical way, and transmission or information storage and retrieval, electronic adaptation, computer software, or by similar or dissimilar methodology now known or hereafter developed.
The use of general descriptive names, registered names, trademarks, service marks, etc. in this publication does not imply, even in the absence of a specific statement, that such names are exempt from the relevant protective laws and regulations and therefore free for general use.
The publisher, the authors and the editors are safe to assume that the advice and information in this book are believed to be true and accurate at the date of publication. Neither the publisher nor the authors or the editors give a warranty, expressed or implied, with respect to the material contained herein or for any errors or omissions that may have been made. The publisher remains neutral with regard to jurisdictional claims in published maps and institutional affiliations.

This Springer imprint is published by the registered company Springer Fachmedien Wiesbaden GmbH part of Springer Nature.
The registered company address is: Abraham-Lincoln-Str. 46, 65189 Wiesbaden, Germany

Contents

1 The Life Course as a Social Construction 1
2 What Is "Life Course Research"? 13
   2.1 A Brief History of Life Course Research 14
   2.2 The Theoretical Concept of Life Course Research. 30
       2.2.1 Life Course: A Substantive Definition 31
       2.2.2 "Time Matters!" 40
3 The Life Course as an Institution 47
   3.1 The Institutionalization of the Life Course. 48
   3.2 Institutionalized Life Course and Biographisation
of Life Organization 60
4 Collective Life Courses: Generations, Cohorts and Social Change. . . . 67
   4.1 Cohort Studies and Social Change 67
       4.1.1 Inter- and Intracohort Conception 67
       4.1.2 From Cohort to Life Course Analysis 75
   4.2 Historical Generations and Social Change 84
       4.2.1 "Generation": A Problematic Term? 84
       4.2.2 The Sociological Problem of Generations 87
       4.2.3 Problems and Potentials of the Generation Concept 96

5 Structures of the Life Course 103
- 5.1 The Basic Tripartite Structure of the Life Course................. 103
- 5.2 Social Structuring Factors of the Life Course.................... 112
  - 5.2.1 "Act Your Age!" – Age-Appropriateness-Ideas and Timetables 113
  - 5.2.2 Institutional Life Course Structures 125
- 5.3 "Normal Life Course" and De-Standardization of the Life Course 140
  - 5.3.1 The Chronologically Standardized "Normal Life Course" 140
  - 5.3.2 "De-Institutionalizing" Individualization of the Life Course?................................. 154

6 Life Course Research: A Conceptual Perspective................... 171
- 6.1 Principles of Life Course Research........................... 172
- 6.2 Analytical Concepts of Life Course Research 181

7 Life Course Research, Quo Vadis? 205

References 217

List of Figures

Fig. 1.1	The two earliest life staircase depictions	8
Fig. 1.2	The "steps of ages" of man and woman (around 1900)	9
Fig. 2.1	The age stratification model of Riley. (Own illustration, based on Riley et al. 1972, pp. 3–26)	22
Fig. 2.2	The emergence of life course research. (Source: Own representation)	29
Fig. 2.3	The "time" dimension in life course research. (Source: Own representation)	42
Fig. 3.1	Average life expectancy. (Germany, 1871–2017)	49
Fig. 3.2	Rectangularization of the survival curve. (Germany, 1871–2017)	50
Fig. 4.1	Age, period and cohort effect. (Fictitious example)	76
Fig. 4.2	Standard cohort table	77
Fig. 4.3	Operational scheme of a cohort study. (Birth cohorts)	78
Fig. 5.1	Age-differentiated and age-integrated (life course) structures. (Based on Riley and Riley 1994, p. 26)	108
Fig. 5.2	Life course-relevant institutional configurations of US, German and Swedish society. (Source: Mayer 2005, p. 38 f)	135
Fig. 5.3	Life course outcomes in the USA, Germany and Sweden. (Source: Mayer 2005, p. 40 f)	138

The Life Course as a Social Construction

Sociological life course research – like biographical research – has developed into an independent and fruitful field of research since the end of the 1960s. It is true that half a century earlier, in their famous study of "The Polish Peasant in Europe and America" (1918–1920), Thomas and Znaniecki had already used life records to examine the connection between social change, social structures, and the life histories of individuals. However, such a research perspective was supplanted by other methodological-conceptual approaches to empirical social research for over fifty years. It was not until the 1960s that sociological interest in life course and biographical theoretical issues reawakened. Today, life course research is considered one of the most important conceptual innovations in sociology in recent decades (Elder et al. 2003; Heinz et al. 2009). This introductory book provides an insight into sociological life course research and informs about its theoretical assumptions, analytical concepts and main results.

A book that introduces students to sociological life course research must first answer the question of what its subject actually is. In everyday understanding, the term "life course" means the course of an individual's life as a stream of – more or less linked – events, states and processes from birth to death. In this context, everyday thinking follows an individualizing understanding of the term: every person has a life course – but every life is different, unique. It is certainly true that every person, especially in modern individualized societies, has a distinctive life course.

However, this everyday understanding of the life course as an individual phenomenon is not a sociological concept of the life course. The object of sociological life course research is not individual life courses as such. But how does sociology conceive the term "life course"?

The philosophy of knowledge and science shows that there is no a-theoretical view of the world and thus no object of research "in itself". Only and at all in the light of a theoretical perspective does something become an object of research. In order to at least hint at this methodological insight into the theory-loadedness of all observation and knowledge: what is problematic about the research object "unemployment" and what is investigated depends on whether this state of affairs is viewed from, for example, an identity or human capital theory perspective, a family or organizational sociology perspective, a business or economic perspective. The fact that our view of things always takes place in a theoretical perspective also applies to everyday thinking, which, however, takes its view of the world unreflectively for granted, as the quasi only possible way of looking at things. In contrast to this, scientific thinking must make sure of its respective theoretical perspective – and thus of its cognitive limits. If it is true in terms of the theory of science that an object of research is always constituted theoretically, then in order to answer the question of the object of sociological life course research it is necessary to clarify what constitutes a genuinely sociological theoretical perspective.[1]

The fundamental way of thinking in sociology[2] can be characterized as "socio-logic", i.e.: sociology describes and explains its respective object of research "socio-logically" (and not, for example, "bio-logically" or "theo-logically"). To describe and explain something sociologically means to describe and explain it by means of social factors (and not, for example, as a product of natural or metaphysical factors) – in short: to understand it as socially constituted. Accordingly, a genuinely sociological concept of the life course conceives of the life course as a social construction. In line with this fundamental disciplinary perspective, Kohli wrote programmatically in one of the first German-language publications on the life course: "The question of the social construction of the life course is central"

---

[1] To illustrate it with the well-known spotlight model of cognition: different "theory spotlights" illuminate different things and areas – what one focuses on and sharply outlines is only blurredly illuminated (or even faded out) by another.

[2] What is at stake here is what constitutes sociology as a scientific discipline – which internally, of course, has a diversity of theories – i.e. the "business basis" of all sociological thinking: what is constitutive for every theory or perspective that is given the predicate "sociological".

(1978a, p. 8). The object of sociological life course research is thus the life course as a social construction. Sociological life course research is concerned with this – historically, culturally comparatively or in relation to the contemporary society of a country. Analytically, three levels can be distinguished.

1. At the level of individual life courses (Chap. 5), the focus is on the one hand on the patterns and structures of life courses that have developed in a sociohistorical formation such as modern industrial society. Corresponding studies – as Back illustrates – "search for systematic regularities in events of unique meaning" (1980, p. 2) and their social constitutive factors. A second strand of research at this level addresses life courses in terms of differentiation and inequality theory as an element of social structure. Since every life course is embedded in social structures in the form of age-related participation in social positions and roles, life courses can be regarded as "patterned dynamic expressions of social structure" (Mayer 2004, p. 165). Corresponding studies examine the social structural positioning of individuals in the various spheres of life and society over the life span.
2. At the level of collective life courses (Chap. 4), the focus is on interrelations between social structure and social change on the one hand and cohorts on the other. The historically specific socio-cultural circumstances in which people live bundle individuals into characteristic collectives. Such cohorts or generations are defined by a formative experience that individuals have together in the same time interval. Generations, however, are not only shaped by social circumstances. Conversely, socio-structural conditions are also changed by collective life courses and cohorts function as carriers of social change. Corresponding studies on these interrelations address not only the succession of generations and differences between cohorts, but also intra-cohort differences.
3. Finally, on a third level, the life course is to be understood as an institution (Chap. 3). The institutionalized life course represents a system of rules for the temporal dimension of life, both with regard to the positions and roles that individuals assume in the course of their lives and with regard to their biographical planning and actions. The life course as an institution "has come to achieve social order by processing people through the social structure and articulating their actions, in other words, by providing the rules by which individuals unfold and conduct their lives" (Kohli 2007, p. 256).

Chapter 2 answers the question of what "life course research" actually is. To this end, the development of this field of research is traced in terms of the history of ideas and then a substantial definition of "life course research" is presented.

Life course research is concerned with the life course or life courses as its object of research; the four chapters just mentioned deal with this. However, life course research also understands itself in the sense of a conceptual orientation: as a kind of "paradigm" of empirical social research. This theoretical-conceptual perspective is discussed in Chap. 6.

The concluding chapter outlines the crucial challenge facing life course research today.

This brief outline of sociological life course research is elaborated below. Its most important results and findings are presented and its theoretical assumptions and analytical concepts for empirical studies are introduced and discussed. Methods of life course research are not the subject of this book, as this would go beyond its scope (in this respect, reference is made to the relevant methodological literature). In addition to knowledge of the essential results of sociological life course research, the reader should also and above all have an understanding of its working methods and possibilities at the end of the book – and perhaps also an interest in working in the field of life course sociology. First, however, the basic idea of sociological life course research, which is strange to everyday thinking, is illustrated by three examples.

The sociological conception of the life course as a social construction may be unfamiliar to everyday thinking. Nevertheless, this conception is certainly present and effective in the everyday world of life. Here, the sociological understanding of the concept manifests itself, for example, in a document that is an essential part of every job application: the "curriculum vitae" (CV). A "curriculum vitae" is a largely standardized document. This standardization points to the fact that there are generally accepted socio-cultural ideas about the course of a life: there are social expectations about the structure of CVs to which applicants (must) orient themselves. For example, with regard to the temporal structure of a CV, there is an expectation that one should have completed a course of study within a certain time frame or by a certain age. The presentation of an individual's life history in a "curriculum vitae" thus follows social conventions that dictate which aspects of one's life history are relevant and how they are to be presented.

> A 'CV' is not so much documenting the life course of an individual in its uniqueness, but rather is organized around the question: "What employers want to see and how to say it" (Bright and Earl 2011). As this subtitle of an English-language job application guide makes clear, the primary concern is to serve expectations on the part of potential employers – about which applicants are often unclear. There is now an extensive body of advice on this problem of unclear expectations, which helps to minimize uncertainties and "optimize" one's own CV. (Hesse and Schrader 2007; Schmich 2013)
>
> - Take a look at such guides and think about "optimizing your CV".
> - Discuss – if accessible – different application CVs.
> - You are applying for a position as a research assistant at the university after completing your sociology studies: write your CV. What would your CV look like if you were applying for a position as a consultant at a social welfare authority or at an NGO or a church foundation or a foundation close to an employer or a trade union?

The basic assumption of sociological life course research can also be illustrated by the "invention" of childhood. In modern industrial societies, life is divided into childhood, adolescence, adulthood and old age (Abels et al. 2008). In everyday thinking, these definable phases of life are regarded as quasi-natural, universal realities. However, these are by no means anthropological universals. Thus, according to Ariès's seminal work, in the Middle Ages there was no "perception of childhood specificity, that specificity which categorically distinguishes the child from the adult, even the young adult. There was no such conscious relation to childhood" (1975, p. 209). Medieval society, in fact, had "no conception of education (…) because, from its point of view, there were no problems here at all: the child took its place alongside the adult as a matter of course immediately after weaning or a little later" (Ibid., p. 559 f.). Children, as soon as they got along without their mothers or wet nurses, belonged to adult society without transition and were regarded as small, "incomplete" adults. There was no separate and institutionalized world of children's lives from adult life. The idea that adolescents should be prepared for adult life and that there should be a specific form of life called "childhood" for this purpose, separate from the adult world, was alien to the Middle Ages – unlike to antiquity: it "saw no such distinction and consequently had no concept of such a transitional period. The great event at the beginning of modern times was therefore the renaissance of educational interest. (…) One now finds that the child is not ready for life, that one must subject it to a special influence, a quarantine, before releasing it into the adult world" (Ibid., p. 550 f.). Only now does the "invention" of childhood as an independent, socially institutionalized phase of life occur. "Childhood" is thus – like "youth"[3] – a socioculturally constituted phenomenon of modern times. Ariès's book, published in 1960, sparked a wide-ranging discussion that led to considerable criticism of his thesis.[4] Nevertheless, his central insight – as Honig sums up – has endured: "Childhood is not an anthropological universal; rather, it must be understood as a historical, changeable phenomenon" (1999, p. 18).

- Look at representations of children in the visual arts from the Middle Ages to the 17th century: what do you notice?
- Has "childhood" now become globally established as an independent, institutionalized phase of life?
- When is a person considered "old"? Are there historically or interculturally different concepts of age?

All cultures are familiar with the division of human life into a sequence of definable age phases. In the European cultural area, such concepts of the life course have been found since Greek antiquity (Rosenmayr 1978; Saake 2006, p. 98 ff.). Solon, for example, divided life into ten seven-year phases as early as 600 BC. In modern times, such age-phase models found popular expression in the image of the staircase of life (Joerissen and Will 1984). The staircase of life, which was widespread from the eighteenth century to the first half of the twentieth century, presents life as a

---

[3] A definable, socially institutionalized youth phase did not emerge until much later: beginning in the second half of the eighteenth century, it formed in the course of the growing division of labor and the associated need for qualifications until it became generally established at the end of the nineteenth century and then expanded strongly in the twentieth century with the expansion of education (Gillis 1980; Mitterauer 1986).

[4] An overview is provided by Cunningham's (2006) comprehensive and readable work on the history of childhood.

1 The Life Course as a Social Construction

gradual process of ascent and descent, maturation and decay.[5] Figure 1.1 shows the two oldest life staircases, created around the middle of the sixteenth century. In addition to the absence of a childhood and youth phase – particularly striking in Breu's woodcut – it is especially noticeable that animals are assigned to the age phases. These symbolize specific behavioral characteristics of the age groups (for example, the third age correlates with the strength of the bull). The animal symbolism familiar to contemporaries points to the existence of culturally shared ideas about characteristic features of different age groups. Here – and this is the crucial point – it is not or not only a matter of "natural" characteristics of different ages, but also of socio-cultural attributions. More clearly than the animal symbolism, which may still permit a purely naturalizing interpretation, this is shown by the aphorisms frequently found in life staircases relating to the individual stages: thus – to quote from a widespread saying – the statement "60 Jahr gets Alter an", (60 years old age starts), for example, may still be due to natural ageing; the statement "40 Jahr wolgethan" (40 years well done), however, can no longer be explained as a consequence of the ageing process or other natural conditions, but is rather a socio-cultural attribution. This social construction of "age" becomes particularly clear with the help of the gender-specific life staircases, because "sex" is not only a biological but also a social category (in English: sex or gender). Figure 1.2 shows male and female "steps of ages" in a chromolithograph created around 1900 (gender-specific life staircases already existed in the sixteenth century).

Particularly in the wake of the third age stage associated with starting a family, the life courses of men and women diverge. The resulting differentiation of the individual age phases, i.e. of peer groups, into typically male or female "stage ages" can be explained neither as a consequence of chronological nor biological ageing, but only by means of social factors. The characteristics associated with certain ages are not "natural" age characteristics, but socio-cultural attributions, i.e.: the behavioral characteristics attributed to the members of an age group reflect social behavioral expectations. The linking of specific individual behavioral characteristics or social behavioral expectations with certain age groups, as shown in the life staircase, shows that "age" is also socially "charged" and overformed in everyday thinking.

---

[5] Besides the division into seven-year steps (Hebdomads) – which is still popular today, e.g. among anthroposophists – antiquity already knew a whole series of other periodizations.

Earlier depictions of life phases were linear (horizontal juxtaposition) or circular (wheel of life). Anthonisz's woodcut is indeed constructed in steps – but in the composition of the picture the idea of a circle of life is still present insofar as it motivates the viewer's eye to a circular movement: the gaze following the steps of the staircase of life is guided at its end via the grave back to the cot, from death back to birth. Significantly, one speaks in this regard of the cycle of life. This term is sometimes used synonymously with "life course" – which is not appropriate, however, because the term "life cycle" implies, in addition to the aspect of maturation and decay, the aspect of generational reproduction, i.e. an idea transcending the lifetime and life course of the individual: "Strictly defined, life cycle refers to maturational and generational processes in natural populations. Alternative conceptions of life cycle, like life span and life course, do not share the same intrinsic reference to generation or reproduction that transcends the single lifetime of the individual" (O'Rand and Krecker 1990, p. 241).

Cornelis Anthonisz: De trap des levens. Woodcut, c. 1540 (Wikimedia Commons)

Jörg Breu d. J.: Die Lebensalter des Mannes. Woodcut, 1540 (Wikimedi Commons)

Fig. 1.1 The two earliest life staircase depictions

1 The Life Course as a Social Construction

Design: F. Leiber, Publisher: Gustav May Sohne
(Wikimedia Commons: http://www.dhm.de/ausstellungen/lebensstationen/1_177.htm)

Ten years old, the best time,
  A boy full of happiness and merriment
At 20 years the handsome suitor
  Inspires the first love fire
At 30 he sees, full of rapture,
  To wife and child with love looks
At 40 years of age at the destination of the track,
  Without fear he says 'Tis well done
At 50, there's a silent stand,
  He checks what comes and what disappears

At 60, the world says,
  The path already noticeably descends
At 70, the stick must be at hand,
  As a greyhead he wanders through the land
At 80, hair bleached,
  Life's day turns to night
At 90, weak, bent and lame,
  The rotten life is only grief
And then, when a 100 years have passed,
  He prays that God will have mercy on him …

Design: F. Leiber, Publisher: Gustav May Sohne
(Wikimedia Commons: http://www.dhm.de/ausstellungen/lebensstationen/1_177.htm)

The child is for life
  An angel of God attached
Ten years, the child in the wing dress
  Enjoy the bliss of innocence
At 20 years of age, blossomed into a maiden,
  In pure love her heart glows
Then, at 30, the joys of motherhood
  To give the woman the highest pleasure
At 40 the children's happiness calls
  The own youth her back
At 50 'standstill' as they say,

A grandson makes her happy now
  At 60 it's all downhill
Slowly walking after the grave
  With 70 year great grandchild
The old mama still freun
  At 80 she is weak,
Leaning on the faithful grandson
  At 90, long since snow-white,
Does she only think of the last rice
  And approach a 100 more,
Beg God to have mercy on them

Fig. 1.2 The "steps of ages" of man and woman (around 1900)

In 1954 the famous New York artist Saul Steinberg draw this life staircase.
• Compare the caricature with the depictions presented before. What strikes your attention?
• How would a life staircase look like that would skewer the conditions in Germany or the US today?

© The Saul Steinberg Foundation / Artists Rights Society (ARS), New York (ink on paper, 14¼ x 23 in. Private collection)

The term "age" has different colloquial meanings. The chronological (calendar) age of an individual indicates the number of years that have passed since birth. Biological age refers – often in terms of standard values – to the stage of development of an organism and its biophysical and biochemical condition. Psychological age refers to the subjective experience, evaluation and coping with one's own age and ageing. Finally, social age refers to the social positions and roles that individuals assume in the course of their life span from birth to death, i.e. to their membership of socially differentiated age phases and groups. These age phases and their sequence are socioculturally formed and constituted. In other words, "age" is also a social category, the life course also a social construction.

In this introductory chapter, a sociological concept of the life course was developed and the reader was familiarized with the basic idea of sociological life course research: to understand the life course as a social construction. But why does the book focus on sociological life course research? After all, life course research is a multidisciplinary field and programme of investigation in which, in addition to sociology, psychology and demography in particular, as well as anthropology, economics, political science and history, and also natural science disciplines are involved. So why, when to this day the multi-, inter- or transdisciplinarity of life course research is repeatedly emphasized – even as a necessity[6] – this focus? The main reason is didactic. This book aims to introduce students of sociology to life course research. The study of sociology is supposed to teach the theories, concepts, and methods of the discipline; students are supposed to grasp the way sociology thinks and learn to master its theoretical and methodological tools – which, in relation to the topic of this book, means: to look at the phenomenon of "life course" from a sociological perspective, that is, to deal with sociological life course research. This

---

[6] "The study of lives is, of necessity, an interdisciplinary and multi-method enterprise" (Settersten 1999, p. 1).

is what this book is all about (although for stylistic reasons the adjective "sociological" will be omitted in the following, i.e. when "life course research" is referred to from now on, this term means sociological life course research).

> Of course, sociological life course research does not ignore the results and arguments of other disciplines, but takes personality psychological variables into account in its analyses, for example, if the research question requires this. But this self-evident fact does not have much to do with (a meaningful concept of) inter- and transdisciplinarity. Their necessity and superiority over disciplinary research is justified by the fact that the problems of this world and its societies are not structured in disciplinary terms. This is probably true – but: what does this mean for the scientific analysis of these problems? At the beginning of the chapter, reference was made to the methodological insight into the theory-loadedness of all observation and knowledge, which cannot be escaped, but only reflexively assured. If one assumes that disciplines are constituted around a fundamental way of thinking or theoretical perspective, disciplinarity is not a matter of putting on intellectual blinkers, but simply an indispensable prerequisite of scientific knowledge. Multidisciplinarity is unproblematic with regard to this methodological insight insofar as a question is merely dealt with here by several disciplines, i.e. considered from different perspectives (a problem – especially one relevant to practice – is, however, the weighting of the diverse results to which these disciplinary perspectives lead with their respective specific view of the problem). Interdisciplinarity and transdisciplinarity differ from this mere juxtaposition of perspectives – there is still considerable ambiguity about both terms – in that they integrate different disciplinary or even non-scientific perspectives. Such a fusion of fundamental theoretical perspectives or ways of thinking may sometimes succeed, but sometimes – and probably more often – it is not possible (see also the concluding chapter). There has been an extensive and controversial discussion on this topic since the 1970s. (Kocka 1987; Klein 1990a, b; Balsiger 2005; Jungert et al. 2010)
>
> - What do you think: do you first have to master the theoretical and methodological tools of your discipline before you can work interdisciplinarily at all?
> - What does the abandonment of disciplinary studies in favor of interdisciplinary courses mean in terms of educational content or goals?
> - What does interdisciplinary science education mean for the transmission of knowledge and cognition?

What Is "Life Course Research"? 2

This chapter answers the question of what actually constitutes life course research and how this field of research can be systematically grasped. In order to gain an initial understanding, the prehistory of life course research is first briefly reviewed. After all, the life course theoretical research approach did not simply fall from the sky towards the end of the 1960s. Rather, the life course perspective has theoretical antecedents in the social sciences. An outline of the history of ideas of the emergence of life course research outlines how this field of research developed in social science discourse (Sect. 2.1). Following this sketch of the history of science, the question of what actually constitutes life course research is addressed from a systematic perspective (Sect. 2.2). In order to answer this question, the basic idea and central research object of life course research will be substantively specified: What exactly is meant by the life course as a social construction? A theoretically sound definition of the life course is presented that substantively establishes the field of life course research. This theoretical conception of life course research goes beyond the widespread understanding, especially in Germany, of life course research in the sense of focusing only on the "external" shape of life courses (Sect. 2.2.1). An essential characteristic of life course research is its principally dynamic research perspective. For this reason, the central role of the complex factor "time" or temporal structures in life course research is discussed in conclusion (Sect. 2.2.2).

2.1 A Brief History of Life Course Research

The idea of life course and age as a social construction was already present in ethnology in the nineteenth century. Schurtz, for example, wrote in his fundamental work published shortly after the turn of the century that a division into age classes, with which specific rights and duties are associated, "had already been understood earlier by experts as the oldest type of social order" (1902, p. IVf). Since early ethnology pursued the programmatic strategy of uncovering universal structural patterns of society by means of the study of so-called primitive social formations, "age" was regarded as a central structural or structuring feature of all societies: it functions – like "gender" – as a universal social ordering principle. The criterion "age" can provide this universal ordering function because it occurs as a natural characteristic of human beings. However: the "simplest natural associations resulting from consanguinity are contrasted with the age classes as the first attempt at a consciously implemented division, albeit also based on natural foundations" (Ibid., p. 83). Thus, Schurtz already understood the structuring of society according to "age" not simply as a purely natural order, but also as a socio-cultural construct.[1] In the meantime, cultural and social anthropological studies have not only provided ample evidence that age groups and phases are constituted as the result of socio-cultural typification and attribution processes, but have also shown that this social structuring of the life course is extremely diverse, i.e. varies interculturally and historically (Kertzer and Keith 1984; Bernardi 1985; Elwert et al. 1990).

This insight can already be found in Linton's work, who – entirely in the universalist perspective of early ethnology – introduced "age" (and "gender") into

---

[1] Nevertheless, "age" as a structuring principle has a naturalizing effect: it makes the existing social order appear not as socially constituted, but natural – and thus depoliticizes it. The social construction of "age" or age groups is – like that of "gender" – one of the "possible forms of the naturalization of society. Naturalization means that social orders created by human beings present themselves as something natural, in other words that self-evidence is gained by recourse to the biological. (…) That every naturalization also contains a natural element is obvious and constitutes its plausibility … But it is only the basic material for the social construction" (Elwert and Kohli 1990, p. 4).

sociology as a social-structural organizing principle.[2] His essay, tellingly titled "A Neglected Aspect of Social Organization," emphasized that "age-sex categories and their derivatives are the building blocks of the society" (1940, p. 872).[3] To be sure, Linton retained that conception of "age" (and "sex") as universal criteria for regulating role behavior and principles of social structuring, and he transferred this universalist notion to sociology. At the same time, however, he clearly formulated the notion of "age" as a sociocultural construct, which had already been established by Schurtz: despite the "close relation which age-sex categories bear to physiological facts, they are by no means divorced from cultural factors. (…) Societies have, therefore, a considerable range of choice with respect both to the number of age-sex categories to be distinguished and to the points in the lifecycle at which transitions from one category to another are supposed to take place" (1942, p. 591).[4]

This idea of socioculturally constituted age categories stands out from the idea of universal patterns of human development that prevailed in developmental psychology at the time (Bühler 1933). Until the beginning of the 1940s, the notion of universal developmental sequences of the individual went hand in hand with a social-structurally based life course perspective in life course studies. It was only in the following period that there was a gradual analytical divorce of that developmental psychological approach to human development from a sociological life course perspective anchored in social structure. In sociology, this initially resulted in the structural-functionalist approach of age differentiation or age groups (see

---

[2] Parsons is often mentioned in this context, but he only dealt directly with "age" (and "gender") as a social organizing principle in a single essay (1942).

[3] Linton explains the neglect of these structuring criteria with their "deceptive appearance of simplicity. The existence of age-sex categories is so obvious that their importance to social structure is likely to be overlooked" (1940, p. 872 f.).

[4] A vivid example of this socio-cultural overforming and construction of "age" or age classes was provided by Prins (1953), who in his study of the age class systems of three East African tribes shows that transitions between age classes do not simply depend on the – approximately equal – chronological age of the individuals, but are also determined, for example, by patrilineality (entry into a new age class system only as the son of a man leaving the highest age class), by marriage, or by the fact that a man no longer has a wife of childbearing age or any uncircumcised children.

below). Within psychology, the growing social-scientific criticism of the idea of general human developmental stages that unfold necessarily and unalterably (Erikson 1959) led to greater consideration of sociocultural factors.[5] In particular, so-called life span development psychology has attempted since the late 1960s to adequately account for sociocultural context (Baltes et al. 1998; Brandtstädter and Lindenberger 2007). Since that analytical divorce in the course of the 1940s and 1950s, a life span development psychology perspective and a sociological life ourse perspective have developed – if not completely independently of each other, then largely side by side (see also the concluding chapter).

Back to Linton, who – himself an anthropologist – referred in his article to another insight of early ethnology: namely, that transitions between age groups, especially the transition to adult status, take place in ritualized form. However "a given society's system of age-sex categories may be, the individual's transfer from certain of these categories to those next in the age series is usually marked by ceremonial observances. However, all the transitions within any system are rarely commemorated in this way. The one transition which is well-nigh universally ritualized is that of entry into the adult group" (Linton 1942, p. 597). It is true that ethnology had been predominantly concerned with the rites of passage into adult status. However, van Gennep's "Les rites de passages", published as early as 1909, was a study of the ritualization of other status transitions and life events, such as "ceremonies on the occasion of birth, childhood, social puberty, engagement, marriage, pregnancy, parenthood, initiation into religious communities, and burial" (1986, p. 15 f.). In doing so, van Gennep's fundamental research interest was directed at the context of the rites of passage framing these events, or more precisely: at the universal "sequence order of ceremonies" (Ibid., p. 20). However, his three-phase structure of separation, threshold or transformation, and affiliation rites developed in this regard is not of interest to the history of life course research. Rather, what is important here is that van Gennep conceptually replaces the fragmented consideration of distinct age groups and statuses with a perspective on the life course as a whole, addressing the interrelation of different events, statuses, and phases across the life span. By conceiving of the life course theoretically as a sequence of ritualized status transitions and directing the analytical perspective to

---

[5] This attempt was initially still "typically from the perspective of a maturing or aging organism. (…) This perspective views the social context as a 'scene or setting' through which the person – loaded with his or her 'natural predispositions' – must pass" (Elder and Shanahan 2006, p. 670).

the linking processes of the diverse statuses, van Gennep formulates – at least implicitly – a dynamic approach to life course research. The potential of this dynamic perspective, however, remained latent for over five decades. One reason for this was the static theoretical perspective of structural functionalism, which dominated sociology until the 1960s.[6]

> Are there still "ritualized status passages" in contemporary German society today, and if so, which ones?

Parsons' structural functionalism adopted the social and cultural anthropological notion of a universal structuring of both society and the individual's life course according to age categories and established it in the form of an age-group sociology. Accordingly, every society groups members of roughly the same chronological age into a series of age groups, the sequence of which the individual passes through in the process of aging.[7] For structural functionalism, which aims at system stability, age groups are a central element of social continuity: they represent a functional solution to the system-threatening problem of permanence, which results from the limited lifespan of the members of society.[8] Why is the fact that people age and die a permanent continuity problem? For its continuity, every society must continuously compensate for the death of members by births. These new members, however, have not already internalized at birth the values and behavioral orientations necessary for the fulfillment of the role requirements placed on them in the course of their lives, i.e. the values and behavioral orientations necessary for

---

[6] "In every society, the life of an individual consists in passing successively from one age to another and from one activity to another. (…) To each of these events belong ceremonies whose aim is identical: to lead the individual from one well-defined situation to another equally well-defined one. Since the goal is the same, the means, … must also be, if not identical in the details, at least analogous. (…) Thus the ceremonies … exhibit a general similarity" (Gennep 1986, p. 15 f.).

[7] Linton had postulated seven universal age groups which "appear to be basic to all systems of age-sex classification …: Infant, boy, girl, adult man, adult woman, old man, old woman" (1942, p. 593).

[8] Under certain circumstances, however, youth age groups in particular can also develop "deviant" behavior and thus prove to be dysfunctional or a problem for system stability.

the functioning of society. In this respect, as Parsons vividly points out, "the 'barbarian invasion' of the stream of new-born infants ... is a critical feature of the situation in any society" (1951, p. 208). Consequently, society must ensure through socialization[9] that its new members internalize the values and orientations essential for the maintenance of social stability. In doing so, its socialization task is not limited to childhood and adolescence. Because the members of the various age groups each have to satisfy specific role requirements, the changes in age groups that accompany the ageing of individuals require preparation for the new age roles to be filled through lifelong socialization (Brim 1966).

A prominent example of structural-functionalist age-group sociology that illustrates the central role of age groups in the context of society's need for socialization for the purpose of ensuring continuity, especially with regard to the important transition to adult status, is Eisenstadt's cross-cultural and historically comparative study of the social phenomenon of youth groups and movements. Using societies with different constitutions, Eisenstadt sought to identify the socio-structural preconditions for the emergence and existence of youth age groups. In the process, it became apparent that these are a product of modern societies with a complex division of labor. In familialistic societies with a low division of labor, the difference between familial and societal role structure is also small. In these societies, family socialization is sufficient for practicing the culturally prescribed adult roles. In modern societies with a complex division of labor, this adult world is characterized by instrumental behavior, universal orientation, specific roles, and status acquisition. The expressive and particularistic patterns of interaction, diffuse roles, and askriptive status that dominate family and kinship relationships are incompatible with these demands. Family socialization, therefore, cannot prepare adolescents, at least not adequately, to assume and fill adult roles. This family socialization deficit in modern, highly differentiated and individualized societies is compensated for by youth groups as an important instance of socialization: due to their composition and role structure, they act as a link between the security of the family context and the instrumental anonymity of the adult world. Youth age groups also emerge "in societies in which the family (or kinship unit) does not constitute

---

[9] The second critical aspect is – as a consequence of unsuccessful socialization – deviant behavior, which Parsons wants to correct by sanctioning.

the main unit of the social and economic division of labor, and in which the individual must acquire and learn various role dispositions which cannot be learned within the family. Age groups, which are usually articulated during the period of transition from the family of orientation, may serve as channels for the learning (of some, at least) of these general role dispositions. Thus it may be said that age groups constitute an interlinking sphere between the family and other institutionalized spheres of society (political, economic, etc.)" (1956, p. 270).

In the mid-1960s, Cain presented an overview of the early approaches to a sociology of the life course and a first systematic account of the state of research in a widely cited handbook article. This essay is sometimes cited as a kind of founding document of life course research because Cain explicitly aimed "to identify, isolate, and systematize a life course, or age status, frame of reference" (1964, p. 273). In this context, however, the life course term is not – as the quote suggests – synonymous with age status. Whereas the term "life course" refers to the quasi-automatic passage through the sequence of different statuses that accompanies the aging of the individual, the term "age status" refers to the "system developed by a culture to give order and predictability to the course followed by individuals" (Ibid., p. 278). This conceptual difference is to be understood in terms of a conceptual priority of the socially institutionalized age-status system over the individual life course. In other words, Cain wanted to formulate an age-status rather than a life-course theoretical framework. Accordingly, his attempted theorization (Ibid., p. 287 f.) ultimately does not go beyond a systematic and concise presentation of the conceptual framework of structural-functionalist age-group sociology.

In this context, the normative approach of temporal life course structuring developed by Neugarten in the 1960s (Neugarten et al. 1965) must be mentioned, which shows great proximity to the structural-functionalist life course perspective. For Neugarten, a pioneer in the developmental psychology of the second half of life and gerontology, norms of age in society function as a system of social control: they determine an individual's social age and constitute a "roadmap" of life, non-compliance with which is sanctioned. Since the normative structuring of the life course through age-role expectations and stereotypes will be dealt with in a separate sub-chapter (see Sect. 5.2.1), it is sufficient here to refer to Neugarten's approach to age norms.

Since the end of the 1950s, criticism of structural functionalism has been growing in the sociological theory debate. Criticism was levelled at its static, ahistorical basic conception, which is oriented towards the stability of an invariant social order, i.e. a real-historical exceptional case, while it cannot explain the ongoing social change of society, i.e. the factual normal case. Related to this, a theoretical neglect of the – individual and collective – actors and their actions was also criticized. As a result of this theoretical critique, structural functionalism lost its dominant position in sociology and was displaced by dynamic and action-theoretical approaches, which conceptually take into account the dimension of time and history as well as the actor. The general theoretical criticism of structural functionalism was also applied to its sociology of age groups. On the one hand, it was criticized that the (members of) age groups are not only role and function bearers, i.e. mere objects of socialization, but also subjects of action: individual and collective actors whose actions have social consequences. Above all, however, the age group model inspired by early ethnology and its interest in universal structural patterns was criticized as conceptually static: as itself a timeless, ahistorical scheme.

In the context of this theory critique, a whole series of life course sociological works emerged in the 1960s and 1970s that attempted to overcome the conceptual deficits of structural-functionalist age group sociology.[10] It is important to see that these works do not converge on the one sociological study of the life course, but rather establish different approaches to an age differentiation or life course sociology. What unites them is a basic conception that is sensitive to actors as well as to time and history, whose motto could have been what Mills – one of the sharpest critics of structural functionalism – said in his book on "The Sociological Imagination", which was hardly received in Germany: it should make it possible "to understand the larger historical scene in terms of its meaning for the inner life and the external career of a variety of individuals. It enables (…) us to grasp history and biography and the relations between the two within society" (1959, p. 5 f.). The various sociological life course studies in those years can be grouped into four relevant strands of research.

---

[10] Nevertheless, the universalistic age-group model of structural functionalism, inspired by ethnology, remained prevalent in sociology for some time (Foner and Kertzer 1978).

Probably the most important life course sociological perspective of the time: the cohort approach goes back to Ryder's essay on "The Cohort as a Concept in the Study of SocialChange" (1965).[11] In it, Ryder systematically relates the dimension of individual lifetime to that of social time, i.e. he relates individuals with their respective ages to the historically specific social contexts in which they are embedded. Due to their anchoring in historically different socio-cultural situations, individuals of approximately the same ages form cohorts that can be distinguished from one another. In this respect, Ryder regards cohorts as a central concept for the study of social change. Ryder's dynamic cohort approach has established its own strand of research in the sociology of life courses and, because of its importance, will be dealt with in detail in a separate sub-chapter (see Sect. 4.1) in the context of the discussion of collective life courses.

A second research strand – taking up the cohort approach – was Riley's further development of the structural-functionalist sociology of age groups. Her "sociology of age stratification" (Riley et al. 1972; Riley 1985) is based on a model that assumes four age-related structural elements. Society consists of a number of different age strata – each constituted by individuals of approximately the same age – that vary in size and composition. The members of the various age strata differ in terms of their action orientations and competencies. While these two age-related characteristics refer to the level of the members of society (population), the other two refer to the level of the role system of society. Corresponding to the various age strata is an age-related societal role structure, i.e. a structure of roles that varies in type and scope and is open to the members of the various age groups. The fourth element represents age-related role expectations and sanctions of society. Riley conceives of these four age-related elements as resulting from distinct but interrelated processes. In terms of the population, these are the two vital processes of permanent cohort flow, which forms the diverse age strata, and individual aging as passing through these age strata. A second set of processes is of a linking nature, "linking people with roles" (Riley et al. 1972, p. 8): socialization ensures that individuals can fulfill the requirements of the diverse roles socially designated for them in the course of their lives; allocation refers to the mechanisms of continuous

---

[11] In his review of the research of those years, Elder concluded that "the dynamic, cohort-historical perspective, with its lifespan framework, stands out as the single most important contribution in recent years to research on age differentiation in the life course" (1975, p. 187).

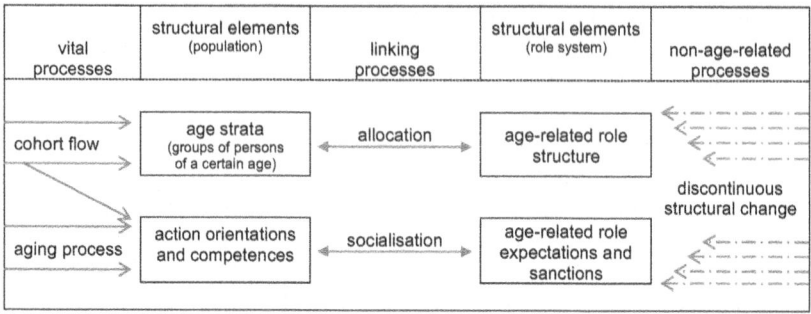

Fig. 2.1 The age stratification model of Riley. (Own illustration, based on Riley et al. 1972, pp. 3–26)

assignment of individuals to these – respectively appropriate – roles.[12] In addition to these age-related processes, there is a third set of non-age-related processes that have a direct impact on the social role system as discontinuous structural change.

Riley's age stratification model (Fig. 2.1) represents a complex feedback system in which a change in one parameter has an impact on all other parameters. The central point in her approach is that there are differences in the dynamics of the three sets of processes, which "arise from the crucial fact that the life span of a society or of its population is far longer than the life span of its members. Not only do aging and cohort succession differ in their timing; but, still more important, there is a fundamental asymmetry or lack of synchronization between the sets of processes affecting people and those affecting roles. The wide range of factors influencing the role structure, though less clearly understood than the population processes, are patently less regular or definably in periodicity. Thus, a constant tension – a potential source of immanent change – inheres in the articulating pro-

---

[12] These two linking processes "enable the role structure to persist and the performance of age-specific functions to continue, despite the succession of role-incumbents" (Riley et al. 1972, p. 8) – a central requirement for stability and continuity of society.

cesses whereby the rhythmic flow of people is channeled through an unpredictable structure of roles" (Ibid., p. 12). This permanent tension exists for both processes of connection, but occurs as inter- or intragenerational conflict primarily in allocations in which actors compete for scarce goods. In this respect, Riley's age stratification theory takes both criticisms of structural functionalism into account: it dynamizes its age group sociology (Ibid., p. 515 ff.) and makes conflicts between actors the social normal case (Ibid., p. 433 ff.). In this respect, her age stratification model represents the most advanced approach of structural-functionalist life course research (but – unlike the cohort concept and the two following perspectives – has not been systematically continued to this day).

- Develop examples of how an inter- or intragenerational conflict arises from a change in a structural feature or process.
- Discuss these examples of inter- or intragenerational conflicts in terms of intervention possibilities and sustainable political solution strategies.

Since the mid-1960s, a third life course perspective emerged with the (re)discovery of biographical research (Fuchs-Heinritz 2009, p. 85 ff.). In the USA, a biographical research approach had become established in the Chicago School (Thomas and Znaniecki 1918–1920; Anderson 1923; Zorbaugh 1929; Cressey 1932; Shaw 1930), but had then been supplanted in the 1940s by procedures for collecting and analyzing mass statistical data.[13] In German sociology – despite a biographical tradition in Germany going back to the late eighteenth century (and unlike in education and psychology) – there were no biographical approaches until the early 1970s (Chanfrault-Duchet 1995). The reasons for the (re)discovery of

---

[13] Thomas and Znaniecki believed that "personal life-records, as complete as possible, constitute the perfect type of sociological material" (1919, p. 6). After the decline of the Chicago School, biographical procedures continued to be used only in (interactionist) deviance research.

biographical research in sociology at that time are not of interest here.[14] What is relevant here is that it was initially primarily a matter of a methodological biographical orientation, i.e. the instrumental use of biographical procedures in empirical social research. Soon, however, a change "from the 'biographical method' to biographical research" (Fischer-Rosenthal 1990) occurred, especially in Germany: going beyond the initial methodological interest, a comprehensive "claim of biographical research as a general sociological perspective" (Ibid., p. 23; Fuchs-Heinritz 1998; Rustin 2000) was postulated. In the wake of this change came the institutionalization of an independent, though far from clearly delineated, field of research. There is agreement that biographical research cannot be reduced to the subjective interpretation of life stories. Rather, biography is considered a social construct in which individual contexts of experience and action are mediated in a unity with the social structural context – and because of this mediatedness, biographical research is not limited to the individual, but can also analyze social processes and circumstances. However, a theoretical consolidation of this branched field of research is still pending. It is obvious that biographical and life course research have points of contact in terms of content, and in some cases even share the same research interests. Nevertheless, biographical and life course research, especially in Germany, have developed and established themselves in sociology rather in distinction to each other. As an introductory presentation of life course research, this book follows this evolved demarcation: biographical research is not addressed here as such, i.e. as an independent field of research, but only in relation to life course research. For more detailed information on biographical research as such, please refer to the introduction by Roberts (2001) or Fuchs-Heinritz (2009).[15]

The fourth perspective, fundamental to the development and establishment of life course research, was opened up by Elder with his study of the "Children of the

---

[14] Although this (re)discovery of biographical research in the various countries "took place roughly at the same time …, it did not spread on the same ground. In each nation, it matched the fields of interest and the sociological – or, more broadly, intellectual – traditions of its practitioners" (Chanfrault-Duchet 1995, p. 209; Bertaux and Kohli 1984). Incidentally, an unbroken continuity of biographical research existed only in Polish sociology (Kohli 1981, p. 283 ff.).

[15] Biographical research is still not defined theoretically, but through specific procedures or data, i.e. merely methodologically: "all research approaches … that have life stories as their data basis (or as data alongside others)" (Fuchs-Heinritz 2009, p. 9).

Great Depression" (1974). In the early 1960s, Elder had come into contact with three longitudinal data sets that had been initiated a good thirty years earlier by developmental psychologists: the Oakland Growth Study examined the life courses and personality development of a sample of the 1920/1921 birth cohorts growing up in Oakland, while the Berkeley Guidance Study and Berkeley Growth Study examined a sample of the 1928/1929 birth cohorts growing up in neighboring Berkeley. The two study groups thus consisted of individuals who experienced the Great Depression at different stages of their childhood. The thematically broad longitudinal data sets of these studies documented their life courses over several waves of data collection well into adulthood, i.e. over more than half a century.[16] To be sure, the Oakland/Berkeley studies had initially been designed for a shorter time period and different purpose, namely developmental psychology questions regarding the childhood and adolescent phases. Elder, however, recognized the life-course sociological potential of their information-rich longitudinal data sets: these made it possible to analyze the effects of the Great Depression on the lives of those Oakland and Berkeley children also over the long term – and across different spheres of life –, that is, to examine the fundamental sociological question of the relationship between society and the individual in its temporal dimension as well. What is the relationship between social context, social change, and the lives of individuals over time? How do societal and biographical development dynamics intertwine over the course of life?

Elder himself emphasizes that "this exposure to longitudinal data encouraged me to think holistically about lives and development over time and across changing contexts" (Elder 1999, p. 304). This simple statement points to a fundamental theoretical shift in research perspective for life course research. Elder shifted the focus away from distinct age groups and conceptually opened it to the entire life course in its internal interrelations and its intertwining with changing social contexts. This shift in perspective involved two conceptual innovations. First, Elder conceptually shifted from a fragmented approach that looked at distinct ages and stages of life to a holistic perspective that looked at the life course as a whole. Such a "life course"

---

[16] The first data were collected from fifth graders around 1930, and the most recent survey took place in the early 1980s. Elder's book on the "Children of the Great Depression" is based only on the data collected by the Oakland Growth Study up to the mid-1960s; Elder did not publish analyses that included the Berkeley data set until later (e.g. 1979).

perspective, truly living up to its name, had already been laid out, over half a century earlier, in van Gennep's[17] study of ritualized status transitions and their linkages in the life course, but had remained latent due to the predominance of structural-functionalist thinking in sociology. Elder's work made this dynamic life course perspective with its analytical potential virulent.[18] The fragmentation of the life course into distinct life phases gave way to a view of the life course as a whole: i.e., of the entire life span and thus, above all, of the internal interrelationship of the various stages of life (the fact that such an interrelationship exists should be familiar and immediately apparent to everyone on the basis of their own biographical experience). The second conceptual innovation of Elder's work was that, in contrast to previous longitudinal studies, whose analyses focused on a specific area of life, it analyzed individual life courses across the various fields: Elder directed attention to the interrelationships between the diverse areas of life (such as family and working life) and their intertwining with the social context and change. Elder's conceptual innovations mark – in short – the transition from age-group sociology to dynamic life course research.

> Illustrate the significance of Elder's two conceptual innovations using concrete examples – empirical or imagined – such as in the area of social inequality or mobility.

---

[17] While Elder did not mention van Gennep's "Les rites de passage", Glaser and Strauss explicitly referred to it at the very beginning of their book "Status Passage" (1971) – although it has little to do with van Gennep's work. Glaser and Strauss attempted to develop a formal status passage theory by listing and categorizing properties of status passages (such as reversibility, temporality, or shaping). However, this theorizing strategy ultimately misses the very thing that makes van Gennep's work conceptually interesting for life course research. To be sure, Glaser and Strauss's book appears in the bibliography of many life course studies and the term "status passage" is widely used. However, their (unsystematic) attempt at theorizing did not have an impact on life course research comparable to Elder's work.

[18] Empirical research, however, is – at least so far – restricted to the analysis of longer trajectories spanning individual life phases, because an investigation of overall life courses presupposes that longitudinal data sets exist in which individual lives are recorded over the entire period from birth to death.

Based on the different economic impairments of the children's families caused by the Great Depression, Elder used this crisis to examine the fundamental question of the "linkages between socioeconomic change ... and its psychosocial effects within the life course" (Ibid., p. 13).[19] The empirical results of his studies show that the Great Depression had different effects on the lives of the children studied and produced divergent patterns of progression and development both within and between cohorts. Elder's diverse empirical findings are not of interest here in detail.[20] One particularly important finding was that the crisis shaped the life courses and personality development of the Oakland and Berkeley children in very different ways, even though the two cohorts were only a few years apart in time. A significant role in these divergent life course effects was played by the fact that "when the economy collapsed, the Oakland children were beyond the years of family dependency and entered adulthood after the economy had begun to revive. By contrast, the Berkeley children ... remained dependent on the family through the worst years of the decade" (Ibid., p. 317). The influence of even such a serious event as the Great Depression on the lives of individuals thus depended crucially on the phase of life in which an individual was affected. Theoretically, Elder's finding points to the fact that the (long-term) effects of societal contexts and changes on individuals cannot be adequately captured and conceptualized without reference to their particular life stage (age). To put it positively: in studies of the relationship between society and the individual, the two dimensions of social and individual

---

[19] It has been said above that since about the middle of the twentieth century psychological life span development research *life course development research* and sociological life course research have developed separately and side by side. As Elder's just quoted talk of psychosocial life course effects shows (see also Elder 1999, p. 318), this of course does not mean that these two life course perspectives are completely sealed off from each other. There have been and still are life course researchers in whose work psychological and sociological concepts and conceptions are intertwined (besides Elder himself, e.g. Alwin 1994, 1995; Clausen 1986, 1991; Diewald 2006; Diewald et al. 2006; Heinz 2003a, b; Sampson and Laub 1997; Shanahan 2000).

[20] An informative overview is given in a paper by Elder and Caspi (1990) translated into German. Two empirical results may illustrate the intra- and inter-cohort variance of life course effects due to the Great Depression. Within the Oakland cohort, for example, severe household economic losses altered the relational and role structure of the family such that girls had to do more household work and boys (and mothers) had to "earn extra income," leading both to these children becoming independent earlier compared to those from less deprived families and to boys from severely deprived families adopting the male breadwinner family model early and maintaining it throughout their lives, while girls' lives followed the female homemaker model. Different life course effects were evident between the two cohorts, for example in "consistently greater developmental handicaps of the Berkeley deprived men in adolescence, the more adverse effect of economic hardship on their education, and a more troubled sense of psychological well-being among these men up to the 50s" (Elder 1999, p. 318).

time must be systematically related to each other – a reference that the sociological classics do not address in their reflections on the relationship between society and the individual, because they assume an "ageless" individual, as it were. In contrast, Elder's studies empirically illustrate that the basic sociological question of the relationship between society and the individual must be answered within the framework of a theoretical and methodological conception that takes into account the interweaving of societal-institutional contexts and dynamics (macro/meso level) with biographical-individual situations and dynamics (micro level).

Elder also attempted to formulate a theoretical basis for life course research by drawing generalizing conclusions from his empirical findings in the form of "paradigmatic principles" (Ibid., p. 302). However, these life course principles do not represent an elaborated theory of the life course (for a detailed discussion of these principles and their problematic theoretical status see Sect. 6.1). Elder does talk about life course theory – without ever systematically presenting it – but wants the concept of theory in this composite term to be understood in a special sense: namely, as a "theoretical orientation that establishes a common field of inquiry by defining a framework that guides research in terms of problem identification and formulation, variable selection and rationales, and strategies of design and analysis" (Ibid.). However his attempted theorization may be evaluated theoretically, in fact Elder's life course principles functioned as a theoretical framework for the developing life course research. His life course principles, together with the analytical concepts of "transition" and "trajectory" (Elder 1985; see Sect. 6.2), were the conceptual platform on which life course research flourished until the turn of the millennium. In this respect, Elder is rightly regarded as the doyen of (North American) life course research.

The following diagram (Fig. 2.2) provides an overview and schematic illustration of the social science roots and the development of life course research.

The history of the emergence of life course research in social science discourse is thus complete: since the second half of the 1970s, life course research has been established as a sociological field of research. This field, with its theoretical approaches, achievements and deficits, its analytical concepts and empirical results, will be dealt with substantially in the following chapters (methods of life course research will – as already stated in the previous chapter – not be dealt with). In this respect, the presentation of the genesis of life course research in terms of the history

2 What Is "Life Course Research"?

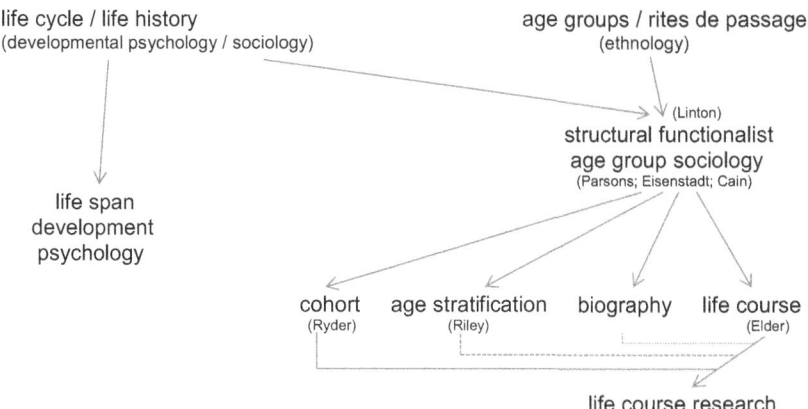

Fig. 2.2 The emergence of life course research. (Source: Own representation)

of ideas ends here.[21] However, the further development of this now established field of research – concluding the subchapter on the history of science – will at least be briefly touched upon.

---

[21] The presentation of the history of science in this subchapter focused on the emergence of life course research within the discourse of the social sciences, i.e. in terms of the history of ideas. In this context, two further aspects internal to science should be mentioned that played a role in the emergence of life course research: firstly, deficits in various fields of empirical social research, the elimination of which suggested a life course perspective, such as in mobility and inequality research (Mayer 1987, p. 55 ff.) or socialization research (Kohli 1980, p. 299 ff.), and secondly, progress and innovations in the field of methodological development and statistics with regard to the consideration of the dimension of "time".

The development of life course research in the 1960s and 1970s was certainly also influenced by external factors, i.e. social conditions, structures and developments: the increasingly rapid social change in the twentieth century (World War I, the Great Depression, World War II, the Cold War, economic prosperity, political and cultural changes as a result of the civil rights, women's, student and hippie movements) with its effects on the lives of individuals and society as well as serious demographic changes, especially increasing life expectancy and falling fertility, i.e. the change in the social age structure in the sense of an ageing population (Elder et al. 2003, p. 5 f.).

Since the mid-1970s, a large number of empirical life course studies have emerged which – taken together – have shown the multiformity of life courses and their historically and culturally varying organization. In particular, the tripartite structure of the modern "normal life course" compared to life courses in pre-modern societies was empirically proven and theoretically justified in relation to the institutional and cultural anchoring of this modern standard biography. At the same time, however, a considerable variance in life course patterns was identified – both within modern societies and in social comparison – and theoretically sharpened in the thesis of the erosion of the normal biography. In the process, operating with abstract contextual concepts such as the well-known welfare state typology "liberal vs. conservative-corporatist vs. social-democratic" ultimately proved insufficient for determining the structuring factors and mechanisms of life courses. As a consequence, these findings led to the insight into the necessity of a detailed specification of the concrete socio-cultural contexts and institutional regimes in which life courses are embedded in each case. After its heyday in the 1980s and 1990s, the discourse on life course research has become somewhat quieter since the turn of the millennium. However, this does not mean that it has lost its relevance. Rather, concepts, methods, and approaches of life course research have seeped into all kinds of fields of empirical social research and are now part of the standard repertoire there – such as longitudinal analyses. This dissemination of life course research is undoubtedly a success story (but it also has a downside – this aspect will be addressed in the final chapter).

2.2 The Theoretical Concept of Life Course Research

The fundamental object of sociological life course research is – as outlined in the first chapter – the life course as a social construction. But what exactly does this basic idea of the life course as a social construction mean? How is the term "life course" to be substantively defined and thus the field of life course research to be theoretically conceived?

First, a delimiting preliminary remark. There is a growing tendency to conceive of life course research not theoretically, but simply methodologically in terms of a micro analytical longitudinal design.[22] There is no doubt that such a research

---

[22] Symptomatic of this is the name of the international journal "Longitudinal and Life Course Studies" (Bynner et al. 2009) or the "Society for Longitudinal and Life Course Studies", which was launched in 2009. One may speculate whether the resort to such an understanding – comparable to the still merely methodological definition of biographical research (see the corresponding note in the previous subchapter) – is due to the lack of an elaborated life course theory accepted by the vast majority of the relevant scientific community.

design, operating with individual-level trajectory data and methods for their dynamic analysis embedded in a multilevel model of social processes, represents a central element for the field of life course research. However, this cannot be defined solely in terms of a specific research design, not merely in terms of methodology or even a specific type of data. Rather, what life course research is must be determined theoretically. There is, in fact, a crucial difference between the use of a micro analytical longitudinal design in empirical life course research and the independent field of life course research: the latter essentially also implies a substantive conception. How is the basic idea of the life course as a social construction to be theoretically specified? How can the constitutive object of life course research be substantively defined? To this end, a theoretically substantial definition will be proposed and explained in the following.

2.2.1 Life Course: A Substantive Definition

There is a whole range of life course definitions in the relevant literature. They all have one thing in common: they deal with sequences of age-related events and positions in social contexts, their connections and temporal structure (sequence, duration, dynamics, etc.) in the course of a life. Apart from that, however, they differ in their accentuation of content and their respective scope, as the three examples of renowned life course researchers cited below illustrate.

A. In their preface, the editors of *the Handbook of the Life Course* define the life course as an "age-graded, socially-embedded sequence of roles that connect the phases of life" (Mortimer and Shanahan 2003, p. XI).
B. Giele and Elder define the life course as a "sequence of socially defined events and roles that the individual enacts over time" (1998, p. 22).
C. Mayer, too, initially characterizes the life course in the sense of this conceptual commonality, but then specifies his understanding of the life course to the effect that the "structures of the life course ... are at least partially institutionalized, that is, independent of individual motives and intentions. (...) The social shaping of the life course occurs primarily through the mapping of social differentiation within and between institutions onto the life course" (1990, p. 10).

With regard to the substantive accentuation of these definitions, it should be noted that (A) and (B) describe the life course essentially as a "'role course': age-related role transitions" (Settersten 1999, p. 6), while the role concept does not occur in (C). In contrast to the two role-theoretically based definitions, (C) is anchored in institutional theory and brings the institutional shaping of life courses into focus, which is again neglected by (A) and (B). The individual as a biographical actor who – intentionally or as a non-intended side effect of his actions – shapes or at least helps to shape his own life is only mentioned in (B). Such different accentuations of content in life course definitions have consequences for research perspectives – and this is the insight we are concerned with here.[23] A fundamentally role-theoretical understanding of the life course suggests different questions, theses, explanatory approaches, analytical strategies and variables for empirical research than an institutional-theoretical concept of the life course. A view that sees the individual only as a passive bearer of socially predetermined roles or only as a person whose life follows institutionally predefined paths implies a different research perspective for empirical life course studies than one that sees the individual as "the architect of his own fortune", i.e. as an actor who has the power to act in and vis-à-vis social structures.

> - For each of the three cited life course definitions, formulate a research question for an empirical life course study suggested by the respective content emphasis.
> - Develop a research design for each of these three empirical life course studies or questions. Compare and discuss the three empirical projects/research designs.

As an aside, it should be noted in this context that the life course definitions cited above were chosen as examples because their different substantive accentuations reflect a characteristic difference between North American and European, especially German, life course research. The former still conceptually implies – grosso modo – clear echoes of the structural-functionalist sociology of age groups

---

[23] For this reason, the differences in content between the cited life course definitions and their conceptual consequences are exaggerated here – even if this means that the explanations do not do justice to the life course understanding of the cited colleagues: for example, the institutional life course shaping emphasized in (C) is not completely irrelevant for (A) and (B), but appears in the formulation "socially-embedded" and "socially defined", respectively; and the individual as a biographical actor mentioned only in (B) is not completely ignored by the authors of (A) and (C).

and roles and accords great importance to the individual and his or her potential for action. For the latter, on the other hand, the moment of institutional structuring of life courses or the "interface between the specifications of large social institutions and individual action" (Mayer 1990, p. 10) is constitutive.[24]

What follows from the outlined facts of the different substantive accentuation of life course definitions and their perspective consequence for empirical life course studies with regard to the attempt of a conceptual specification of the basic idea of life course research? The first conclusion to be drawn is that a theoretically sound and useful conception of this field of research must not ignore any substantially relevant moment of the complex phenomenon of "life course as social construction". This then raises the question of which moments are substantively relevant to the concept of the life course. First and foremost, of course, there is what is common to all definitions found in the relevant literature: it is about sequences of age-related events and positions in diverse social contexts, their interrelationship and temporal structure in the course of a life. Secondly, if the definitions presented above are taken as a basis, it must be taken into account that these age-related chains of events and positions are socially structured and, above all, institutionally preformed. However, the social pre-structuring of life courses is not to be understood deterministically: people are not – comparable to pawns – institutionally directed through their lives along predetermined paths. Thirdly, this means that individuals are to be understood as biographical actors who shape their own lives within the framework of socio-structural conditions. According to what has been said so far, these are the three substantial and indispensable moments for a theoretically substantial and useful concept of life course. A definition that includes these three essential moments has been proposed by Heinz. He defines the life course as a "flexible, time-dependent social configuration that is co-constructed by individuals and institutions, a configuration that evolves in a loosely coupled relationship between social structure and the outcomes of individual decisions. At the same time, life courses are still path dependent because they are related to a society's institutional fabric" (2003b, p. XIII).[25]

---

[24] More generally, on the differences between North American and European life course research, see Hagestad (1991); Heinz and Krüger (2001); Marshall and Mueller (2003).

[25] However, the aspect of age-related event and position linkages is formulated somewhat tersely in this life course definition as "time-dependent social configuration".

Nevertheless, this life course definition also remains deficient in that it inappropriately narrows the scope of life course research. With regard to the scope of this field of research, it was stated in the previous chapter that life course research addresses its subject matter on three analytically distinguishable levels: on the level of individual life courses, on the level of collective life courses, and on the level of the life course as an institution.[26] The latter refers to the life course as a system of rules for the temporal dimension of life, which encompasses both its "external" course in the form of sequences of events and positions and the "internal" biographies and life plans of individuals. None of the definitions cited takes this moment of the life course as an institution into account conceptually. They suggest empirical research at the level of individual life courses, i.e. on life course patterns as well as on differentiation and inequality theory. They also suggest empirical research on the level of collective life courses, i.e. on questions and phenomena related to generation and cohort theory. However, like most of the definitions found in the literature, they conceptually ignore the life course as an institution. This is remarkable – after all, it is precisely this moment of the life course as an independent regulatory system of the temporal dimension of life that is the core idea of an essay by Kohli (1985) that is fundamental to the field of research. This moment of the life course as an institution,[27] established by Kohli in life course research – and in a certain sense establishing it – will be presented in detail in the following chapter. The definition of the life course now proposed here starts from this fundamental level of the life course as an institution, which encompasses the other moments. It conceives of the life course as a – historically variable – socio-culturally and politically constituted institution that produces social continuity and social integration through the structural embedding and, above all, institutional preformation of age-related event and position configurations in the diverse social fields, which also represents an orientation for the biographical actions of individuals.

---

[26] In this sense, Dannefer and Uhlenberg also see life course research as a field that "encompasses phenomena representing at least three levels ... of analysis: (1) the individual level ..., (2) the level of social aggregation ..., and (3) the cultural or symbolic level" (1999, p. 313). This third level describes the life course as an institution: as a "set of social rules and practices and as a socially objectified idea that has plausibility in a given societal context as a set of publicly shared meanings and expectations for the course of human lives" (Dannefer and Kelley-Moore 2009, p. 404).

[27] This is neglected by North American life course research in particular (but critically, e.g. Dannefer 2011).

This life course definition, which may seem somewhat complicated at first glance, is briefly explained below. It consists of four segments of meaning: First, it is about the life course as an institution for establishing social integration and social continuity (1). The institutionalized life course fulfils this function by means of a social-structural, in particular institutional embedding or preformation of age-related events and positions (2). This socio-structural framing refers to the "external" life course in the form of event and position configurations in the various social spheres (3). Finally, the pre-programming of life courses thus given also affects the "inner" orientation, i.e. the biographical planning and action of individuals (4).

1. When talking about the life course as an institution, it is important to remember what institutions actually are and what they do. In general, institutions are understood to be relatively permanent structures of meaning with a regulatory and orientation function with regard to central, recurring societal challenges.[28] Institutions represent culturally coagulated answers to such societal needs and problems, which collectively and individually relieve the burden of action and produce (action) security. The life course as an institution represents – as already mentioned – a regulatory system for the temporal dimension of life. But to which social challenge does this regulatory and orientation function respond? Since the beginning of the modern era, people have been increasingly freed from traditional ties. This process of individualization led, among other things, to the fact that societalization solely through social collectives (e.g. family, class, village community) became problematic. With the growing individualization, the necessity arose to compensate for the reduced social integrative power, i.e. the reduced integrative capacity of the traditional form of societalization. This could only be achieved by a form of societalization that was based on the individual himself: the life course. The life course as an institution, as a system of rules for the temporal dimension of life, represents a new mode of societalization that complements the traditional form of integration. Or to put it with Kohli (repeating the quotation from the first chapter): "the institutionalized life course has come to achieve social order by processing people through the social structure and articulating their actions, in other words, by providing the rules by which individuals unfold and conduct their lives" (2007, p. 256). This would briefly explain the meaning of the first part of the proposed life course definition

---

[28] To put this in concrete terms, a society, for example, is constantly faced with the challenge of reproducing itself and integrating future generations. In the course of socio-cultural evolution, the institution of the "family" – in whatever concrete form – has evolved to deal with this task.

("a – historically variable – socio-culturally and politically constituted institution that produces social continuity and social integration").[29]
2. The second segment of the definition's meaning answers the question of how the institutionalized life course fulfills its societalization function, i.e. produces social integration and social continuity: "through the structural embedding and above all institutional preformation of age-related event and position configurations". Individuals and their life courses are embedded in a multitude of economic, political, social and cultural contexts, from whose totality and interaction a social-structural, above all institutional pre-programming of life courses results. This socio-structural pre-programming of life courses can easily be illustrated by the example of school as the – to take up a well-known, almost sixty-year-old formulation by Schelsky – "first and thus decisive, central point of setting the course" (1957, p. 17) for the occupational positioning, social security and life chances of individuals. The structure of the school system and its institutionalized regulations channel students into different school careers that lead to the acquisition of, for example, a Hauptschulabschluss or the Abitur. These school-leaving qualifications are in turn linked to different educational and labor market-related follow-up options (such as apprenticeships vs. university studies) and biographical options in general. In this respect, the institutional choices made in the school system direct individuals not only into certain school careers, but much more far-reaching: into predetermined "life course paths" with different occupational statuses, social risks and life chances in general. The second segment of meaning emphasizes this social-structural, especially institutional framing of life courses. Yet, the socio-structural embedding and preformation of life courses is not to be understood deterministically. To stay with the school example: those who were directed into a secondary school career do not necessarily end up in a vocational training course or in an unskilled job in the labor market or in unemployment; it is possible to change from secondary school to a post-secondary school and thus to expand the spectrum of follow-up options – but this is anything but unproblematic and easy.[30]

---

[29] The fact that this system of rules of the temporal dimension of life – like any other institution – is historically variable (institutional change) and socio-culturally and politically constituted needs no explanation.

[30] In Germany's tripartite school system, this institutional setting of the course, which implies serious consequences for the further course of life, already takes place after primary school or orientation stage (exception: integrated comprehensive school), i.e. comparatively early at the age of ten to twelve.

> - Give further examples of the social-structural, in particular institutional, shaping of life courses (a) within the education system as well as (b) in other areas of society (e.g. in relation to the occupational system or in companies).
> - Does the socio-structural pre-programming of life courses also extend to the area of family life?
> - From the point of view of institutional pre-programming of life courses, discuss the individual duration of studies (BA degree after six semesters or much later).

3. The third segment of the definition states what is embedded in the social structure and institutionally shaped: the "age-related event and position configurations in the various social fields". In terms of their "external" shape, life courses can be depicted as a stream of age-related events and positions that reflects an individual's social-structural localizations over a lifetime, which exist primarily in the form of "memberships in institutional orders" (Mayer and Diewald 2007, p. 515). This stream, i.e. the "external" trajectory of a life, is not an empirically random accumulation of events and positions in the process of individual aging. The age-related events and positions do not simply stand unconnected next to each other, but rather in a temporal and content-related context: they are interconnected as a result of their social-structural, in particular institutional, embedding, linked to configurations. This socio-structural embedding and framing of life courses defines age-related rights and obligations, events and transitions, roles and positions, and in this respect largely shapes the "external" course of life or group-specific life course structures (e.g. with regard to gender, milieu of origin or educational status). These configurations of events and positions can be limited to one area of life, but they can also cross the various social fields. For example, the typical educational path of academics (school enrolment at the age of six → transition to lower secondary school after four years of primary school → transition to upper secondary school after a further five or six years → Abitur after a total of twelve or thirteen years of school → subsequent start of university → acquisition of an academic degree after at least three or five years of study) is an illustrative example of an age-related configuration of events and positions within a social field. The pattern of "education → career entry or employment → marriage → starting a family", which was widespread in men's life courses until the 1970s, is an example of a cross-field configuration: in this sequence of events and positions, completion of vocational training first acts as a prerequisite for starting a career, and this successful transition to employment then in turn acts as the economic basis and prerequisite for marriage and subsequent starting a family.

In this context, another disciplinary remark is in order: since the age-related configuration of events and positions in life courses very often encompasses different social spheres, life course research is conceptually at odds with well-rehearsed research claims and "hyphenated sociologies" (such as the sociology of education, occupation or family).[31]

4. Finally, the life course as an institution also extends to the "inner" orientations of individuals, their biographical plans and life designs. This is – as has already been pointed out – not to be understood deterministically: the social-structural embedding and, in particular, institutional framing of life courses does not mean denying the moment of innovative subjectivity of the individual, his freedom of action and creativity.[32] The individual, however, does not think, make his biographical decisions and act in a completely subjective inner space that is sealed off from society. They do not plan their lives detached from socio-structural contexts and influences, quasi only out of themselves. Rather, the socio-structural, in particular institutional framing of life courses, as well as the resulting event and position configurations that become manifest as the "external" course of life, are present to the individuals who are certainly – perhaps not comprehensively, but to a large extent – conscious of them. They form a background foil on which the individual shapes his life plan and acts biographically. This would also briefly explain the last segment of the definition's meaning ("which also represents an orientation for the biographical actions of individuals").

---

[31] Occupational and employment histories, for example, can only be analyzed comprehensively if family and relationship contexts and dynamics are not ignored. In this respect, Moen and Han criticize the conceptual segmentation of sociology: "Scholars have been victims of the very social institutions they purport to study, using taken-for-granted classifications and definitions to frame the focus of their research (…): occupational and organizational sociologists (as well as economists) have charted work careers …; family sociologists have concentrated on 'family' careers" (2001, p. 425). In contrast, life course research stands for a conceptual "reframing of life paths, from a concentration of either work or family transitions and trajectories to considering work lives and family lives as lives in tandem" (Ibid.).

[32] Without such a moment, the structural preformation of life courses would indeed be deterministic – and social change would not be possible: the demographic metabolism would then be exhausted in the identical reproduction of existing social structures. This point touches on a fundamental problem for the social sciences: the question of human freedom of will and action within the framework of given social structures. This fundamental theoretical or philosophical question cannot be dealt with in detail here – those interested in the topic are referred to an essay by Beckermann (2012), which offers an overview of the various philosophical positions on the subject.

In the previous subchapter, it was pointed out that life course and biographical research, despite overlapping content, have developed and established themselves methodologically as well as institutionally rather in demarcation from one another. Conceptually, this has led to a situation in which life course research is often understood only as (quantitative) "external" life course research, i.e. in the sense of an analytical focus solely on the "external" configurations of events and positions in life courses. Such an understanding, which evacuates the analysis of individuals' "internal" biographical orientations into the sphere of responsibility of (qualitative) biographical research, was shaped in Germany primarily by the large-scale "German Life Course Study" (GLHS) conducted from the early 1980s to 2010 and works produced in its environment (Mayer 1990; Blossfeld and Huinink 2001). In contrast, the life course definition proposed here establishes an understanding of life course research according to which this field of research includes both the quantitative analysis of the "external" shape of individual life courses (course dimension) and the qualitative analysis of the "internal" life plans of individuals (biography dimension). The definition presented here stands against the conceptual narrowing of life course research to "external" life course research, which is widespread – especially in Germany. Theoretically, a conception of the research field in terms of mere "external" life course research is to be criticized as reductionist, because the life course as an institution: as a system of rules for the temporal dimension of life refers not only to the "external" sequences of events and positions, but also to the biographical structuring of a life (Schmeiser 2006). And from a methodological point of view, it is to be criticized that ignoring the biographical dimension – as leading representatives of the life course approach themselves concede – "can lead to false causal attributions" (Blossfeld and Huinink 2001, p. 24; Mayer 2002, p. 53).[33]

Why the division of life course research into (quantitative) "external" life course research and (qualitative) "internal" biographical research, which is particularly common in Germany, is wrong, becomes clear in the explanations on the life course

---

[33] To illustrate this with the example given by Blossfeld and Huinink themselves: "An unmarried couple could, for example, first decide to marry and then decide to have a child. The woman could then become pregnant and, before the birth of the desired child, the couple could marry. In this case, as part of quantitative life course analyses, we would observe the pregnancy event prior to the marriage event and, on this basis, calculate the probability that the onset of pregnancy increases the marriage event. In fact, however, the marriage decision was made before the pregnancy event occurred, so there is no causal relationship between the pregnancy event and the marriage event. The analysis would lead to erroneous conclusions" (2001, p. 24).

as an institution (see Chap. 3). In order to clarify the theoretical conception of the research field, the central role of the factor "time" in life course research should be briefly discussed here.

2.2.2 "Time Matters!"

The previous section presented a substantial definition of the sociological term "life course" and a theoretical conception of the sociological field of "life course research" based on it. The research logic of life course research is based on the basic theoretical assumption that individual life courses and social structures, especially institutional structures, are closely and inseparably intertwined. In examining this reciprocal interweaving of individual life courses and societal structural contexts, two opposing directions of causality can be distinguished analytically: one analytical perspective is concerned with the effects of societal structural contexts on the biographies and life courses of individuals; the other analytical perspective illuminates the effects of changing life courses on the socio-structural conditions and institutional regulations of a society.

The vast majority of empirical life course research follows the first analysis perspective and deals with the effects of socio-structural framework conditions and institutional regulations on life courses. Studies on the effect of the duration of parental leave on re-entry into the labor market or on the effects of different economic situations on the transition into the employment system or on the consequences of belonging to low or high birth rate cohorts for professional careers or on the influence of the level of state transfer payments to private households on the life planning of the respective persons are examples of this perspective. Much less frequently, empirical studies pursue the opposite perspective of analysis and examine the effects of changing life courses and biographies on social structural contexts and institutional regulations. Examples of this perspective include studies on the consequences for the institution of "family" and "marriage" of a changed lifestyle in the wake of the sexual revolution since the 1960s, or on the consequences of the increased age of women at first birth from an average of 24 years in 1970 to 31 years today for the demographic structure of German society.

> - Formulate further examples or questions for the two directions of analysis.
> - Consider and discuss why empirical life course research seldom deals with the repercussions of changed biographies and life courses on sociostructural contexts or why its predominant analytical perspective is directed towards the influence of societal structural contexts on the life courses of individuals.

With its basic theoretical assumption of the mutual interweaving of individual life courses and social structures, life course research takes up a problem that has accompanied sociology since its beginnings: the question of the relationship between structure and action.[34] In this context, the mutual constitutional relationship between action and structure is split into single-track relationships by the two analytically distinguishable opposing directions of causality, so that either the structural aspect (structure → agency) or the moment of action (agency → structure) is prioritized in the analysis. However, it is crucial that the basic assumption of life course research theoretically postulates an inseparable entanglement of individual life courses and social structures, i.e. a reciprocal constitutional relationship. Against a determination of action by structures or a reduction of structure to action, it emphasizes the complex structure-agency interplay, which must be concretely investigated in each case as an empirically principally open question.[35]

It is characteristic of life course research that it examines the complex structure-agency relationship from a dynamic, time-sensitive analytical perspective. "Time matters" – this programmatic title of a collection of essays by Abbott (2001), which is addressed both as a statement and as a conceptual challenge to sociology in general, also and especially applies to the field of life course research. For, like few other sociological concepts, the life course concept refers directly to the dimension of time: after all, the very notion of "life course" is, by its inherent reference to the process of individual aging, a time-related, explicitly processual concept. According to Wingens and Reiter, it is the "systematic consideration of 'time' – to be precise: the conceptual integration of the time-dimension into the structure-agency interplay – which makes the particular theoretical quality of the sociological life course

---

[34] The ongoing debates on this structure-agency problem in the sociological theory discussion (and the connection of this ontological question with the methodological micro-macro problem) cannot be further discussed here.

[35] In such empirical studies, the two directions of causality are then – obviously on theoretical grounds – given different and alternating weightings.

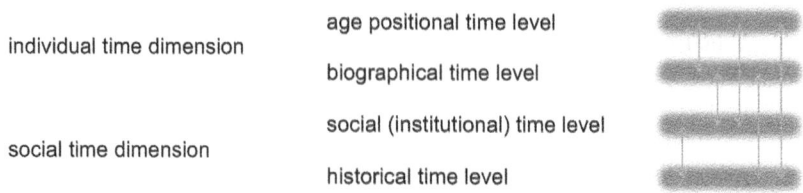

Fig. 2.3 The "time" dimension in life course research. (Source: Own representation)

approach" (2011, p. 189).[36] This time-sensitive, dynamic perspective represents an essential moment of life course research. In this respect, its basic idea can be summarized in one simple sentence: it is about relating the dynamics of social structures to the dynamics of life courses and analyzing their interactions. The moment of time and temporality, which is essential for life course research and its dynamic analysis perspective, has not yet been explicitly addressed in the previous section. In the following, therefore, the relevance of the dimension of "time" for this field of research will be briefly outlined, concluding the remarks on the theoretical definition of life course research.

Analytically, four socially constituted time levels (in two time dimensions) can be distinguished, which take account of the moment of time and temporality both with regard to individual life courses and with regard to social structural contexts (Fig. 2.3). In the individual time dimension, an age-positional and a biographical time level can be distinguished, and in the societal time dimension, a social (institutional) and a historical time level. In the reality of life, these four time levels interpenetrate each other and are intertwined. This empirical interweaving of the age-positional, biographical, social (institutional) and historical time levels must be taken into account theoretically and methodologically by life course research.[37]

---

[36] Accordingly, their essay is entitled "The life course approach – it's about time!"; similarly programmatic titles can also be found, for example, in Alwin (1995) or Hendricks (2001).

[37] Of course, individual and social life is also influenced by a natural time dimension (e.g. by day-night changes or the human biological "internal clock"; the best-known example of the relevance of the human biorhythm is the discussion that has been going on for years about the start of school or the chronobiologically based demand for a later start of lessons). Although the natural time dimension, especially chronobiology, also has sociologically relevant implications (see the highly readable introductions by Zulley and Knab 2003 and Roenneberg 2010), sociological life course research is less interested in this natural time dimension than in socially constituted time levels.

At the age-positional time level, the focus is on the age-related event and position configurations that individuals experience and adopt in the course of their lives in the various social fields. Of particular importance for the analysis of these "external" life course configurations are their temporal internal structures, i.e. questions about the time of occurrence of events, the duration of stay in positions, the sequence of position changes and the dynamics of such status transitions. The biographical time level is concerned with an individual's "inner" life-historical experience to date, his further life plans and his current biographical actions, i.e. the concrete way in which he is currently shaping his life. In this context, an individual's life history and life plans (past and future reference) are relevant above all with regard to his current biographical action (present reference), because "reality exists in a present" (Mead 1932, p. 1).[38] Even if the present has a primacy of meaning in principle, the question of how the present, past and future relate to each other biographically remains an empirically open one (whereby age is likely to be an important determinant). At the social (institutional) level of time, it is a question of the structurally and politically anchored concepts of time in society with regard to the course of life. The social-structural embedding and institutional framing of life courses implies their time-structural preformation. In this respect, one can speak of normative "social clocks" that define time- and age-related events, positions, roles and status transitions in the life course. The life courses of individuals can – both in terms of their course and their biographical timing – correspond to these socially prescribed points in time and time periods or deviate from them, i.e. be on-time or off-time – which is then sanctioned positively or negatively accordingly. The two individual levels of time can therefore (and usually do – to varying degrees) stand in tension with the time and process structural specifications of the social (institutional) level of time. At the same time, however, the time-structural norms of the "social clocks" are also a relieving frame of reference for biographical life plans and the individual life course. Finally, the historical time level is concerned with social-historical epochs. The historical circumstances and events that make up different epochs shape the life courses of individuals as well as their biographical plans in a specific way (whereby age in turn functions as a moderator variable).

---

[38] According to Mead, past and future have meaning, indeed exist, only in relation to a present that is event-related, i.e. emergent as well as ephemeral (Flaherty and Fine 2001).

> - The characterization of the four time levels to be considered by life course research is deliberately kept general: formulate concrete examples that can be used to illustrate the life course relevance of the age-positional, the biographical, the social (institutional) and the historical time levels respectively.
> - Then discuss – also with the help of concrete examples – the interrelationships of the time levels shown in Fig. 2.3 in terms of their significance for life courses.

In relation to the four levels of time relevant to the life course, "time" is not to be understood in the usual sense of the monotonously constant passage of time, as represented by the tick-tock of a clock – rather, it is about "time" in the form of different and varying time structures. The fact that time does not always run uniformly, that there are different kinds of time structures, is familiar to everyone with regard to the biographical level of time: probably everyone has already had the experience in life that time sometimes flows slowly and almost does not want to pass, while at other times it flies by in a flash and runs away. At the age-positional time level, there are both eventful life course phases associated with various positions and status changes and, in terms of the "external" course shape, uneventful times (e.g. transition to and early adulthood phase vs. older age). On the social (institutional) time level, there is a multitude of different and varying temporal (pre-)structuring of the life course, which results from the institutional structure and the organizations of a society. With regard to the historical time level, there are phases of slow, barely perceptible social change, evolutionary standstill, so to speak, on the one hand, and phases of revolutionary upheaval, i.e. dynamic or even abrupt social change, on the other.

> Give concrete examples of different and varying time structures on the social (institutional) time level, i.e. of institutionally or organizationally determined (pre-)structuring of the life course.

To conclude the remarks on the relevance of the time dimension for life course research, it should be pointed out that time-structural incongruities result from the different and varying time structures in and between the four life course-relevant time levels, since these are interwoven in the empirical reality of life. Such asynchronies present themselves in the actor's perspective as a synchronization problem with which the individual is confronted and which he has to "solve". Life course research is primarily interested here in the asynchronies or synchronization problems between the social and the individual time dimension.[39] An illustrative example of this is the much-discussed problem of reconciling family and work, which arises as a result of the time-structural incongruities between the time constraints or requirements of the institution of gainful employment, of the company in which one is employed, of the occupation and professional position that one holds or has to fulfill, of the day-care center that looks after one's child, of the offices that one sometimes has to visit, of the institution of the family, of a partnership, of the needs of one's child, of one's own needs and biographical plans, etc. – in other words, as a consequence of time-structural asynchronies that – a paradoxical task, so to speak – the individual must somehow synchronize.

> This attempt at synchronization was described in a ZEIT article (6/2014) under the heading "Geht alles gar nicht" ("It's all impossible") as follows: "So we work out a plan with our partners, synchronize our diaries, every half hour for the week. Who will look after the children and when? Who's taking them to the friend's birthday party? Who will drive them to the tournament on the weekend? Here we squeeze in another hour of sports, on Thursdays she goes to choir, you have to be there at seven! The family becomes a carpool, couples become partners in the logistics business."

---

[39] Of course, synchronization problems also exist within the individual time dimension: for example, if someone has not yet reached a certain professional position in the company, although according to his professional biographical planning and assessment this would be long overdue and deserved. Or vice versa: someone considers himself not yet "mature" enough to really be able to fill the professional and social position to which he has been promoted – the new position comes too early in relation to the professional biographical planning of the promoted person himself.

- Discuss whether this really "all doesn't work at all" or whether there are successful synchronization strategies – and if so: which ones.
- A couple (both 30, married for two years, both graduated from high school and subsequently trained as bank clerks, both employed since then, both in a comparable professional position with good career prospects) has a child. Play out the synchronization problem of reconciling family and career for this couple:
  - What time-structural constraints and options do they have to deal with after the birth of the child?
  - The career and life histories of the two are largely the same until the birth of the child. Use your sociological imagination to further develop the (probable) career and life trajectories for both of them after the birth of the child. Discuss the circumstances that set the course for their respective further careers and lives: why are they decisive? What options do the two actors have with regard to these trend-setting moments?
- Formulate further concrete synchronization problems that result for the individual from asynchronies between the social and individual time dimensions, i.e. from the time-structural incongruities of the historical or social (institutional) time level on the one hand and the age-positional and biographical time level on the other.

The Life Course as an Institution 3

Life courses were and are always influenced and structured by the specific sociocultural formation in which people live. The sociological concept of the life course developed in this book does not, however, conceive of the life course as a universal historical phenomenon. The conceptual definition developed in the previous chapter fundamentally describes and conceives of the life course as a social institution: as an independent system of rules for the temporal dimension of life (temporal mode of socialization). However, the life course was only formed into an independent system of rules that regulates the temporal dimension of life – both with regard to its "external" course and with regard to the "internal" biographical perspectives and decisions of individuals – in the course of the social structural change of the last two hundred and fifty years. The "institutionalization of the life course may be regarded as a concomitant of the rationalized and individualized society" (Buchmann 1989a, p. 18). The life course as an institution for the production of social continuity and social integration is a product of social modernity.[1]

The understanding of the life course as a social institution was decisively developed by Kohli. In his fundamental essay "The Institutionalization of the Life Course" (1985),[2] he outlines how, in the context of the structural transformation of the pre-industrial way of life of the eighteenth century into the life course regime of modern industrial society, the life course emerged as an independent system of

---

[1] This statement and the following remarks refer geographically to social modernization processes in (parts of) Europe and North America.

[2] Kohli developed and elaborated his conception of the life course as an institution in a whole series of essays (e.g. 1978b, 1983, 1986a, 1986b, 1988).

rules for the temporal dimension of life, i.e. as an institution. Kohli's talk of the institutionalization of the life course refers not only to this very process, but uno actu also means its result: the institutionalized life course or the life course as an institution.

3.1 The Institutionalization of the Life Course

That transformation of the way of life, which Kohli[3] outlines in terms of structural history, can be characterized quite generally as a "transition from a pattern of randomness of life events to one of a predictable life course" (ibid., p. 4 f.). An important moment of this structural change of the way of life and at the same time a condition of its possibility was a demographic development affecting life span. In order for the institutionalization of the life course to get underway at all and for a predictable, i.e. institutionalized life course to emerge, there had to be – as Imhof vividly titles it – a demographic change "from an uncertain to a secure life course" (1988). What is meant by this is that people are no longer overtaken by death at any age, but normally die at an older age. This transition from a random death pattern, in which the times of death are widely scattered over the (biologically possible) human lifespan, to the normal case of dying at an older age is shown in the following two figures. First, the change in life expectancy at birth in Germany since 1871 is shown (Fig. 3.1). While representative data from the Imperial or Federal Statistical Office are available for this period, life expectancy for the period before the foundation of the German Empire can only be estimated on the basis of individual regional studies. According to Imhof's data from a region in northern Hesse, life expectancy from the beginning of the seventeenth century to the end of the nineteenth century was between 25 and 35 years (1984a, p. 178 ff.).

As the figure shows, life expectancy has more than doubled since the foundation of the German Empire (from over 35 and 38 years for men and women respectively to – according to the model calculation of the Federal Statistical Office – a good 78 and 83 years). The figure only shows an average life expectancy of at least 65 years for those born since the middle of the twentieth century. The low average life

---

[3] The various historical findings that Kohli uses to illustrate this structural change do not need to be repeated here; what is important here is merely the direction in which it has developed. Incidentally, this also applied to Kohli's now classic essay, which was not intended to provide a detailed historical tracing of structural change and an analysis of its causal factors, but rather to show the "contrast between before and after and thus the direction of structural change" (1985, p. 3).

3.1 The Institutionalization of the Life Course

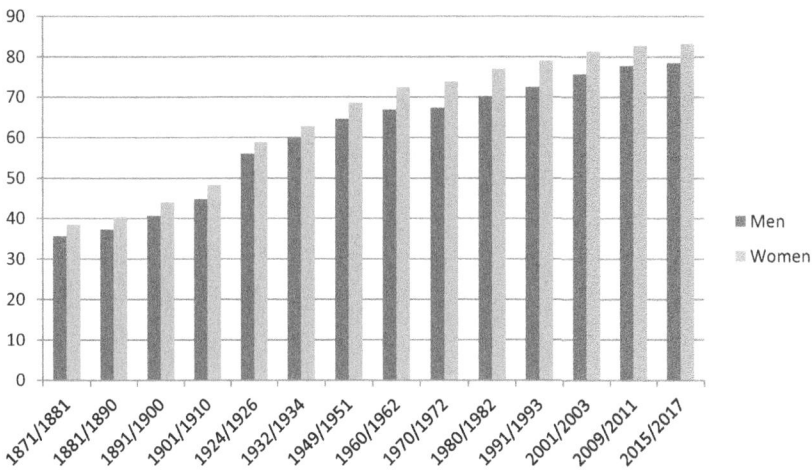

Presentation based on: Federal Statistical Office (2018): Life expectancy of men and women at birth in Germany from 1871 to 2017 (in years). Statista. Statista Ltd. Accessed 11 October 2019. https://de.statista.com/statistik/daten/studie/185394/umfrage/entwicklung-der-lebenserwartung-nach-geschlecht/

Fig. 3.1 Average life expectancy. (Germany, 1871–2017)

expectancy, historically the normal case until the twentieth century, resulted above all from the high infant and child mortality rate: as late as the beginning of the 1870s, about a quarter of all live births died before the end of a year, at the beginning of the twentieth century it was about a fifth; by the beginning of the 1930s it had been possible to reduce infant mortality to below 10%; today the corresponding figure is only 0.3%.[4] As the life-staircase depictions in the first chapter, made in the mid-sixteenth century, show, it was possible for people to live to a ripe old age in earlier centuries – as long as they survived the childhood and youth phases. At the same time, however, Death, enthroned above the staircase of life in both woodcuts, makes it clear that he is to be reckoned with at all times: in one depiction, he throws a whole bundle of arrows over all ages, without taking aim; in the other woodcut, significantly, he aims his bow in the direction of the younger ages. This is a striking expression of the random pattern of death that was widespread until the twentieth century. Even more clearly than Fig. 3.1 on the continuous

---

[4] Source: Federal Institute for Population Research: Infant Mortality in Germany, 1872 to 2016 (BIB 2018). Accessed October 11, 2019. https://www.bib.bund.de/DE/Fakten/Fakt/S10-Saeuglingssterblichkeit-ab-1872.html/

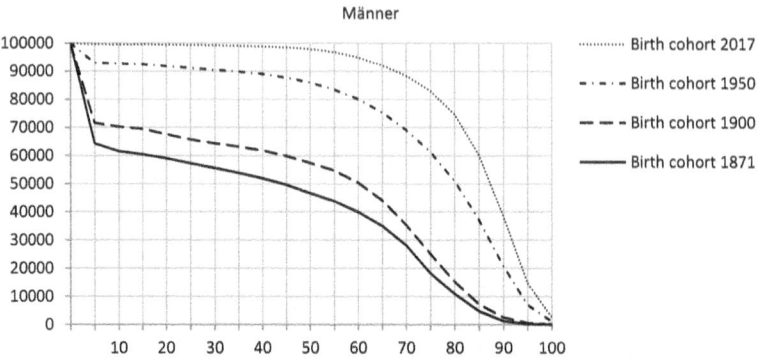

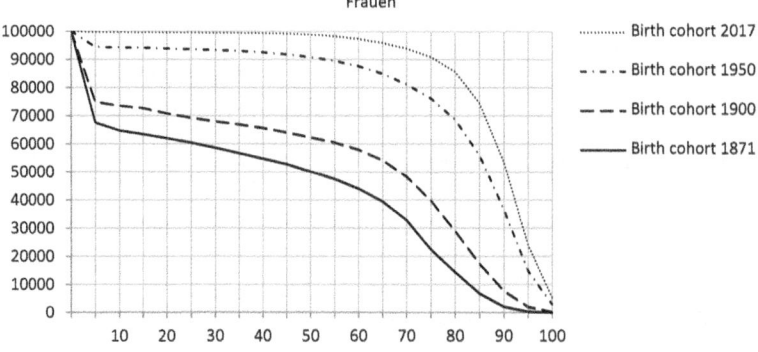

Fig. 3.2 Rectangularization of the survival curve. (Germany, 1871–2017)

increase in life expectancy, the next figure shows the transition from this random death pattern to a death pattern in which deaths are concentrated at higher ages (Fig. 3.2).

The pronounced infant and child mortality among the older birth cohorts is clearly visible: a good third of the 1871 birth cohort and more than a quarter of the 1900 birth cohort did not even reach today's school enrolment age. At the age of less than 45 and 50, respectively, the oldest male and female cohorts were already halved; only a good third of the men and just under two-fifths of the women in this cohort lived to the age of 65 or older. In contrast, infant and child mortality in the youngest cohort no longer plays a statistical role. According to the model calculations of the Federal Statistical Office, this birth cohort 2017 will not have shrunk by half until it is over 87 years old (men) or almost 91 years old (women); over 92% of the men and over 95% of the women in this cohort will be over 65. Since the foundation of the empire, the survival curve has continuously changed in such a way that it increasingly takes on the form of a right angle (rectangulation), i.e. deaths have become increasingly concentrated in the older age groups. As long as the pattern of deaths was random, i.e. people died at very different ages, it was impossible for a socially and individually expectable life course to emerge.[5] Only the demographic transition to a "safe" lifetime, to the normal case of a long life, made the institutionalization of the life course possible.

Now, the general characterization of the structural change of life as a transition from the event pattern of randomness to an expectable, institutionalized life course does not only refer to the age at death. Not only the lifespan, but rather all possible life events have become temporally "predictable" in the course of the past two and a half centuries. This is exemplified here by the standardization of the age of first marriage. Imhof's data on marriages in a Hessian village from the late seventeenth century to the end of the nineteenth century show that the average age of men and women at first marriage has hardly changed (men: 25.8 and 25.4 years, respectively; women: 24.1 and 24.3 years, respectively). However, the almost identical average values conceal the fact that marriage has undergone a substantial change in time structure during these two hundred years. At the end of the seventeenth century, the age at marriage was still widely spread (from 16 years to over 40 years) and considerable age differences between spouses were not uncommon (mind you: even for first marriages). In the course of time, first marriages became increasingly concentrated in a narrower and narrower age range, until "finally ... towards the end of the 19th century, a focal point-like condensation around a mean value became apparent. Individual age at marriage and 'average age at marriage' begin to coincide more and more" (1984b, p. 57). Age differences between married couples were also increasingly leveled out and eventually reduced to a narrow age band of only a few years. By 1900, in fact, unlike in the 1700s, marriages were normally contracted at the average age of about mid-20s mentioned above. In the course of these two hundred years, therefore, an enormous temporal standardization and norming of marriage took place.

---

[5] "Representative life histories have existed only since we all reached a fairly equal and advanced age, which has not been the case for very many generations. Before that, one died as an infant, another as an old man, the third sometime in between; one mother died in her first childbed, another long after she had buried all her own children" (Imhof 1984b, p. 17).

> - "At the time of the 'unequal couples' it would have been unwise" – according to Imhof – "if mutual physical attraction had been made the foundation of a marriage. The flash in the pan of physical love could have been over all too quickly. (...) In today's partnership relationships, on the other hand, we may ascribe a greater role to sex appeal, for today similarly old, or rather young, bodies stand opposite each other for many years. The intimacy of marriage and the family, their increasing affectivity in the course of modern times, seem to me to be closely connected with this standardization of marriage ages ..." (1984a, p. 184). Discuss Imhof's conjecture.
> - Imhof draws the conclusion from the fact that only today "individual and average life data are almost identical" (1984b, p. 56) that "today, whether we like it or not, we are all much more 'average' than our ancestors ever were" (ibid.) or that "every life course was more unique, more distinctive, more colorful then than it is today" (ibid., p. 18). What do you think about this?

The temporal standardization illustrated by the example of the age of death and marriage can be observed for all possible life events within the framework of the social structural change of the past two hundred and fifty years. Life courses became increasingly predictable: a socially and individually expectable "normal life course" emerged. This institutionalized ("normal") life course was "driven by the newly emerging age-stratified systems of public rights and duties ... By introducing criteria linked to chronological age, they constitute binding age boundaries. In the course of historical development, the central benefit systems (schooling and old-age security systems) have proliferated, leading to a homogenization of life courses" (Kohli 1985, p. 8). Kohli's quote addresses two aspects: chronologization and the central structuring factors of the life course. The latter are the education and pension system as well as the employment system (not mentioned in the quotation, but to be considered as an implicit reference), which is preceded and followed by the aforementioned benefit systems. These three central structuring factors result in the three-part basic structure of the life course. The institutionalized tripartite structure of the life course will be dealt with in detail in a separate sub-chapter (see Sect. 5.1); here we are concerned with the aspect of the chronologization of the life course.

3.1 The Institutionalization of the Life Course

The Civil Code, enacted by Napoleon Bonaparte in 1804,[6] was the first to establish a differentiated structure of chronological ages under civil law, which was also applied in other areas of law (e.g. the age of majority was set at 21 or the age of marriage at at least 18 for men and 15 for women). Today, such legally constituted age boundaries, i.e. legally anchored age-related entitlements and obligations, exist for all areas of society and life (e.g. active or passive voting rights, driving licenses, civil service employment, school enrolment, retirement, age of criminal responsibility, juvenile criminal law, child benefit, educational assistance benefits, admission and fare reductions, etc.). Particularly relevant for the institutionalization of the life course were – as already mentioned – the introduction of the school system and the old-age security system. In Germany, there was no uniform regulation before the introduction of compulsory schooling in the German Empire in 1871. An important milestone, however, was the compulsory schooling of 5–12 year-olds in Prussia in 1717, which initially met with manifold resistance and refusal. Only after the foundation of the German Empire did (almost) all children actually attend school.[7] Today, compulsory schooling generally begins at the age of six and lasts for at least twelve years (of which nine or ten years are full-time compulsory schooling in primary and lower secondary education),[8] i.e. compulsory schooling extends until the child reaches the age of majority. The school or education system as a whole today is age-oriented in many ways, above all through the year groups and the specified time periods or transition rules for the various stages of education. For example, one usually acquires the "Abitur" at around 18 or completes a BA degree at almost 26. The introduction of compulsory schooling and the further expansion of the school and education system constituted – and this is what we are concerned with here – a new phase of life oriented towards chronological age, which for most people did not exist before.

In 1889, workers' pension insurance was introduced in the German Empire – as the first public old-age pension system. Before the introduction of this old-age security system, people worked as long as they could (and mostly died shortly after-

---

[6] The Code Civil (also: Code Napoleon) forms the first of Napoleon's five codes and is one of the great works of law in legal history: it represents the first comprehensive and uniform regulation of civil law.

[7] In 1816, only a good half of school-age children in Prussia attended elementary school; by the middle of the nineteenth century, this figure had risen to about four-fifths, and in 1871 the proportion was 86.3% – it was not until "the 1880s that school attendance by all school-age children was enforced despite child labor" (Schmeiser 2006, p. 59).

[8] Those who do not attend a general or vocational school in full-time form thereafter in the upper secondary level are subject to compulsory vocational schooling, which as a rule comprises three part-time school years.

wards). The retirement age at the time was 70, which, given the life expectancy at the time, meant that only about a fifth of workers were even eligible for pensions. However, the establishment of statutory pension insurance – comparable to the introduction of compulsory education – laid the foundation for the emergence of a distinct new phase of life: retirement. In the meantime, not only is the vast majority of the population actually entering this phase of life; the retirement phase today also encompasses a considerable period of life – the average pension drawdown period today is almost 20 years.[9] The introduction of statutory pension insurance based on chronological age thus constituted a new phase of life and thus standardized people's life courses. Whereas previously, for example, there was no specific age at which the farm was normally handed over to the son and the retreat to the old age home took place, the statutory retirement age imposes a temporal standardization of the withdrawal from working life. Since the introduction of the statutory pension insurance, the state has taken over more and more social security functions and – especially in the course of a massive welfare state expansion between the early 1950s and the mid-1970s – has woven a tightly meshed social policy net encompassing all areas of life. Today, "there are almost no transitions in the life course that are not framed in some way by social policy" (Behrens and Voges 1996, p. 18). These welfare state frameworks and regulations are often age-oriented, i.e. they link entitlements and obligations to age (such as compulsory schooling and pension entitlement) and thus promote a chronological standardization of the occurrence of life events.

A chronological standardization of the life course presupposes that the chronological age of people is known to society or state institutions as well as to the individuals themselves – which is by no means a matter of course. The Tuareg, for example, do not count years of life; when asked about his age, a Tuareg – Spittler vividly points out – would initially reply that he "did not know. If you insist as a European and ask the man approximately how old he is, he might say 30 years. If you note this incredulously and tell him he must be older, he suggests 100 years to satisfy the European. If you estimate him to be 70 years old and give him that figure, he readily accepts it and will repeat that age of 70 years in subsequent years if another European asks him about it" (1990, p. 108). The chronological age has no relevance for the Tuareg – who can of course count -; decisive for the assignment of an individual to

---

[9] The fact that today the majority of the population enjoys retirement is due firstly to the significant increase in life expectancy and secondly to the inclusion of further population groups (e.g. salaried employees in 1911) in the pension system or the other (compulsory) standard systems of old-age provision (e.g. civil servants' pensions or social insurance for artists). The employment rate of those employed in Germany today beyond the age of 65 who are subject to social security contributions is just over 5% (Microcensus 2013; own calculation).

3.1 The Institutionalization of the Life Course

an age or better: life stage is rather his biological state of maturity. Until the nineteenth century, large parts of the European population did not know their own age exactly. Thus, the ages given in official documents of the time are mostly estimates, which, especially at the beginning of the modern era, were often rounded off to ten or five years (i.e. one was 30 or 40, perhaps 35, but not 33 or 39 years old). Societies in Europe and the West were also, until about the middle of the nineteenth century, "not a place where age played a vital part in people's everyday lives and associations. The ... institutions were not structured according to age-defined divisions, and ... cultural norms did not strongly prescribe age-related behavior" (Chudacoff 1989, p. 10). The general knowledge of chronological age is thus – like the reference to exact chronological year dates in general – the result of a protracted process extending into the nineteenth century. Only since then has chronological age become a generally known individual and socially relevant structural characteristic.

At the beginning of this chapter it was said that life courses are always structured by the socio-cultural formation in which people live. Our modern structuring of life courses is temporally oriented to chronological age. However, the temporal structuring of life courses can certainly take place without reference to age, as the following example shows, in which a Tuareg born in 1905 at the age of 81 describes his life course: "The first thing I did was goat herding. We are there, we are there, we are there, then I gave up goat herding and entered the garden. I gave up the garden and started the madrasa. I left the madrasa and returned to the gardens. During that time I wore my first trousers, ... I had my years for that. I was there, I was there, I was there until I begat my children (...) I left the garden, we went on caravan, we went on caravan, we went on caravan, we went on caravan, we went on caravan, we went on caravan. The last few years, as the children grew up, I left them to their own devices. I returned to herding goats. Here I am now in the bush" (Spittler 1990, p. 116 f.).

- What definable phases of life are discernible in the narrative? What gives this Tuareg life story its temporal structure?
- How and by what does the Tuareg life course structure differ from that in modern Western industrial societies? How from that in pre-industrial Europe?
- Assign the chronological age of the narrator you assume to each of the distinguishable phases of life and compare these ages with the actual respective age of the narrator – which can be reconstructed from Spittler's essay.

The institutionalization of the life course has so far been presented as an increasing chronological standardization of the occurrence of life events, i.e. with a view to the "external" life course. However, the life course as a system of rules for the temporal dimension of life refers not only to the "external" sequences of events and positions, but – according to the definition of the life course in the previous chapter – also to the biographical perspectives of individuals. The "life course as an institution means … on the one hand, the regulation of the sequential course of life, and on the other, the structuring of the lifeworld horizons or bodies of knowledge within which individuals orient themselves and plan their actions" (Kohli 1985, p. 3). The institutionalization of the life course in the latter sense is only hinted at in Kohli's seminal essay.[10] Empirical findings in this regard were provided twenty years later by Schmeiser (2006) in his complementary structural history of the individual's biographical interpretation and action perspective. He vividly describes the change and structuring of the biographical perspective, of the interpretation and conceptualization of one's lifetime by the individual himself, which has taken place in social modernity, as the "inner" institutionalization of the life course. This "inner" institutionalization is exemplified here by the transformation and structuring of the biographical orientation of the student body in the wake of the establishment of the year-class system.

As Ariès (1975, p. 285 ff.) shows using the example of higher educational institutions in France, instructional differentiation historically took place initially only with regard to the level of knowledge of the pupils: they were taught together spatially, but were grouped according to their respective level of knowledge, the composition of which varied according to the subject taught, and then group specifically addressed. Since this classification of pupils was based on varying levels of knowledge and development depending on the subject, the respective groups were not age-homogeneous. Until the eighteenth century, there was an "indiscriminate mixing of students and grammar school pupils, of immature children and young men in the same classes" (ibid., p. 328). It was not until the beginning of the nineteenth century that the link between age and class level, which is taken for granted today, had become established. In Germany, the replacement of the subject class system first took place at the Gymnasien, where the year class system had already been established in the 1830s (Schmeiser 2006, p. 59). The elementary schools, which were attended by more than 90% of the pupils at that time, introduced year classes much later: in urban elementary schools the changeover had largely taken place by 1920, in some rural areas it lasted until the 1960s (ibid., p. 61 f.). With the

---

[10] Kohli blamed this on a sparse body of research and pointed to the need for independent analyses of relevant biography-related phenomena (1985, p. 10 ff).

3.1 The Institutionalization of the Life Course

extensive spread of year groups at the end of the nineteenth century, "genuinely pedagogical tests such as annual and half-year reports and promotion decisions" (ibid., p. 63) came into being.[11] What does this have to do with structuring the biographical orientation of pupils?

This can be easily illustrated in contrast to the conception of time and development of the already mentioned Tuareg, for whom not the chronological age but the biological maturity of an individual is important. For if one "does not start from an abstract annual count ... then it makes no sense to speak of precocious or retarded. One can perhaps state that one grows quickly and the other slowly, but the yardstick for too-early or too-late is missing" (Spittler 1990, p. 108).[12] In contrast, the school year-class system automatically links learning goals to the chronological age of the students. Thus, for each year group, there are scholastic, i.e., societal, ideas about age-appropriate levels of subject knowledge and intellectual development in general, the attainment or failure of which is documented in report cards that determine whether a student advances or falls behind in school. On an annual basis, students are subjected to assessments that generally classify their knowledge and intellectual levels as age-appropriate or underdeveloped (or even: advanced). However, when schooling is organized as an annual sequence of developmental stages and advancement to a higher (grade) level is contingent upon successful completion of the previous (grade) level, students inevitably perceive their (school) lives from the (time-)biographical perspective of coming along, falling behind, or getting ahead. The comprehensive establishment of year classes leads to "collective biographical socialization into the logic of a career" (Schmeiser 2006, p. 53). The system of year classes with career-relevant certificates functions as a kind of

---

[11] The "elementary school or dismissal certificates that can be traced in Germany from 1825 onwards were police rather than educational test certificates, since the school supervisory authorities used the dismissal certificates to monitor the fulfilment of compulsory education" (Schmeiser 2006, p. 63).

[12] How (fast/slow) an individual develops "depends on many influences. Once on the individual peculiarity of people. 'People are not alike' is a standard answer when one asks about differences. The natural diversity of people ... is accepted as a matter of course and gives no cause for alarm. But the process of maturation also depends on external influences. Early work makes people mature faster, but under certain circumstances it also makes them age earlier. Times of famine in the wake of droughts and wars make man and animal grow slower than in normal times. This too is met with serenity. There are fast and slow times, but slow does not mean too slow. (...) Today, not only the state administration but also other Western-influenced institutions are pushing for the date of birth to be recorded in writing, such as medical development services. They ... are oriented towards an abstract scheme of development. It irritates them that they often cannot tell whether a child is malnourished or not, because they cannot judge that without precise age information" (Spittler 1990, p. 109).

"hidden curriculum": in addition to subject matter, the student "learns" above all to understand his or her (school) life from the perspective of "career".[13] The internalized logic of career functions as a behaviorally relevant biographical orientation framework.

> According to Luhmann, "career" is the universal form of life in modernity. Careers emerge "as a social inevitability" (1989, p. 232) in the wake of the transition from stratificational to functional differentiation: "To the extent that social-structural determinations of life courses are regressed, that is, reduced to conditions for careers, careers become a universal form of life" (ibid., p. 235). Under conditions of stratificational differentiation, a person's life course is still largely determined by his or her social-structural position qua birth. In the functionally differentiated society of modernity, on the other hand, life courses are formed as a sequence of events, "each of which combines (but with a different distribution of weight) self-selection and selection by others" (ibid., p. 232; Luhmann formulates here in his terminology the basic assumption of life course research mentioned in the previous chapter, according to which life courses represent the result of a complex *structure-agency interplay* over time, the causalities of which are to be analyzed empirically in each case). Accordingly, careers or life courses are structurally completely contingent: "All career events are contingent selections of further selections. From each event, the prehistory becomes the necessary precondition, the subsequent future the consequence" (ibid., p. 233 f.). From the point of view of individuals who are not unburdened of taking action in the reality of their lives, this makes careers highly uncertain. Now uncertainty "is always ever-present uncertainty. It accentuates the importance of the present; and all the more so because the present … becomes relevant in the career context as a past of the present future. One might miss something that cannot be made up later. One might have omitted to prepare for an opportunity that happens to occur. As a result, one tends to overestimate the relevance of one's beginnings, especially one's educations (or, to choose another example, one's efforts to strengthen the health of one's still healthy body). One tries to

---

[13] For their practice in and through the educational system in general, see. Luhmann and Schorr 1979, pp. 233 ff. (esp. 277–283).

gain time-binding effects from the present, especially in view of the high uncertainty, i.e. to capitalize on time. There are hardly any objective limits to meaningful effort: One can never exclude the possibility that more or different preparation will ultimately tip the balance" (Luhmann 1989, p. 234 f.).

- Discuss Luhmann's considerations. How do you solve the problem that there are "no objective limits to meaningful effort"? Do you agree with the statement that the relevance of training is overestimated? How do you generally see the relationship between one's own performance and preparatory effort (i.e.: self-selection/agency) on the one hand and the resulting opportunities, luck and favorable or adverse circumstances (i.e.: external selection/structure on the other?)

Kohli's concept of the institutionalization of the life course refers – to briefly summarize what has been said so far – to a process of the formation of a chronologically standardized "normal life course" in the sense of normally given, expectable event and position sequences and configurations that are anchored in the social structure and, in particular, institutionally pre-programmed ("external" institutionalization). This standard life course, as a life-time process model, represents a culturally provided scheme to which individuals orient their biographical planning and life plans ("inner" institutionalization). The institutionalization of the life course is thus – according to Weymann in reverse order – "a contribution to the production of biography and identity and ... at the same time a contribution to the constitution of social structures" (1989a, p. 1). The institutionalized life course represents a system of rules for the temporal dimension of life, i.e. it has a socializing function. As a temporal mode of socialization, it compensates for and supplements the reduced integration capacity of the categorical mode of socialization, which is based on a traditional and stable membership of individuals in social collectives. Since the traditional integration of individuals into social collectives has become fragile in modernity, modern individualized society requires a form of integration that also and above all focuses on the individual himself. This is precisely what the life course does as an institution: as a system of rules for the temporal dimension of life, it constitutes a life-time programme of events that individuals can and must follow and orient themselves to.

3.2 Institutionalized Life Course and Biographisation of Life Organization

Kohli sees the institutionalization of the life course as part of the broader process of social individualization that began with modernity. The prominent individualization thesis[14] refers first of all to the detachment of individuals from traditional collective ties (release dimension). At the same time, this release – which is often overlooked – necessitates a renewed and novel social integration of individuals (reintegration dimension). In modern individualized society, this can only take place by means of a mode of socialization that "starts with the individuals as independently constituted social units" (Kohli 1985, p. 3). This is precisely what the institutionalized life course does. It is obvious that it cannot function in the sense of a deterministic system of rules for the temporal dimension of life, since with the growing release of individuals from traditional ties, their biographical "scope for action" (Weymann 1989b) inevitably grows to the same extent. It is true that this newly won biographical freedom to shape one's life is at the same time pre-structured and preformed by the life-time process model that is culturally provided in the course of the institutionalization of the life course.[15] What is decisive here, however, is that the life course as an institution does not function in the sense of a deterministic steering of quasi-passive individuals who do not make use of their biographical scope for action. Rather, the institutionalized life course forms "a new template for the individual conduct of life while remaining open for interpretation and action and even normatively prescribing such an openness in the sense of a 'biographization' of life as a project" (Kohli 2007, p. 255). What does this concept of biographization mean (Fuchs 1983; Fischer and Kohli 1987; Brose and Hildenbrand 1988)?

The biographisation of the shaping of life can be characterized as "imposed freedom", i.e. the term refers to a paradoxical state of affairs. Like the institutionalization of the life course, its biographisation is part of the broader social individualization process. This individualization "has indeed had a liberating effect. (…) It has opened up previously unknown choices and trajectories of mobility for

---

[14] The individualization theorem was fundamentally formulated by Beck (1983, 1986). For an introductory overview, see Junge (2002); for a discussion of the individualization thesis, see Berger 1996; Kron 2000; Berger and Hitzler 2010.

[15] Like every institution, the institutionalized life course can also fulfil the basic – practically necessary – performance of institutions: namely, relieving individuals of uncertainty of action or reducing complexity, only by "restricting" the possibility space of individual freedom of action.

3.2 Institutionalized Life Course and Biographisation of Life Organization

the individual" (Berger et al. 1975, p. 168). People's lives are no longer largely predetermined by the structure of society, but the individual himself has advanced to become the planner and designer of his life. At the same time, this liberation means a compulsion to shape one's own biography: that the course of life "is placed as a task in the actions of each individual. (…) In the individualized society, the individual … must learn to understand himself as a center of action, as a planning office in relation to his own life course" (Beck 1986, p. 216 f.). Life becomes a biographical project to be shaped individually. The concept of biographisation means precisely this reflection on one's own biography imposed on people by the process of individualization, the "I"-centered interpretation and planning of life demanded of the individual by society, and the shaping of life organized around one's own "self".[16]

Contrasting two illustrative examples, the phenomenon of biographization may be briefly illustrated in terms of structural history. In his aforementioned studies in northern Hesse, Imhof came across a farm that had always been owned by a Johannes Hooss for more than four hundred years since the sixteenth century (with a single exception). How was that possible, given the enormous infant mortality during that period? Imhof's research revealed that several sons were given the name "Johannes" in each generation (a total of three-quarters of the male descendants; 1984b, p. 148). This multiple naming was intended to ensure that at least one "Johannes" survived the childhood phase, so that "there was always a descendant named Johannes Hooss ready as a role bearer to guide the fortunes of the farm … In this way the farm was not merely owned by Johannes Hooss for ten or twenty or thirty years, but continuously for four and a half centuries" (1984, p. 188). It was not the owner of the farm, but the farm and its continuity that mattered. It was not as an individual, but as a role-bearer that Johannes Hooss was relevant: only one link in the long chain of family or generational connection, the respective Johannes temporarily represented the ideal of the continuity of the farm as a livelihood spanning generations. In contrast to such supra-individual life-guiding values and ideas that outlasted the uncertain life of the individual, social individualization moved the individual to the center, i.e., made the "I" the reference point of one's life and

---

[16] In this context, reference should be made to the concept of biographicality, which is used more in the context of educational science (Alheit 1995; Alheit and Dausien 2000), as well as to the concept of self-socialization (Heinz 2000; Zinnecker 2000). In this context, Meyer's reflections on the parallel "institutionalization of life course and self" (1986, p. 201) are also interesting in terms of life course theory. For him, both the structurally embedded life course and the individual (private) self are "institutions and both sides are institutions of individualism" (ibid.; on the historically deeply rooted individualism of Western culture and on the individual actor as its basic unit and central figure, see also Meyer and Jepperson 2000).

the individual "self" its director. This transformation of the way of thinking and behaving can be vividly illustrated by the change in the life-time structure of autobiographies. Until the eighteenth century, the representation of individual life memories followed an annalistic logic (Niggl 1977): the temporal structure of life resulted from recurring seasonal and historical[17] events – from an external sequence of events. In the course of the eighteenth century, this form of representation increasingly gave way to the logic of a history of the development of the individual, who matures into an individual, distinctive personality in confrontation with the social structural contexts. Modern autobiographies thus follow – and this also applies with regard to the integration of external structural contexts into personal development – an inner logic that is "determined by the individuality of the self" (Alheit and Brandt 2006, p. 17).

The individual "self" as the director of one's own life is obviously in a state of tension with the institutionalized life course. This tension between a biographical shaping of life and the institutionalization of the course of life can no longer be addressed in an analytical perspective that focuses solely on the "external" shape of the course of life. This is because life course research of this kind implies the theoretical assumption that individuals as biographical actors can be neglected or even ignored.[18] The individual is not understood as a shaper, or at least a co-shaper, of the course of his life, but "exclusively as a biographically processed unit" (Kohli 1985, p. 20), i.e. it is assumed that the individuals, themselves quasi-passive, are channeled through their lives by social structures and institutional regulations. It is true that the term "life course research" already linguistically emphasizes a focus on the "external" sequences of events and positions in life; but even in relation only to this "external" course of life, the idea that this is largely or even directly the result of structural-institutional external control is hardly plausible. Not to be mis-

---

[17] Whether it be big history (e.g. wars), local history (e.g. a devastating conflagration) or one's own family history (e.g. death of parents).

[18] "Life course research is concerned with the social shaping of life courses" (Mayer 1987, p. 54), and the "social shaping of the life course takes place primarily through the mapping of social differentiation within and between institutions onto the life course" (Mayer 1990, p. 10). Accordingly, it is primarily (only) the socio-structural mechanisms and institutional regulations that generate life courses and life course patterns that are to be analyzed – biographical knowledge schemata and orientations are at best "socializing amplifiers of these regulatory mechanisms, which also act independently of them" (ibid.). Mayer does concede that the biographical interpretations and perspectives of individuals can also be in contradiction to this and "must then be understood as independently effective knowledge repertoires" (ibid.) – however, it is puzzling how an analytical perspective that conceptually excludes the biographical level from the outset can register this contradiction at all.

understood: the widespread life course research has produced a large number of important and also innovative empirical findings. And it is precisely its conceptual exclusion of the biographical level of reflection and action that makes it empirically "easier" to implement and thus attractive for social research. In terms of life course theory alone, the issue here is the tension between the biographization and institutionalization of the life course, which can no longer be addressed in a narrowed perspective of the "external" course of life.

Problematic in this respect is also a life-course theoretical model, in which the tension relationship is not faded out, but is harmonized in a functionalist way. Such a model takes account of the fact that "an individualized society depends on individuals fulfilling their part (which also means that there is the possibility that they do not do so). Subjectivity is conceived here as a necessary component of society" (Kohli 1985, p. 21). The biographical reflexivity and orientation of the individual is acknowledged as an independent factor in this model – however, at the same time its principle parallelism to the structurally shaped, standardized life-time sequence programme is asserted: individuals want biographically what they should structurally in society. The possible tension between biographization and institutionalized life course is not denied, but it is relativized and put in brackets, i.e. dismissed as a negligible factor compared to the functional fulfillment of roles as a result of the socio-structural internalization of socio-structural requirements.

In contrast to the conceptual fading out or harmonization, life course theory would have to maintain the tension between biographisation and the institutionalization of the life course. According to Kohli (and Beck), it is the institutionalization of the life course that enables individuals to understand life courses as biographical projects to be shaped individually: the institutionalized life course, as a standardized life-time process model, forms the basis and prerequisite on which, or under which, individual life planning and shaping that stands out from this expected "normal life course" can take place at all. However, the institutionalization of the life course not only enables individuals to plan and shape their lives around their own "I". As part of the social individualization process – and as a result of the non-deterministic character of the life course as an institution – it simultaneously implies the social demand of biographisation on the individual. The institutionalization of the life course thus simultaneously enables and requires its biographization. Biographical reflexivity is an indispensable correlate of the institutionalized life course. In terms of life course theory, then, as Kohli rightly emphasizes, a conception would be appropriate in which "the tension between life course as a pre-ordered (heteronomous) reality and biography as a subjective construction is preserved and can be questioned as to its consequences" (ibid.).

Here it becomes clear once again that – as already mentioned in the previous chapter – life course research must not conceptually tear apart the constitutive coherence of the "external" course and "internal" biography dimensions of its subject in the form of separate life course research on the one hand and biography research on the other. Such a division into two separate analytical perspectives may facilitate empirical research work, but it is conceptually problematic. For the tension inherent in the institutionalization of the life course or the life course as an institution: the constitutive interaction between the socio-structurally and institutionally envisaged life course model and the subjective biographisation of the shaping of life would then be completely lost from view and could be captured neither in its historical nor intercultural nor intragovernmental (i.e. between different life phases or areas) variation.

To conclude the chapter, three aspects related to the biographization of life design will be briefly addressed. Even if people in the individualized society of modernity reflect on, design and shape their lives around their own "I" – this does not mean that individuals have unlimited biographical freedom of action in a space that is, so to speak, free of society. On the contrary: modern society in particular is covered by a close-meshed (welfare) state regulatory network and bureaucratically "regulated" from the cradle to the grave. Precisely for this reason, however, the biographical freedom to shape one's life can also become a problem, because individuals, "in view of the high complexity of social contexts, are in many cases hardly in a position to make the decisions that become necessary in a well-founded manner, weighing up interests, morals and consequences" (Beck and Beck-Gernsheim 1994, p. 14 f.). The biographisation of the shaping of life can thus lead to a biographical overload.

- Discuss the problem of biographical overload using specific empirical or imagined examples?
- Have there been situations in your life in which you have experienced such biographical overload? How did you deal with it?

Nevertheless – and this is the second, directly related aspect – the individual has to take responsibility for his biographical decisions and their consequences. If – as in the individualized society of modernity – the individual himself is regarded as the planner and designer of his life, then all life events and developments in life, successes as well as failures, are no longer to be blamed on any social circumstances, but are also to be answered for individually. This is true not only with regard to society, which attributes the consequences of one's actions to the individual, and

3.2 Institutionalized Life Course and Biographisation of Life Organization

with regard to the attribution of responsibility on the part of other individuals. The individual himself, who sees himself or is supposed to see himself as the master of his own destiny, also attributes positive and negative life events and developments (tending above all to the former, the latter rather unwillingly) to himself (Wohlrab-Sahr 1997).

> - Which biographical "successes" and "failures" were you responsible for in your life so far? How did you experience them and how did you deal with them? Did discrepancies occur between the attribution of responsibility by others and by yourself?
> - In general, how do you judge the societal external and internalized self-attribution of individual responsibility for events and developments in life?

The last aspect to be briefly addressed concerns the temporal horizon of biographical reflection and planning. In his theory draft concluding the studies "On the Process of Civilization", Elias emphasizes that the enormous increase in social interdependencies on the part of individuals has inevitably led "to the subordination of short-term impulses to the imperative of a habitual long view" (1992a, p. 338). Does this civilizational "compulsion of the self to take the long view" with regard to the biographization of the shaping of life mean that individuals today develop and attempt to realize long-term biographical plans encompassing longer phases of life or even the entire life span? Or, in view of the complexity of social conditions and the decision-making situations in which the individual finds himself, is "only incrementalist biographical self-direction promising" (Schimank 2002, p. 12)?[19] Or is it not rather the case that the biographical reflexivity of individuals today has to be both long-term, even in the sense of an overall concept of life, and short-term and situationally (re-)acting? And what do these forms of biographical reflexivity and life design mean for the identity of the individual?

---

[19] Mayer and Müller argue similarly: if it is true that the welfare state's institutional differentiation of spheres of life entails a great "heterogeneity of individual logics of action, then it seems extraordinarily unlikely that individuals are able to unfold and sustain comprehensive and long-term life plans. The institutional structure supports a logic of the present situation rather than a logic of the overall biography" (1989, p. 53 f.). Thus – it is to be feared – the substantial biographical rationality that guarantees an independent life orientation gives way to a functional rationality that is only opportunistically focused on external incentives.

- In your current life situation, is your life planning and design more long term or short term? Do you think that the time horizon of your biographical planning can or will change in the further course of your life? If not: why not? If yes: why and how?
- Schimank justifies the necessity of biographical incrementalism in terms of systems theory with the functional differentiation of modern society. Do you agree with the thesis derived from this social (macro-)structure that "those who do not approach their lives incrementalistically run the risk of serious identity crises for themselves" (Schimank 2002, p. 12)?

4 Collective Life Courses: Generations, Cohorts and Social Change

There are two sociological concepts for capturing collective life courses and social change: cohort and generation (Alwin and McCammon 2003). The two terms are often used interchangeably, but are by no means synonymous. The cohort concept is theoretically simple, clearly defined, and to that extent empirically manageable. In contrast, the (sociologically older) concept of generation is more presuppositional in terms of content, i.e. a theoretically demanding but also problematic concept. This has led to the fact that cohort studies today not only belong to the standard repertoire of life course research, but are its central instrument for surveying socio-structural change, while the generation concept has been neglected (or even explicitly discarded).

4.1 Cohort Studies and Social Change

4.1.1 Inter- and Intracohort Conception

The critique of structural functionalism and its age group concept, which dominated life course research until the 1960s, also led to innovations in life course theory and methodology. The most important conceptual innovation is considered to be the cohort approach, which Ryder – a demographer[1] – introduced into life course research with his paper on "The Cohort as a Concept in the Study of Social Change" (1965). However – the idea of studying social change through cohort

---

[1] In population science, cohort analyses have been part of the standard arsenal of methods for several decades.

analysis was not really new in sociology. Comte, who coined the name of the discipline, had already said in 1839 with regard to the dynamics of social change that "the ordinary duration of human life ... has more effect on the rapidity of development than any other discernible influence. Social progress is essentially based on death, i.e. the successive steps of humanity demand an equally rapid renewal of the carriers of the general movement.[2] In the course of an individual life this is hardly noticeable, but only at the transition of one generation to the following" (1974, p. 140 f.). This quotation not only contains two assumptions that are also fundamental for Ryder's cohort concept (as well as the generation concept): demographic metabolism, i.e. permanent population exchange qua birth and death, is a necessary precondition of social change and[3] the new birth cohorts entering society are only its "carriers" (but not: "causers"). Comte already establishes here the basic methodological idea of the cohort approach: social change only becomes clearly visible in the succession of generations. A century and a quarter later, Ryder says: "The new cohorts provide the opportunity for social change to occur. They do not cause change; they permit it. If change does occur, it differentiates cohorts from one another, and the comparison of their careers becomes a way to study change" (1965, p. 844).

Ryder defines cohorts as "aggregate of individuals (within some population definition) who experienced the same event within the same time interval" (ibid., p. 845). The cohort-defining event is usually birth or the year of birth, i.e. the vast majority of cohort studies work with birth cohorts. However, other events such as educational qualifications, marriage, acquisition of residential property, illness, change of occupation or business, unemployment, etc. can also define cohorts. For example, the event "divorce" constitutes the cohort of those who were divorced at a defined time, e.g. in 1993. In principle, any event can be cohort-defining. For example, the event "flat tire" would create the cohort of those who had a "flat tire" with their vehicle at a defined time. However, the cohort-defining event should be "meaningful," that is, constitute a cohort relevant to a sociological question. This is the case with the "1993 divorce cohort": how many divorced people remarry, how

---

[2] That Comte speaks not simply of social change but of a general movement of human progress is due to his philosophy of history perspective (and not relevant here).

[3] Comte's speculative reasoning: if people were to live forever, "the movement of progress would almost completely cease" or a significantly longer lifespan would "slow down social development, because then the natural struggle between the preservation instinct, the characteristic of old age, and the instinct for innovation, the characteristic of youth, would be in favour of the former" – and conversely, "an excessively short existence ... would also be an obstacle, since the instinct for innovation would then acquire too great a power. (...) A fruitful and lasting development could not emerge from this" (1974, p. 141).

4.1 Cohort Studies and Social Change

long it takes to remarry, what role socio-demographic factors play in this are sociologically relevant questions. On the other hand, it is not evident for which sociological questions the "flat tire cohort 1993" could be relevant.[4]

Each cohort is homogeneous with respect to its defining event and the corresponding socio-demographic condition, but otherwise heterogeneous. A divorce cohort, for example, is homogeneous with respect to marital status, while a birth cohort is by definition age homogeneous. Except for birth cohorts, age varies to a greater or lesser extent in all other types of cohorts: an apprenticeship or retirement cohort, for example, is still relatively age homogeneous, but in marriage, unemployment or career change cohorts, age varies greatly. Although the birth cohort is age-homogeneous, it is heterogeneous with respect to other socio-demographic characteristics such as gender, educational and occupational status, marital status, health, wealth situation, etc. and "more random in composition than any other cohort type" (ibid., p. 848). Ryder does not further differentiate between birth and other cohorts in his paper, but focuses exclusively on the birth cohort.[5]

Successive birth cohorts – according to Ryder's basic thesis quoted at the beginning – are formed into distinct cohorts by ongoing social change (whatever its causes may be). Conversely, this means that processes of social change can be read off from different life course patterns of birth cohorts. The instrument of comparative cohort analysis can thus be used to identify processes of social change. How does Ryder justify his thesis that social change shapes the life courses of different birth cohorts in a specific way, so that distinguishable, distinct cohorts are formed? Ryder argues that "each new cohort makes fresh contact with the contemporary social heritage and carries the impress of the encounter through

---

[4] The cohort-defining events mentioned as examples, such as graduation, marriage or unemployment, are individual life course events that individuals experience in the same historical time interval. Serious historical events such as economic crises, wars, political upheavals, cultural revolutions, environmental catastrophes, etc. can also define cohorts, whereby such a historical event – because it affects all members of society, i.e. people of all ages – must be related to the same time interval in the life courses of the individuals. By means of the historical event of German reunification, for example, different cohorts can be constituted – depending on the research question: e.g. the cohort of East German education graduates or an East German retirement cohort or various cohorts of unemployed women in East Germany at different ages. Frequently, the "formative phase" of adolescence and young adulthood is used as a lifetime interval and linked to a historical event; in these cases, the cohort definition approaches the concept of generation (see Sect. 4.2).

[5] Ryder's "exclusive attention to the birth cohort" (1965, p. 848) may be due to his disciplinary socialization as a demographer. In this context, Mayer and Huinink point out that the term "cohort analysis" in demography, sociology, psychology, and political science referred to "something very similar methodologically, but very different in content" (1990, p. 443).

life. (...) The members ... participate in only one slice of life – their unique location in the stream of history. Because it embodies a temporally specific version of the heritage, each cohort is differentiated from all others" (ibid., p. 845). Accordingly, each birth cohort has a specific historical-social location, i.e. a birth cohort is historically embedded in a very specific social, cultural, economic and political context that is unique to it. For example, those born in the mid-1920s lived through most of their adolescence during World War II, whereas those born in the early post-war years experienced their adolescence at the time of the "economic miracle." According to Ryder, the unique sociohistorical positioning of birth cohorts leads to correspondingly unique, distinctive experiences and appropriations of "social heritage" among their members. As social change continuously transforms society, each birth cohort is "embedded" in a specific social context and is shaped by it in a characteristic way.

According to Ryder, the most important cohort-differentiating shaping factors of the social context are changing educational content (formal education), informal peer group influences, and idiosyncratic historical experiences. The first two factors mentioned already indicate that Ryder's previous justification of his intercohort-theoretical conception needs to be made more precise in life-time terms. Before that, however, we will briefly discuss another cohort-differentiating factor, as well as subsequently address the sociodemographic heterogeneity of the birth cohort already mentioned. The social context has a cohort-differentiating effect not only through its content-related determination of those three factors. The characteristic coherence of a birth cohort also follows "from its own macro analytic features" (ibid., p. 843) – such as the number of its members, its gender ratio, the distribution of its milieus of origin, its educational level, etc. – which are also determined by the social context: "Each cohort has a distinctive composition ... reflecting the circumstances of its unique origination" (ibid., p. 845).[6] Perhaps the most important compositional feature of a birth cohort itself is its relative size, that is, its size in relation to other birth cohorts. The relevance of this factor was highlighted by Easterlin in his much-discussed study of "Birth and fortune: The impact of numbers on personal welfare" (1980).[7] In it, he analyses the impact of relative cohort size on the basis of

---

[6] This sociodemographic characteristic composition of the birth cohort does change over time (for example, through death or out-migration), but "many statistical facets of cohort composition ... differ at age zero from one cohort to the next, and remain approximately unchanged throughout the cohort's history" (Ryder 1965, p. 845).

[7] On the "relative cohort size effect" with regard to individual life courses as well as macro-sociologically with regard to societal changes, see Macunovich (2002) (see Pampel and Peters 1995 for criticism of Easterlin's thesis).

4.1 Cohort Studies and Social Change

the "baby boomers" (USA: birth cohorts from 1946–1964) and claims that the members of these large "baby boom" cohorts are economically and socially disadvantaged compared to the members of the numerically smaller birth cohorts before them: "For those fortunate enough to be members of a small generation, life is – as a general matter – disproportionately good; the opposite is true for those who are members of a large generation" (ibid., p. 3 f.). It is easy to see why this is so according to Easterlin: when very large birth cohorts start school, for example, their members have to learn in overcrowded classrooms – unless educational institutions are (or were) expanded with foresight; when they have completed their education, they encounter a labor market that does not offer enough jobs suitable for all cohort members – unless corresponding jobs are newly created or other employed persons are displaced from such jobs. However, a large birth cohort is not only confronted with "unfavorable" social conditions – it also generates (as indicated in the example) social pressure for changes and social, political, economic and cultural change. Of course, this does not only apply to cohorts with a high birth rate: experiencing and coping with their social embeddedness, each birth cohort can – sometimes it has to – develop innovative behavioral reactions which – in the sense of the repercussions of changed life courses and biographies on social structures and institutions (see Sect. 2.2.2) – change the social context so that later birth cohorts are "stored" in this changed, new social context (Modell 1989).

- How do you think about the role of school (and university) educational content and the role of peer groups in terms of cohort differentiation or shaping?
- Play through the idea formulated in the two sentences following the illustration example for the (West) German "baby boomers" (i.e. the birth cohorts from the mid-1950s to the late 1960s) with regard to institutionalized transitions in the life course and other important life events (e.g. starting school, working, retirement, marriage, starting a family, etc.) as well as life attitudes, behaviors, and values:
    - What economic, cultural, social and political circumstances do these "baby boom" cohorts face?
    - Did these "baby boom" cohorts change social, cultural, economic, or political realities (indirectly or directly)?
    - How do the life courses of these "baby boom" cohorts differ from those of, say, the 1945–1955 birth cohorts, and why?

Ryder is well aware of the socio-demographic heterogeneity of a birth cohort. Nevertheless, his remarks often give the impression that it is a monolithic social entity possessing a kind of "macro-life course". He even says explicitly, "The cohort record, as macro-biography, is the aggregate analogue of the individual life history" (1965, p. 859). According to this statement, he indeed seems to hold that the life histories of birth cohort members aggregate to form something like a (homogeneous) cohort life history. Such a view assumes that members of a birth cohort uniformly experience the social context in which they are "embedded" and cope with it in the same way and are consequently homogeneously shaped by it. Ryder also explicitly states that the "attractive simplicity of birth cohort membership as signified by age cannot conceal the ways in which this identification is cross-cut and attenuated by differentiation with respect to education, occupation, marital status, parity status, and so forth. (…) The meaning of sharing a common historical location is modified and adumbrated by these other identifying characteristics" (ibid., p. 847). However, if the meaning, i.e. the socializing imprint of the social context is thwarted, attenuated, modified and superimposed by the socio-demographic heterogeneity of a birth cohort, the question of the scope and relevance of this inevitably arises. That is, it would have to be clarified empirically for each case whether the members of the birth cohort experience the social context uniformly despite their socio-demographic heterogeneity, so that this has a uniform imprinting effect – or whether and to what extent the socio-demographic heterogeneity of a birth cohort leads on the part of its members to different experiences of the social context, so that no homogeneous imprinting results from this. In any case, a (homogeneously aggregated) cohort life course cannot simply be assumed theoretically as the macro sociological counterpart of an individual's life course. Rather, the sociodemographic heterogeneity of the birth cohort must be taken into account – if not conceptually, then at least methodologically in empirical studies.

Ryder's argument that social change produces distinct cohorts through the mechanism of "imprinting qua sociohistorical storage" must necessarily be specified in terms of life-time, because individuals are ultimately embedded in and influenced by social contexts throughout their lives. His intercohort concept implies two essential life-time assumptions: first, that an imprint on individuals' life courses occurs at an early age that is so fundamental that – second – it persists and manifests itself over the rest of their lives. Ryder locates this fundamental imprinting in adolescence and young adulthood. The differentiation of distinct cohorts thus results from the (always specific) social contexts in which the birth cohorts are "embedded" in adolescence and young adulthood and whose socializing imprints are assumed to have lifelong effectiveness. This is the core of Ryder's cohort concept: ongoing social change, by embedding birth cohorts in unique social contexts, has "variant import for persons of unlike age, and … the consequences of change persist in the subsequent behavior of these individuals and thus of their cohorts" (ibid., p. 844).

4.1 Cohort Studies and Social Change

> - What would be the consequences in terms of content and methodology with regard to Ryder's cohort concept if there were no significant social change over decades? What would be the consequences if processes of serious social change occurred in very rapid succession?
> - A birth cohort is confronted with an incisive social event in high adulthood, so it has an idiosyncratic sociohistorical experience. How do you see the significance of this experience in relation to the experience of the sociohistorical context in which the cohort members were "embedded" during their adolescent and young adult years?

The fact that people are open and receptive to the socializing influences of the social context, especially in their younger years (at least in societies with a differentiated phase of adolescence that allows for "playful" experimentation and shaping of identity and personality), is largely a consensus in developmental psychology.[8] But what about the second assumption, according to which the socializing imprints of adolescence and young adulthood permeate all other phases of life? Do the ways of thinking and behaving, views, convictions and values formed early in life remain stable over the life course? This assumption of stability is – as said – essential for Ryder's intercohort-theoretically conceived approach: "Implicit in the foregoing account of the interdependency of social change and cohort differentiation is the assumption that an individual's history is highly stable or at least continuous" (ibid., p. 851). This assumption, however, is controversial in developmental and personality psychology. There is empirical evidence both for the existence of stable personality traits (e.g. the so-called "Big Five" or certain cognitive abilities and aspects of identity), but also for a lifelong variability of personality structures.[9]

---

[8] The adolescent and young adult years are the crucial formative period because, as Ryder vividly points out, people at this age "are old enough to participate directly in the movements impelled by change, but not old enough to have become committed to … a way of life" (1965, p. 848).

[9] Summarizing, perhaps one should refer to permanent change amid relatively stable structures and that the "stability patterns of individual differences are capable of following any number of different trajectories" (Alwin and McCammon 2003, p. 36; Ardelt 2000; Caspi et al. 2005; Roberts et al. 2006; McAdams and Olson 2010; Specht et al. 2011). Moreover, a meta-analysis of longitudinal studies of personality development has shown that most personality traits build their stability in discontinuous processes and do not reach stability until older adulthood (Roberts and DelVecchio 2000). Adolescence and young adulthood should therefore not be overestimated in terms of their "life course shaping potential".

Interestingly, towards the end of the article Ryder himself relativizes the assumption of stability that is essential for his intercohort concept. In a section entitled "Sources of flexibility: individual and group" (ibid., p. 859) he says that socialization in complex modern societies "continues throughout the whole of life. (…) Socialization need not mean rigidification" (ibid.). However, if individuals can change, develop and learn throughout life, social change does not only take place through cohort succession and differentiation, i.e. inter-cohort, but can also take place through changes in the life histories of members of a birth cohort, i.e. intra-cohort. This intracohort dimension of social change plays no role in Ryder's article. In the concluding section of his essay, he does say that the cohort concept implies and enables two research orientations, namely "first, the study of intracohort temporal development throughout the life cycle; second the study of comparative cohort careers, i.e., intercohort temporal differentiation" (ibid., p. 861). His explanations, however, focus intercohort-theoretically on the succession and differentiation of "new" birth cohorts and conceptually ignore the intracohort dimension of social change. In this respect, Ryder's intercohort conception represents a major advance over structural-functionalist age-group sociology with its implicit assumption of socio-structural statics, because it takes account of ongoing social change, the normal case of permanent change and dynamics in the social context. However, his conceptual omission of the intracohort dimension of social change, the neglect of individual learning, adaptation and development processes over the lifespan, has the consequence that the individual – in contrast to the social context – is not understood as a dynamic, but (after his imprinting in early years) as a "static" person. This is problematic in terms of life course theory, because – as Neugarten criticized early on – such an intercohort conception "does not analyze lives but presents the statistical histories of cohorts" (1985, p. 297).

> Discuss the question of whether social change is "inter-cohort" (i.e. as a result of the continuous replacement or displacement of older birth cohorts by younger ones) or "intra-cohort" (i.e. as a result of adaptation and learning processes in the birth cohorts), firstly using the example of changes in job profiles and occupational requirements and secondly using the example of changed family forms and forms of cohabitation.

4.1.2 From Cohort to Life Course Analysis

Ryder's essay was the starting signal for an incalculable number of cohort-analytical studies; by now there is probably no aspect of social change to which the cohort approach has not been (and continues to be) applied. In the methodological implementation of the cohort theory approach, empirical studies face the problem of having to distinguish and identify age, period and cohort effects. As shown, social change can occur inter- as well as intra-cohort. According to the intercohort concept, social change takes place through cohort exchange, whereby this mechanism assumes distinct historical experiences of birth cohort members in their younger years, resulting in a stable, lifelong shaping of behavior and attitudes (e.g., an economic crisis after years of social prosperity might lead to distinct material value orientations among people who are in the final stages of their education and transition to employment). In this respect, one speaks of cohort effects. In contrast, according to the intracohort concept, social change occurs precisely through personal-biographical changes in individuals. On the one hand, this mechanism is based on life cycles, i.e. it is a consequence of the individual aging process; in this case, one speaks of age effects (e.g. the age-related decline in learning ability could lead to a lower acceptance of innovations). Secondly, personal-biographical changes can also be based on the individual's reaction to a serious historical event; in this case, we speak of period effects (e.g. with regard to the effects of the Second World War or the collapse of the GDR). Since period and cohort effects are based on the experience and processing of historical events by individuals, it is often unclear which type of effect is present; theoretically, the dividing line between the two effects refers to the individuals affected by such an event: if it has an impact on (almost) all individuals in a defined population, we speak of a period effect; if, on the other hand, it only affects certain birth cohorts, we speak of a cohort effect.[10] Age, period and cohort effects can be theoretically distinguished from each other and clearly defined. In social reality, however, they never occur in isolation and independently of each other, but in different combinations and virtually "amalgamated" – as the following figure illustrates (Fig. 4.1).

---

[10] The Great Depression, for example, certainly represented a period effect, because it had effects on society as a whole, i.e. consequences for all members of society. However, because the consequences of even such a serious event – as Elder's study of the "Children of the Great Depression" has shown (see Sect. 2.1) – also depend crucially on the phase of life in which an individual experiences it, it can also produce cohort effects.

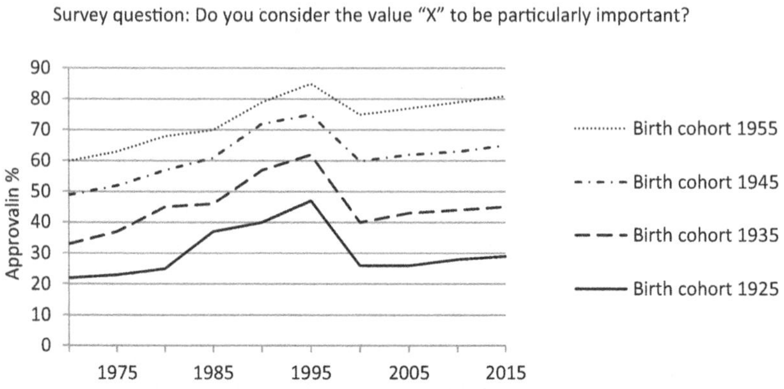

Survey question: Do you consider the value "X" to be particularly important?

[Chart showing approval % from 1975 to 2015 for four birth cohorts: 1955, 1945, 1935, 1925]

Fig. 4.1 Age, period and cohort effect. (Fictitious example)

The figure shows the fictitious results for the fictitious question posed in a fictitious empirical study on the change in social values as to whether one considers the value "X" to be particularly important. The first thing to note is that – especially in the younger cohorts – there has been a change in values related to "X" (agreement was higher in 2015 than in 1970 for each cohort, by 7% for the oldest cohort and by 12%/16%/21% for the younger cohorts). How can this social change be explained? A causal analysis must be able to separate age, period and cohort effects and identify the impact of each. Assuming that this prerequisite is statistically fulfilled: an age effect is then clearly discernible – in every birth cohort the approval ratings have been rising continuously since 1970, i.e. with increasing age, with the exception of the year 2000. A period effect is clearly discernible in this – the approval trend collapses dramatically at the turn of the millennium and then resumes, albeit at a slower rate. A cohort effect is also clearly discernible – the marked differences in approval between birth cohorts that existed in 1970 remain throughout the survey period. In this example, the statistical separation of age, period and cohort effects and the identification of these separate effects (as well as possible interaction effects) was taken for granted. However, this is precisely the basic methodological problem of cohort studies. This methodologically fundamental identification or APC problem can be illustrated by a standard cohort table (Fig. 4.2).

A standard cohort table contains both the intercohort and intracohort theoretical perspectives. Cohort effects are represented by differences between diagonals, age effects by differences within columns and period effects by differences within

4.1 Cohort Studies and Social Change

Age	Year				
	1970	1980	1990	2000	2010
20-29	60	50	40	30	20
30-39	62	52	42	32	22
40-49	66	56	46	36	26
50-59	72	62	52	42	32
60-69	80	70	60	50	40

Cohort effect ⟶   Age effect ⟶   Period effect ⟶

Fig. 4.2 Standard cohort table

rows. In the figure, the period effect can be seen, for example, in the continuous decline in cell values for those aged 60–69 at the individual survey dates from 80 in 1970 to 40 in 2010. An age effect can be seen, for example, in the cell values for the various age groups in 2010, which increase at an increasing rate from 20 for those aged 20–29 to 40 for those aged 60–69. And a cohort effect can be seen, for example, between the 20–29 year-olds and the 30–39 year-olds, for whom there are different cell values at the first survey time in 1970 (60/62), whose difference does not diminish in the following period, but remains the same or even increases here (to 42/50 in 2000). To illustrate the identification problem: figuratively speaking, a period effect, an age effect and a cohort effect arrow overlap in the cell at the bottom right of the table. The cell value 40 could therefore result from a societal development process, i.e. be a characteristic of a period effect. But it could also result from individual aging processes, i.e. be a characteristic of an age effect. And it could also result from a specific, distinct cohort process, i.e. be a feature of a cohort effect. Methodologically speaking: in the standard cohort table, period, age and cohort effects are confounded.[11] Reason for this confounding can be illustrated using the operational scheme of a cohort study (Fig. 4.3).

In empirical studies, the variable "cohort" (C) is operationally determined by the time of the cohort-defining event (here: birth/year of birth).[12] The variable "period" (P) is determined by a relevant observation time (usually on an annual

---

[11] Namely, in a standard cohort table, cohort and age effects are confounded in each column, age and period effects are confounded in each diagonal, and period and cohort effects are confounded in each row.

[12] Often, the variable "cohort" does not only include one birth cohort, but refers to several neighbouring birth cohorts – as in the standard cohort table in Fig. 4.2.

	Period (year)				
Age	1970	1980	1990	2000	2010
25	C 1	C 2	C 3	C 4	C 5
35		C 1	C 2	C 3	C 4
45			C 1	C 2	C 3
55				C 1	C 2
65					C 1

Fig. 4.3 Operational scheme of a cohort study. (Birth cohorts)

basis). And the variable "age" (A) is defined as the length of time between the cohort-defining event and the observation time point.[13] The confounding of age, period and cohort effects, i.e. the identification problem in empirical cohort studies, results directly from this operational definition of the three variables. A, P and C are not independent of each other, but each of the variables is always already contained in the other two, i.e. if the values for two variables are given, the value of the third variable is also determined – in other words: A, P and C are in a linear relationship to each other: A = P-C (Mason et al. 1973; in the operational scheme shown, the cohorts C 1, C 2, C 3, C 4 and C 5 are therefore the birth cohorts 1945, 1955, 1965, 1975 and 1985). It is true that the question of an empirical study may sometimes allow one of the three variables A, P and C to be declared irrelevant and thus eliminate the identification problem. But apart from the fact that for this one would have to know in advance that a variable – and which one – is ineffective: in by far the majority of cases such a non-effectiveness imputation is not possible.

The ongoing methodological discussion on the identification problem will not be referred to in detail here. The consensus now seems to be that the so-called APC problem cannot be solved purely statistically (but see O'Brien et al. 2008). A definitive identification of the separate effects as well as possible interaction effects – as Glenn sums up the decades of discussion – "through statistical model estimation is not possible. Belief that the effects can be separated statistically has led to much pseudo-rigorous research" (2003, p. 475). The identification problem can only be

---

[13] For the purposes of this definition, the variable name should generally be 'duration', as 'age' is an appropriate term only for birth cohorts (for an unemployment cohort, for example, the definition does not indicate how old a person is, but rather how long the person has been unemployed).

4.1 Cohort Studies and Social Change

solved theoretically. One such conceptual-level solution has been proposed by Rodgers, according to whom "a solution to the dilemma lies in the specification and measurement of the theoretical variables for which age, period, and cohort are indirect indicators" (1982, p. 774; Renn 1987; Beekes 1990). Rodgers conceives of A, P, and C as indicator variables for complex theoretical constructs whose meanings or contents are only fuzzily and above all: inadequately captured as "age," "period," and "cohort". His theoretical-conceptual approach to solving this problem therefore consists in explaining A, P and C as precisely as possible in conceptual terms in order to capture all relevant influencing factors and to be able to specify statistical analysis models accordingly: "we must ask ourselves what it is we are really interested in estimating. Age, period, and cohort ... are used only because they are convenient and readily measurable indicators of more basic concepts ... Our problems arise because these indicators are confounded; the underlying concepts are not confounded. Moreover, our problems arise when we try to do our analysis when we have only the three indicators. If we are to replace even one of them with a set of more directly relevant variables, the parameters all become estimable" (Rodgers 1982, p. 786). Thus, in a cohort study examining, for example, a labor market sociological topic, the variable "period" could be broken down into several directly relevant variables – reflecting both specific time periods and events as well as longer-term trends – such as the phase of the economic miracle or the oil price shock, relevant changes in legislation, the development of the unemployment rate, the gross domestic product, consumer demand, the industry structure, etc. (Rodgers 1982, p. 886).

The most common approach to the identification problem in empirical cohort analyses today follows the solution strategy proposed by Rogers. The identification problem, which is based on the linear relationship A = P-C, is thus restricted – or, so to speak: dismissed – to the operational level. Ultimately, however, this also abandons conventional cohort analysis with its three-factor design and transforms it into a dynamic (time-related) multivariate multilevel analysis model. The specification of the inadequately coarse indicator variables "age", "period" and "cohort", i.e. their replacement by a bundle of directly relevant variables marks a research perspective shift towards a – temporally as well as in relation to the subject area – multidimensional modelling of life courses, with which the "rigid categories of the cohort-analytic paradigm ... are (dissolved): age into a multidimensional bundle of state durations in the life course, cohort membership into an accumulating, multi-dimensional, multilevel 'life history', period into an equally multidimensional, multilevel space of current life conditions and opportunities" (Mayer and Huinink 1994, p. 109).

Such dynamic, multidimensional, multilevel life course analyses require longitudinal data on individuals. Only by means of such data[14] is it possible to relate the changes taking place in the various areas of life and society to one another at the micro level of individual life courses, the meso level of organizations and the societal macro level. Today, there is a whole series of such data sets – such as the German Socio-Economic Panel (SOEP; Wagner et al. 2008; Schupp 2009) – that are relevant for life course research and can be used.

> - Find out about other longitudinal data sets in Germany, Europe or the USA that are of interest for life course research.
> - Make clear – possibly with the help of a graphical representation – the advantages of longitudinal data over cross-sectional data by means of concrete examples (e.g. occupational histories or partnership biographies).

Finally, a few examples of such cohort studies are given. The most prominent German example of a dynamic, multidimensional, multilevel cohort study is the "German Life Course Study" (GLHS; Mayer 2015). This large-scale project, conducted from 1979 to 2010, collected and analyzed life histories of German birth cohorts whose members were born between 1919 and 1971. Methodologically, the GLHS was quantitative, i.e. only the "external" life course was collected in the form of age-related event and position configurations and sequences in the various social and life domains. These data were collected retrospectively in personal interviews or via computer-assisted telephone interviews (for the most part) and are available on a monthly basis. The observation period, for which a total of more than 12,000 life histories are available, spans a good eight decades and extends to 2005. The GLHS thus maps social change in Germany during almost the entire twentieth century in a unique way.[15]

---

[14] And, of course, appropriate statistical analysis techniques such as event history analysis, sequence pattern analysis, or latent class analysis (Abbott and Tsay 2000; Aisenbrey 2000; Aisenbrey and Fasang 2010; Blossfeld and Rohwer 1995; Cornwell 2015; Macmillan and Eliason 2003; Mills 2011; Windzio 2013).

[15] The West German subproject covered the birth cohorts 1919–21, 1929–31, 1939–41, 1949–51, 1954–56, 1959–61, 1964, and 1971 (two surveys); the East German substudy (two-wave panel) covered the birth cohorts 1929–31, 1939–41, 1951–53, 1959–61, and 1971. A large number of publications resulted from the GLHS; only a few important monographs are mentioned here: Blossfeld (1985); Allmendinger (1994); Lauterbach (1994); Huinink (1995); Huinink et al. (1995); Solga (1995); Wagner (1989, 1997); Konietzka (1999); Hillmert (2001); Jacob (2004); Mayer and Schulze (2009).

4.1 Cohort Studies and Social Change

To record life courses retrospectively that a person's life course is recorded in retrospect in a one-off survey. In this process, memory problems and dating errors can occur among the respondents – especially with regard to phases of life that occurred longer ago. However, the retrospective survey is now a well-functioning survey instrument that provides reliable data (Brückner and Mayer 1998; Reimer 2005; Matthes et al. 2007). Life histories can also be collected prospectively in panel studies. A panel study records the further course of a person's life, starting from the initial survey point, by means of repeated interviews (panel waves) over a certain period of time. Both survey methods have their advantages and disadvantages (Scott and Alwin 1998; Solga 2001).[16]

A prominent current example of dynamic, multidimensional, multilevel cohort studies in the form of a prospective panel study is the "National Educational Panel Study" (NEPS; www.neps-data.de/). Launched in 2008 as the largest project in German educational research, the NEPS has been a permanent research infrastructure facility since 2014. The aim of the NEPS is to collect, describe and analyze long-term educational trajectories with regard to competence development, different learning environments, social inequality and educational decisions, educational outcomes, motivational and personality psychology aspects and persons with a migration background. Unlike retrospective surveys, in a prospective panel study analytical results can only be obtained over time.[17] For this reason, i.e., in order to nevertheless obtain results as quickly as possible, the NEPS works methodologically with a multicohort sequential design: it comprises six starting cohorts that are representative initial samples for persons of certain ages or in certain stages of the educational system. These starting cohorts are new-borns, four-year-old kindergartners, fifth graders, ninth graders, first-year students, and 23- to 64-year-olds. The educational trajectories of these cohorts, which cover a total of more than 60,000 individuals, are collected and tracked in repeated surveys. In this respect, the NEPS with its data is a unique research-based infrastructure institution worldwide (Blossfeld et al. 2009, 2011, 2016).

---

[16] An important problem with panel studies is panel mortality, i.e. participants of the initial sample cannot be interviewed again for whatever reason, which can lead to a systematic distortion of the representativeness of the sub-samples of further survey waves for the initial sample and thus also for the population to which the study ultimately refers (Rendtel 1995).

[17] If the initial sample of such a study consists of school beginners, for example, it will take at least ten years before initial analyses are possible, e.g. with regard to the transition from the education system to the employment system, whose results, moreover, only refer to the secondary school graduates – corresponding statements about the entire cohort could only be made after almost 20 years because some of them will go to university.

Another example of a dynamic, multidimensional, multilevel cohort study in the form of a prospective panel is the "Occupational History Study East Germany" (Sackmann et al. 2000).[18] In this study, the educational, occupational and family histories of three cohorts of East German graduates were examined: in a representative random sample, persons who completed their vocational training or university studies in the regions of Leipzig and Rostock in 1985, 1990 and 1995 were recorded. These cohorts were confronted with very different conditions with regard to their transition from the education system to the employment system: the 1985 cohort had completed their education, guaranteed career entry and first years of work under the social framework conditions of the GDR; the 1990 cohort had been educated during GDR times, but their transition into the employment system coincided exactly with the turbulent "Wende" (fall of the Berlin wall) period; finally, the 1995 cohort had already undergone their education under the new market economy conditions and encountered a shrunken but again consolidating labor market when entering the employment system. In the baseline survey, the life histories of 3743 persons were surveyed retrospectively and then followed in two further panel waves until the year 2000; a total of 2202 life histories documented without gaps on a monthly basis are available. Methodologically, the project was designed as both a quantitative and qualitative panel. A sub-sample of 67 persons was constructed from the initial sample using labor market theory criteria. Qualitative interviews were conducted with these persons; 47 of these skilled workers and academics took part in a qualitative occupational biographical interview again five years later. In contrast to the GLHS, the focused quantitative sample and the in-depth qualitative interviews made it possible to conduct differentiated analyses of the social change in the new federal states resulting from the reunification of Germany and the abrupt system change.[19]

A final example of a dynamic, multidimensional, multilevel cohort study is the "Kölner Gymnasiastenpanel" (KGP). In contrast to the three examples just mentioned, this panel study was an intracohort project. The KGP began in 1969/1970 with a survey of 15-year-old tenth grade students at 68 high schools in North Rhine-Westphalia (n = 3240). Repeat surveys were conducted in the mid-1980s and 1990s as well as in 2010; this last survey still comprised about two-fifths of the initial sample. The KGP collected cohort members' educational, occupational, and personal life histories, as well as their attitudes toward a variety of social phenomena and issues, on a monthly basis. Its four surveys document the life histories of

---

[18] The research project was carried out within the framework of the DFG Collaborative Research Centre 186: "Status Passages and Risks in the Life Course" (1988–2001).

[19] Publications from this project include: Sackmann and Wingens (1995, 1996); Sackmann et al. (2001); Windzio and Wingens (2000); Wingens (1999); Wingens and Sackmann (2000); Wingens et al. (2000).

4.1 Cohort Studies and Social Change

1301 high school students over four decades up to age 56 (Meulemann 1995; Meulemann et al. 2001; Meulemann and Birkelbach 2012).[20]

Dynamic, multidimensional, multilevel intracohort studies collect and analyze the life histories of the members of a singular cohort. Their analytical focus is on the consequences resulting from the sociodemographic heterogeneity of this cohort in the course of the aging of its members. With regard to the analysis of processes of social change, however, studies based on intracohort theory harbor a danger: longitudinal analyses of only one singular cohort can easily be subject to "cohort-centrism" (Riley 1988, p. 26), i.e., they can inadmissibly generalize empirical findings on the life courses and patterns of this cohort. Only by comparing cohorts, i.e. with an intercohort-theoretical research design, can general patterns of development – e.g. with regard to the institution of the "family" in the direction of a pluralization of life forms – and thus social change be established.

Almost 40 years ago, in a short article entitled "What is a cohort and why?", Rosow described three basic problems of the cohort approach. One of them is the "boundary problem": "The basic problem is a paradox: how to create a series of discrete cohorts from a continuous flow of people. (…) What we are really unclear about is whether cohort is only a conceptual or also an empirical unit. If cohort is only a concept without any empirical meaning, then it does not matter where we divide cohorts as long as we do not disturb their order. (…) So cohorts could be divided arbitrarily or for convenience into as many or as few equal intervals as we wish. But this is purely a technical decision that completely misses the point about cohorts. If cohorts are differentiated by events and experience, then they must have an empirical as well as conceptual basis. These events differ in kind, so that cohorts are distinguished more by qualitative than quantitative differences. They are intrinsically discrete, they do not function as continuous variables, nor do they reflect such effects" (1978, p. 68).

- Discuss the "boundary problem".

---

[20] In addition to the KGP, the "Hamburg School Leaver Study 1979" should also be mentioned here (Friebel et al. 2000). This quantitative and qualitative intracohort study investigated the educational biographies of Hamburg secondary school graduates. In 1980, the educational biographies of 354 school leavers were collected; the further biographies of these persons were then followed in several repeat surveys until 1997 (131 persons still took part in the last survey).

4.2 Historical Generations and Social Change

4.2.1 "Generation": A Problematic Term?

In 1928, Mannheim published his theoretically fundamental work on "The Problem of Generations" (1964). Although the concept of generation is thus sociologically considerably older than that of the cohort – and Ryder clearly borrowed from Mannheim's classic essay – the concept of generation plays virtually no role in life course research. One reason often cited for this is the ambiguity of the concept of generation. When, for example, the war generation, the parents' generation, the students' generation, the generation of the young old, or the "internship generation" (or even the next generation of electric shavers) are mentioned, the term is used in very different frames of reference: it refers to socio-cultural collectives shaped by historical circumstances, to genealogical relationships, to phases of life, to age groups, or to cohorts (or to technical product lines). Kertzer rightly complains that this polysemantic use of terms is "guaranteed to sow confusion. The confounding of generation as a principle of descent relationship with concepts related to age and historical time has resulted in studies that are methodologically flawed" (1983, p. 142) – which he convincingly proves with a number of examples. Only – who or what is to be criticized then: the concept of generation or the sociologist who uses it inconsistently?

In order to avoid the inadmissible conflation of historical generations, descent relations, life phases, age groups and cohorts in the term "generation", some researchers (after the cohort concept had found its way into sociology), especially from the USA, propagated a restriction to genealogical relations: "generation" should be understood solely in the sense of familial generations (Ryder 1965; Riley et al. 1972; Glenn 1977; Kertzer 1983). The fact that this attempt at terminological regulation was not able to gain acceptance points to the fact that, in addition to descent relations, the concept of generation contains a further social phenomenon which, due to its social relevance, cannot simply be suppressed from its semantics – and which should also not be defined away, because this would waste an analytical potential of this concept. This social phenomenon is – as a brief look at the history of meaning of the concept of generation shows – about historical generations.

"Generation" was borrowed in the early sixteenth century from the Latin "generatio", i.e. "generation, procreation".[21] The original concept of generation was thus "without doubt a biological-genealogical one" (Jaeger 1977, p. 430) and

---

[21] For an overview of the meanings and uses of the term generation, see e.g. Sackmann (1992); Weigel (2002, 2006, p. 107 ff.); Fietze (2009, p. 23 ff.).

4.2 Historical Generations and Social Change

referred to familial reproduction. In addition, the term also had generic connotations, i.e. it also referred to the human race (Latin "genus"): analogous to familial genealogy, human history was also assumed to have a biologically determined rhythmicity that existed at intervals of a good 30 years. The idea that history and social change are subject to a biologically determined generational rhythm is now obsolete – only the familial concept of generation is biologically based.[22] At the end of the eighteenth century, there was a semantic shift in the concept of generation: in the course of that century, accelerating social change led to the concept of "generation" moving from the horizon of a continuous generative sequence into a perspective of discontinuity. "The one course of time" – according to Koselleck – "becomes a dynamic of multi-layered times at the same time. What progress had brought to the concept, that – to put it briefly – old and new collide ... had become an experience of everyday life since the French Revolution. The generations lived in a common space of experience, but this was fractured in perspective according to political generation and social standpoint" (1979, p. 367). Everyday life and present-day experiences of people existing at the same time were no longer the same, but were shaped by their social position and, more importantly here, their membership of different generations. In reaction to this novel experience of historical-social discontinuity, a new conceptual understanding emerged in the sense of historical generations (Riedel 1969). The relationship between generation on the one hand, history and society on the other is thus reversed: the genealogical understanding of the concept saw the biologically determined rhythm of the familial succession of generations as the cause of social change – the historical concept of generation sees in these social changes the cause of the formation of distinct generations (which in turn can have an effect on social change).[23]

Despite this essential relationship between historical generations and historical-societal discontinuity, the term "generation" plays virtually no role in life course research for the recording of collective life courses and social change. The reason for this is that neither familial nor historical generations, unlike cohorts, can be precisely defined in time. As far as familial generations are concerned, analyses of intergenerational data do not permit any statement about social change because considerable age differences exist within generations (as Blau and Duncan already

---

[22] The biologically determined rhythm of the familial succession of generations cannot be transferred to history and society, because the succession of births in larger social formations represents a continuously flowing stream.

[23] Only "in the concept of historical generations is the experience of the temporalization of history, the simultaneity of the non-simultaneous as the specific experience of modern times, integrated" (Fietze 2009, p. 40).

showed in their classic mobility study (1967, p. 82 ff.)). If, for example, one were to compare the value orientations of 16-year-olds with those of their parents and grandparents, there would – assuming that the mothers were 19–39 years old at the time of the children's birth (for the fathers an even greater time frame can be assumed) – already be age differences of at least 20 years in the parents' generation, which would double to at least 40 years in the grandparents' generation. As a result of such age differences, empirical studies that work with the familial generation concept cannot provide any insights into general social change. As far as the familial generation concept is concerned, only this much: it refers to genealogical stages, whereby this familial generation sequence is biologically constituted. Family generations have no constitutive relation to history and society, but are simply "given" as biologically conditioned social facts – in this respect, the question of the conditions and causes of the formation of a generation does not arise here. From a research perspective, the familial generation concept rather aims at the relations between familial generations as well as their relation to the welfare state (Lüscher and Schultheis 1993; Bengtson and Harootyan 1994; Wissenschaftlicher Beirat für Familienfragen 2012) and examines the familial as well as welfare state transmissions of cultural, social and economic services and capitals (Szydlik 2004).[24] In this respect, it can be generally stated that familial intergenerational relationships are "per se characterized by ambivalence. However, generational ambivalence does not lead to a drifting apart of the family generations. (…) The keyword 'lifelong solidarity' describes the relationship between family generations much better" (Szydlik 2000, p. 233). Anyone interested in family generations or the sociological relevance of the family generation concept is referred here to the relevant literature;[25] the following is concerned solely with the historical generation concept.

---

[24] According to Kaufmann, generational relations are "the observable consequences of social interactions between members of different, usually family-defined generations"; in contrast, generational circumstances refer to "the connections between the living situations and collective destinies of different age groups or cohorts, which are not directly experienced by those involved and are essentially mediated by institutions of the welfare state" (1993, p. 97). In this context, the transmission of educational capital (influence of the parental home on educational opportunities) has been and continues to be extensively researched; the transfer of wealth and home ownership has been increasingly discussed for some time. The transmission from the children's to the parents' generation is primarily concerned with care and domestic support services. With regard to generational relations, the focus is on the question of whether family-generational solidarity is undermined or supported by the welfare state (crowding out vs. crowding in).

[25] In addition to the publications already mentioned, e.g. Liebau (1999); Kohli and Szydlik (2000); Lüscher and Liegle (2003); Pillemer and Lüscher (2004); Lange and Lettke (2006); Blome et al. (2008); Ette et al. (2010).

For historical generations, Berger has framed the complaint of precise temporal locatability in the question "How long is a generation?" (1960). His programmatic question about the beginning and end of a generation, about the birth cohorts belonging to it, alludes to the fundamental problem of the historical concept of generation, that of having to clarify the constitutive reference of a historical generation to history and society: how and why do distinct historical generations form out of the continuous stream of the sequence of births, ageing and death? In his classic essay, Mannheim attempted to solve this problem. As far as the criticized precision of the temporal localizability of a historical generation is concerned, his essay (and the subsequent generation sociological discourse) leads to the insight that historical generations cannot be localized temporally with the same precision as birth cohorts. But – is this enough to declare the concept of generation irrelevant in life course research?

4.2.2 The Sociological Problem of Generations

In his work, Mannheim first criticizes the two perspectives under which the generational phenomenon has been thematized so far. The positivist way of thinking is to be criticized because it "seeks to understand the formal change of intellectual and social currents directly from the sphere of biology" (1964, p. 511 f.), i.e. it attributes social change to the biological fact of man's limited lifespan and consequently asserts a biologically conditioned rhythmicity as a general law operating in history. There is no need to go further into this way of thinking: neither is it possible to see how social, political, economic and cultural discontinuities could result directly from the continuous flow of births, ageing and death, nor can the specific form of social change be derived from this biological fact, which is always the same. The romantic-historical perspective, which is only interested in the sphere of cultural change, is to be criticized because with the generation concept it replaces "the usual, only external framework of the course of mental movements" (ibid., p. 516), i.e. the quantitatively measurable chronological concept of time, with the idea of "only qualitatively ascertainable inner time of experience" (ibid.), i.e. a subjective and only by means of understanding accessible "inner temporality". Following Dilthey, Mannheim emphasizes that this gives the circumstance of "simultaneity ... a deeper than merely chronological meaning. Individuals growing up at the same time experience ... the same guiding influences both on the part of the intellectual culture that impresses them and on the part of socio-political conditions" (ibid.).[26] Whereas in 1875 Dilthey had related this relationship of simultaneity to those growing up together in their similar socialization and assumed a chronological succession of the respective cultural generations, half a century later Pinder emphasized precisely "the 'non-simultaneity of the simultaneous'.[27] Different generations live in the same chronological time" (ibid., p. 517). Mannheim adopts Dilthey's and Pinder's reflections for his generational sociology, but rejects their way of thinking because it "(covers) the fact that between the natural sphere and the spiritual still lies the level of socially forming forces" (ibid., p. 519). His critique of the positivist and the romantic-historical perspective leads to the demand for an "investigation of what lies closer and can be investigated, the transparent texture of social events and their effects on the generational phenomenon" (ibid., p. 521 f.) – i.e.: a sociological perspective. Mannheim develops this perspective by elaborating the "most elementary facts of the generation phenomenon" (ibid., p. 523) by means of a formal sociological analysis.

What now constitutes, in formal sociological terms, "the specific togetherness of the individuals linked in the generational unit" (ibid., p. 524)? First of all, these do not represent a concrete grouping in the sense of the sociological concept of group, but rather "a mere connection" (ibid.), which can be explained by analogy with the concept of class. Class position refers to a "fatefully related embeddedness (Lagerung) … in the economic-power structure" (ibid., p. 525) of society: individuals who are in

---

[26] Dilthey's classic formulation is: "Generation is … a designation for a relationship of simultaneity of individuals; those who grew up, as it were, side by side … we call the same generation. From this then follows the linking of such individuals by a deeper relation. Those who experience the same guiding influences in the years of receptivity together make up a generation. Thus conceived, a generation forms a narrower circle of individuals who, through dependence on the same great facts and changes that occurred in the age of their susceptibility, are united into a homogeneous whole, in spite of the diversity of other factors added" (1961, p. 37).

[27] Pinder, an art historian, attempted to explain the simultaneous existence of different art styles with the help of the generation concept in a much-discussed work on "The Problem of Generation in the History of European Art" (1926). His often quoted talk of the "'non-simultaneity' of the simultaneous" (ibid., p. 11) problematized the "idea of the all-valid, 'uniform time' with its uniform 'progress'; of the compelling 'present' that rolls over the existences" (1926, p. 13). A generational-historical view, on the other hand, "replaces the too clumsy pseudo-accord of the 'Gegenwarten' (presents) with the notion of a polyphony that possesses greater clarity for the sharpened ear, but demands this sharpening. (…) It teaches to differentiate historical time from the subjects' angles, and thus to feel its relative nature: that for artists as for people there is not 'the time' at all, but 'their time'. In the – objective – image of the multidimensionality of historical moments in time, this relativization is expressed as the – subjective – difference of each chronologically uniform 'moment in time', as the hidden non-simultaneity of the simultaneous" (ibid., p. 163).

4.2 Historical Generations and Social Change

similar socio-economic positions are objectively, i.e. whether they are aware of it or not, in the same class position. Analogously, the concept of generation also initially merely refers to a related embeddedness[28] of individuals in social space. While in the case of the class situation this refers to the hierarchical structuring of a society and is economically based, in the case of the generation phenomenon its frame of reference is the temporal structure of the course of history and is based on the biologically determined demographic metabolism: by belonging to a birth cohort "one is embedded in a related way in the historical stream of social events" (ibid., p. 527). In this respect, the generation concept is also biologically based in Mannheim. However, the fact of birth, aging and death is merely the precondition for the formation of generations. These are not contained in the biological fact of limited lifetime, and thus cannot be derived from it either, but can only be determined sociologically: on the basis of historical-social structures and processes.[29]

In this respect, the sociological relevance of the biologically based generational embedding must be further questioned. Like every embedding of individuals in social space, it shapes their experience and thinking in a certain way: by limiting the possibilities of experience and action and positively by "suggesting" certain ways of experiencing, thinking and behaving. Mannheim speaks of the "tendency inherent in every embedding ... which is determinable from the peculiarity of the embeddedness itself" (ibid., p. 528). What tendency is inherent in generational embeddeedness, or what specific effects does the demographic metabolism that underpins it produce? In formal sociological terms, five elementary aspects can be identified. Firstly, demographic metabolism brings about the "constant insertion of new cultural carriers" (ibid., p. 530). These social "newcomers" also bring with them a new kind of access to the social and cultural heritage and are therefore, for Mannheim, the most important innovation factor of a society. A second effect is that of the "steady departure of earlier bearers of culture" (ibid., p. 532). Their death enables cultural and social forgetting as a necessary condition of societal advancement. Third, the moment of gen-

---

[28] However, their "fate" with regard to the class position is to be relativized in contrast to the generational embeddedness (as will become clear in a moment): individuals can leave their class position (upward or downward mobility).

[29] Like every phenomenon that is founded by another, the phenomenon of generation could not "exist" without this foundation, but it contains within itself a qualitatively peculiar super-additive that is incapable of being founded. If there were no social interaction between people, if there were no structure of society of a certain kind, if there were no history based on continuities of a specific kind, the structure of the generational connection based on the phenomenon of embeddedness would not arise, but only birth, aging, and death. "The sociological problem of generations thus only begins where the sociological relevance of these conditions is emphasized" (Mannheim 1964, p. 527 f.).

erational embeddedness implies that individuals can always "participate only in a temporally limited section of the historical process" (ibid., p. 535). This aspect is particularly important for Mannheim's theory of generation and will therefore be discussed in more detail in the next paragraph. A fourth consequence is the "necessity of the constant handing down ... of the inherited cultural heritage" (ibid., p. 538). This transmission takes place less in pedagogical form as education or by means of the consciously taught than in socializing form as the unquestioned "letting grow into" of the adolescents. Finally, fifthly, it is about the "continuity in the generational change" (ibid., p. 540). This mostly enables smooth processes of social change, because it is not the young who confront the old, but as a rule neighboring birth cohorts of the cohort continuum between old and young who interact.

> - Discuss Mannheim's view that the sociocultural innovation potential inherent in the biologically conditioned "constant reintroduction of new culture bearers" is greater or more radical than that resulting from the biographical or personality development of individuals in the course of their lives.
> - How does Mannheim's statement "One is old primarily because one lives in a specific, self-acquired, formative context of experience, whereby every possible new experience is assigned its shape and its place to a certain extent in advance, whereas in the new life the formative forces are still forming and the basic intentions are still able to ope with the formative force of new situations in themselves" (1964, p. 534) relate to his statement: "Nothing is more incorrect than to think ... that youth is progressive and old age eo ipso conservative" (ibid., p. 534) to his statement: 'There is nothing more incorrect than to think ... that youth is progressive and old age eo ipso conservative' (ibid., S. 535)?

The aspect of participation in a limited, i.e. specific, section of history is of particular importance because it specifies the moment of generational embeddedness, which Mannheim had initially defined as merely belonging to a birth cohort. However, this moment is not already constituted by the fact that individuals are born in the same chronological period. Thus, for example, with regard to Chinese and German youth around 1800, there could obviously be no question of a related embeddedness. Rather, a generational embeddedness only exists "insofar as it is a matter of potential participation in events and experiences that connect them together.

4.2 Historical Generations and Social Change

Only a common historical-social habitat makes it possible for birth-related embeddings in chronological time to become sociologically relevant" (ibid., p. 536). In this context, Mannheim formulates a developmental psychological thesis with generational sociological consequences: "The first impressions have the tendency to become fixed as a natural world view" (ibid.). According to this, a fundamental imprinting of consciousness occurs early in the course of life, especially in adolescence, which marks out the individual's possible horizon of experience, thought and relevance in his further life, i.e. all biographical experience and processing of subsequent life events and circumstances are always preformed in perspective by this fundamental layer of consciousness. This "predominance of first impressions remains alive and determining even when the whole subsequent course of life should be nothing but a negation and dismantling of the 'natural world view' received in youth" (ibid., p. 537). According to Mannheim, neighboring birth cohorts internalize a fundamental and, as a result of growing up together, also a common, similar world view during childhood and especially adolescence.

The five aspects that can be derived formally sociologically from the biological fact of demographic metabolism do not, however, constitute the generation phenomenon in its entirety; it does not only exist in the moment of generational embeddedness. Mannheim's talk of a potential participation in unifying events already points to a further moment that can be analytically distinguished in the generational phenomenon: the generational coherence (Generationszusammenhang). Just as the objective class situation implies only the possibility of the formation of a class that is self-aware of its social situation (class "in itself" → "for itself"), the generational embeddedness holds only the possibility of actual generational formation. For a generation to constitute itself in real terms, "some concrete connection … must still be added (…). This connectedness might be called, in short, a participation in the common destinies …" (ibid., p. 542). What is to be understood by this? Mannheim's explanations are ambiguous on this central point. His developmental-psychological argument suggests a socialization-theoretical understanding in the sense of individuals being shaped in the same way because of their common experience of the same historical-social events and circumstances during their adolescent phase. However, this understanding, which is widespread in generational sociology (Fogt 1982), again undermines the analytical differentiation of generational embeddedness and coherence, because the latter would then automatically result from the former. Consequently, every youth or birth cohort would also be a generation – and the decisive question in generational sociology, how and why distinct historical generations are formed out of a continuous stream of births, ageing and death, would no longer make sense to ask (or could only be answered decisionistically in the sense of the sociologist's decision to declare certain youth/birth cohorts a "generation" and others not).

Mannheim's remarks on the boundaries of the social (embeddedness) space relevant for the formation of a generation suggest a different understanding of this concrete coherence in the generational context. His example of Chinese and German youth around 1800 names as an upper limit the "belonging to the same historical community of life" (ibid.), i.e. mostly to a national society.[30] As for the lower limit, Mannheim asks whether urban youth around 1800 and young peasants in remote rural areas belonged to the same generational coherence – which he denies, since the latter "were not caught up in those social and intellectual upheavals that moved these urban youth. We will therefore only speak of a generational coherence if real social and spiritual contents create a real connection between the individuals in the same generational stratum precisely in that area of the loosened up and becoming new" (ibid., p. 543). Accordingly, the generational coherence does not arise directly as an inevitable consequence of socialization, but mediated: Mannheim assumes here an interaction between generational embeddings and ongoing social change. Individuals must react to the social changes resulting from this change, and it is only in this concrete confrontation with the changed circumstances as well as their various social attempts and forms of coping that the bond can form among individuals in common. Mind you: can – a generational bond does not necessarily arise in the confrontation with new social situations.[31]

Within this concrete coherence through factual participation in the "becoming new", generational units (Generationseinheit) can then form – as a third moment that can be analytically distinguished in the generational phenomenon. These are (as often erroneously assumed) "not present in the form of a concrete group, even if their core is formed by a concrete group" (ibid., p. 548). Rather, generational units stand for specific forms of coping with that fateful new situation that crystallize in the confrontation with it: for "a unified reacting, a resonating and shaping formed in a related sense" (ibid., p. 547). A generational unit is formed if and to the extent that the concrete confrontations with the changed circumstances take on an innovative shape. Generational units represent cultural and social contents con-

---

[30] It should only be noted here that this upper limit of generationally relevant social space can no longer be taken for granted in (generational) sociology today.

[31] For Fietze – who has presented a precise account of Mannheim's generational sociological considerations and an interesting further development of his approach – historical generations therefore represent "social emergence phenomena" (2009, p. 17): their genesis lies "in the interference of age-specific socialization experiences and overarching processes of social change. They arise, so to speak, through 'friction' between social change and age-specific selectivity of reality perception, but – one could formulate – not as a friction loss, but as a 'friction gain' of social emergence" (ibid., p. 79).

4.2 Historical Generations and Social Change

densed into an identifiable style in the sense of innovative forms of reaction and responses to a fatefully changed situation. Mannheim gives the example of romantic conservatism and liberal rationalism as "polar forms of intellectual and social confrontation" (ibid., p. 544) with the fateful situation at the beginning of the nineteenth century. The example shows that a generational coherence does not have to correspond exactly to a generational unit; several, different generational units can also form in the same generational coherence; it is also possible that no generational unit arises in a generational coherence.

Although Mannheim does not understand the generation unit in the sense of a concrete group, he sees such groups as a decisive condition for the emergence of generation units. For these do not form "for the most part freely floating, without personal contact, but in concrete groups, where individuals meet in vital proximity, increase each other's soul-spiritually" (ibid., p. 547). It is in the dense, intense interactions of a concrete group that the first beginnings of an innovative response to a fateful change develop. If such impulses formulate an interpretation of the situation that corresponds to the experiences of individuals belonging to the same generational embedding, if they offer appealing perspectives for action in dealing with the fateful circumstances – in short, if they meet and give expression to the attitude to life of a larger number of individuals of roughly the same age, then these impulses can take on a coherent form and develop into an innovative response. This is less a matter of correctly reproducing the contents of experience and consciousness than of shaping them. It is crucial that these initial approaches take on a formative, collectively effective shape: symbolically condensing an attitude to life, an attitude to and interpretation of the world through a catchword, a gesture, a work of art, etc., bringing it to the point. Such symbols (such as "1968" or "Y") have "the deeply 'emotional' meaning ... that with them one absorbs not only the contents, but also the formative tendencies and collectively unifying basic intentions sunk into them and through these connects with the collective wills" (ibid., p. 545).[32]

---

[32] To summarize in Mannheim's words: it is "not the contents that connect in the first place; but even more connected are those formative forces through which, shaped, these contents first really receive a character and a directionality" (1964, p. 544 f.). The fact that "the basic intentions that initially rise out of a concrete group ... possess unifying force beyond the concrete group ... is due ... to the fact that they are more or less adequate expressions of the generational embeddedness in question" (ibid., p. 548). "Basic intentions and design principles are the most essential ... because only these have a truly socializing effect; and, perhaps more importantly, these are truly perpetuable" (ibid., p. 545). Also, "by them ... spatially separated individuals, who never come into personal contact with each other, can be connected" (ibid., p. 546 f.).

As already mentioned, a concrete coherence or even a generational unit does not automatically emerge from a generational embeddedness. For Mannheim, whether or not a generational unit is formed depends "first and foremost on the peculiarity of the particular social dynamics in each case. Whether every year, every 30 years, every 100 years, whether a new generational style comes into being rhythmically at all, depends on the triggering force of the social-spiritual process" (ibid., p. 552 f.). The decisive condition for the formation of a generational unit is thus the dynamic of ongoing social change. If the social changes take place only insidiously, the individuals can gradually grow into them without frictions – if the dynamics are only slight, there is no occasion for innovative reactions. If, however, the "latent continuous alteration of the traditional forms of experience, thought and design is no longer possible ... then somewhere the new starting points crystallize into an impulse that stands out as new and into a new formative unity" (ibid., p. 550). Such a new generational style, a generational unity thus emerges when the ways of thinking and behaving of the older birth cohorts no longer function from the point of view of the younger cohorts in the confrontation with a fatefully changed situation, have become problematic for them. It should also be noted that the dynamics of social change must not be too great, because then innovative impulses cannot develop further and be formulated, i.e. approaches to innovative contents and forms are virtually overrun by the rapid succession of social changes. Only if the dynamics of social change are neither too low nor too high will "new generational impulses condense into a forming unit" (ibid., p. 553).[33]

So much for the presentation of Mannheim's classic work, which is fundamental to generation theory. His essay offers a complex argument concerning the basic generational sociological problem of the constitutive relation of historical generations to history and society. This problem exists because the biologically determined demographic metabolism is a continuous process, but the time structure of history and social change is discontinuous. Despite Mannheim's sophisticated argumentation on the fundamental question of how and why distinct historical generations (can) form out of a steady stream of births, aging, and death, some generation-theoretical ambiguities and problems remain.

---

[33] See also Comte's thought experiment outlined in a footnote at the beginning of the chapter.

4.2 Historical Generations and Social Change

In recent times, the topic of "intergenerational justice" has boomed (Tremmel 2012), also luridly dubbed the "war of the generations" in the mass media. The background to this is the crisis of the welfare state, which became apparent at the latest towards the end of the 1980s. This had led to a situation in which the older "welfare state generations", who had benefited from the development and enormous expansion of welfare state services since the 1950s, were now confronted with a "post-welfare state generation" (Leisering 2000, p. 60 ff.) of younger people who had little to expect from the welfare state. With regard to New Zealand, Thomson had already spoken at the end of the 1980s of those older socio-political generations pointedly as "selfish generations" (1996) and of welfare state winner and loser generations (1989). In Germany, the focus is primarily on the statutory pension insurance and its so-called "intergenerational contract" (Hardach 2006). While for the generation of the great pension reform of 1957 the welfare state presented itself as a guarantor of a socially secure life horizon with relatively low contributions yesterday and relatively high returns today, the generation of the various pension reforms of the 1990s saw itself as the maneuvering mass of an old-age security policy for which only one thing was certain: that they would be the net payers of a generational solidarity pact, without being able to assume that it would still apply in their "own old age" (Bude 2005, p. 42 f.).

- Are these welfare state generations (historical) generations at all, or rather age groups or birth cohorts?
- Is the "war of the generations" really about generational conflicts? What are the roots of the conflicts? What role do demographic change and economic development play in this?
- Discuss the so-called intergenerational contract.
- Can the older "welfare state generations" be accused of having preserved the blessings of the welfare state and taken them with them? Or have they even shaped it in their favor and without consideration for future generations?
- When older "welfare state generations" are described as profiteers of the welfare state, they often counter by pointing to the enormous transfers of wealth from the elderly to the benefit of the younger "post-welfare state generation". What do you think about this?

4.2.3 Problems and Potentials of the Generation Concept

Mannheim's argumentation on the formation of a historical generation (unit) is inconsistent, as it implies two readings. On the one hand, the formation of a generation is seen as a direct socialization consequence of events and circumstances experienced at a young age. This is the common view – although it undoes Mannheim's differentiation of the generational phenomenon into the three analytically distinguishable moments of generational embeddedness, coherence, and unit. This widespread reception restricts the concept of generation to the moment of generational embeddedness and thus reduces it to the cohort concept. For this reason alone, it will not be discussed further; also, the problematic assumptions of this common reception have already been discussed in connection with the cohort concept. In relation to this comparatively simple reading, therefore, only two further problems will be addressed. The first is the focus on youth generations, which is argumentatively conclusive.[34] His conception of generations as youth generations shows Mannheim to be a child of his time: in Germany, a veritable youth myth had developed since the late nineteenth century, revolving around the idea of a political mission of youth to renew society (Koebner et al. 1985; Rosemann 1995; Stambolis 2003). In the meantime, however, as Zinnecker states, "the 'youth myth' has faded badly" (2003, p. 50). An understanding of generations only in the sense of youth generations is therefore obsolete and no longer convincing.[35] A conception of the common reading appropriate to the present would rather have to assume that "the phase of life in which experiences constitutive for the formation of a generational context are made ... can range from early childhood to later adulthood" (Rosenthal 2000, p. 165).

A second problem relates to generations as (supposed) collective agents of social change. If – according to the common reading – a socializational automatism turns the generational embeddedness into a generational coherence or a homogeneously shaped generational unit in the sense of a concrete group, it is natural to expect that "generational consciousness leads to collective behavior" (Schulz and Grebner

---

[34] See also Ryder: "The potential for change is concentrated in the cohorts of young adults who are old enough to participate directly in the movements impelled by change, but not old enough to have become committed to ... a way of life" (1965, p. 848).

[35] Adhering to this concept of the youth generation, which is bound to contemporary history, would also mean perpetuating that questionable idea of its political mission: "Even more problematic is the 'sense of mission' committed to the youth myth of the 1920s in a 'heroic' or 'tragic' concept of generation, which can be found in the revolutionary self-mission of 'political generations' to this day" (Weisbrod 2005, p. 5).

4.2 Historical Generations and Social Change

2003, p. 7). This implicit expectation that historical generations act as collective agents, i.e. as relevant factors of social change, represents a basic problem of mainstream generational sociology: namely, to prove empirically that a common historical-social embedding, or a homogeneous imprint supposedly caused by it, leads to collective action on the part of the individuals concerned. That such an assumption of causality is based on theoretically untenable assumptions has already been shown. But also empirically there is no convincing evidence for it, at least not for causality in the strict sense – whereas the dubiousness of such a causal relationship can very well be shown empirically (with regard to political decision-making, see e.g. Best 2003). This notorious difficulty – not to say aporia – of the current sociology of generation can be conceptually eliminated by linking it to the other generation-theoretical understanding contained in Mannheim's argumentation.[36]

This second reading is more complex (and complicated). In it, the emergence of a generation (unit) is understood as a mediated process coupled to a specific modality of the dynamics of social change. However, Mannheim only says under which modalities no generational formation takes place (the pace of social change may be neither too high nor too low) – a positive, informative determination of generational dynamics is missing. In this regard, his essay contains only one hint: "decisive collective events can have a 'crystallizing' effect in this respect" (1964, p. 552).[37] The fact that Mannheim saw major historical events as triggers of a generational formation can be understood from his contemporary historical ties. World War I was experienced (quasi climax of the modern historical experience of discontinuity) as a historical caesura and civilizational trauma and had "a generational effect like hardly any other historical event" (Jureit 2006, p. 25; see Wohl 1979). More important here, however, is a methodological aspect: reference even to such severe major events does not explain the constitution of historical generations.

---

[36] In this context, Mannheim is often criticized for the indeterminacy of the social carrier group of a generation. The question about the social carrier group of a generation is quite justified. However – and apart from the fact that he did not understand generation units as concrete groups – Mannheim does not answer the question of the impulse-givers and social bearers of a generation unit theoretically a priori for good reason: these can only ever be determined with regard to the generation unit in question through empirical sociological studies of knowledge.

[37] This hint was gratefully received by the common Mannheim reception, because in connection with their assumption of an imprinting ("formative") youth phase this means methodologically that the difficult task of empirically identifying historical generations "can be avoided. By checking with the individual cohorts which significant major historical events they experienced during the youth phase, generations can be designed at the desk" (Rosenthal 2000, p. 163 f.).

Such an event, more than other events or circumstances, can become the starting point for the formation of a historical generation – only (the mere reference to) its existence says nothing at all about the factual formation of a generation (unit). Precisely this process of formation, however, would have to be precisely traced, clarified, proven empirically in its reference to the supposedly constitutive major event – only then would the emergence of a historical generation be convincingly explained. This applies in general: methodologically, it is absolutely important not simply to derive generations from historical events or social circumstances, but to empirically reconstruct or prove their connection, i.e. the process of generation formation on the basis of an event or situation experience.

- Consider what major events there have been in Germany since the founding of the Reich and what historical generations there should then be according to the view criticized here.
- Discuss whether there is an "89 generation" (Leggewie 1995). Afterwards, reflect on your discussion: what were the arguments in favor or against?

Such empirical studies show that generations socially construct themselves ex post as "believed communities".[38] Bude (1995), for example, used the example of the "68 generation" – like the two World War generations one of the three important political-historical generations of the twentieth century in Germany (Herbert 2003) – to show that and how generations retrospectively form themselves as communities of experience and memory. According to Bude, generations represent "a social construction with a vague reference to events and little obligation to participate" (2000, p. 25). The event reference is vague precisely because the event itself is not formative, as such not a forming factor, but only the starting or crystallization point for the actual generation forming process. Most of the later so-called "68ers" were not present at the demonstration against the Persian Shah on that symbolic "June 2, 1967 in Berlin … when Benno Ohnesorg was shot" (Jureit 2006, p. 81).[39] Rather, the formation of a generation did not occur until the 1970s and especially the 1980s, in which "a considerable retrospective multiplication" (Bude 2000,

---

[38] This formulation goes back to Weber, who already wrote in the early 1920s with regard to the ethnic community that it is "in itself only (believed) 'commonality', but not 'community' … whose essence includes real community action" (1980, p. 237).

[39] This also applies to the two war generations: "even the material battles of the First World War were really experienced together by very few of those who in retrospect saw themselves as the war generation" (Jureit 2006, p. 81); on the "flak helper generation" see. Bude (1987).

4.2 Historical Generations and Social Change

p. 26) of the "68ers" took place.[40] This means that it is only in retrospect that a generation is formed; it is socially constructed within the framework of a complex web of event-related communication. In these interactions, the different experiences of individuals are interpretatively unified: "The more time passes, the more clearly common moods, basic feelings and problems behind different political and ideological orientations emerge. (...) People talk about the past ..., and all by themselves, the first-person narratives come under the dominance of the we-perspective" (ibid., p. 27 f.). Generations form themselves to the extent that the factual heterogeneity of individual experiences is (re)formed into a unified memory in diverse, networked communications, is preserved in the narrative of a common (life) history and condenses into a kind of collective identity. It is this retrospective unification of experience into a "sense of we" (Corsten 2001, p. 41) through which "generations constitute themselves as life-time 'communities of experience and memory'" (Bude 2000, p. 30).

In this process of social ex post construction of a "sense of we" or a kind of collective identity, it is not the objectivity or authenticity of the experience of a historical (major) event or certain social circumstances that is important. Rather, it is about the "act of construction itself, that is, the fact that ... the person remembering wants to see himself or herself integrated into certain factual and personal contexts" (Schulz and Grebner 2003, p. 22). Interpreting and communicating individual experiences in a generational perspective, putting one's life-historical self-placement in a generational frame of reference, serves to produce "we-sense", generates a kind of collective identity. The formation of generations is thus about the retrospective construction of felt community, believed commonality. This is true, of course, even if the frame of reference is a national, ethnic, gender, class, or professional one. Why and how do individuals feel they belong to a generation[41] (in general as well as in relation to nation, ethnicity, gender, class or profession)? Only corresponding empirical studies can provide concrete answers to this question –

---

[40] In this – Weisbrod says with a slightly cynical undertone – "it is more a matter of a miraculous catch-up multiplication of the generation of narrators than of a generation of experience in the narrower sense. In fact, at the time it was 'a small radical minority' that was involved in the production of immediate, emphatic difference in demonstrations and counter-publics" (2005, p. 7).

[41] The central question of the reason for the feeling of belonging (who feels and declares themselves to belong to a certain generation, when, in which context, in demarcation from whom or what, with which diffuse expectations or concrete interests, etc.) is to be supplemented by the question of how this is made tangible or demonstrated to the outside world?

which, especially today, would also have to take into account the role of the media.[42] In any case, it should be noted that the concept of generation "since Romanticism and increasingly since the end of the 19th century ... has obviously served collective needs for social positioning, for social reassurance and orientation in an extremely convincing way. Alongside nation and class, the generational self-description has proven itself as a variable of identity, and it has since been part of the fixed repertoire of modern societies" (Jureit 2006, p. 124).

> - Compare the statement just quoted with the following: "The contingency category of biography needs an anchor in collective references to experience. (...) This requires a reference point of comparability and imputability. Since 'class' and 'nation' are no longer suitable as self-evident collectivization variables, 'generation' offers itself as a category of social embedding ... The everyday concept of generation combines biblical archaism with pop-cultural topicality. (...) In any case, the community of origin of those of approximately the same age forms a 'natural' hold in the flow of time" (Bude 2000, p. 19 f.).
> - Consider how generational belonging is experienced within the "felt community" and how it is demonstrated externally.

If one understands generations as believed communities that are socially constituted retrospectively, the generational sociological perspective changes. Historical generations are then no longer understood as an (explanatory) factor of social change (a – as mentioned – problematic assumption), but rather as a possibility and means of social self-positioning of individuals. Historical generations are the result of collective self-thematizations, the expression of a social change in experience; they represent not so much collective actors as collective units of interpretation. The concept of generation is not an analytical category for explaining social change, but serves in modern societies to interpret and cope with its experiences. Is it therefore irrelevant for life course research? The fact that the latter largely ignores the theoretically and methodologically more complicated concept of generation –

---

[42] Generational "communities need publicly available objects of identification so that potential commonalities can be negotiated and transmitted at all. Such objects make it possible to make believed commonalities emotionally tangible ... This is true not only for political generations, but also for generational self-interpretations that are oriented towards cultural or social living conditions" (Jureit 2006, p. 17).

4.2 Historical Generations and Social Change

quite in contrast to the cohort concept[43] – contrasts strangely with its public and also academic boom (Jureit 2006; Künemund and Szydlik 2009), which has been going on since the end of the 1980s.

> Since then, the term "generation" has been used in an inflationary manner in the arts pages: Generation Golf, Generation Gulf War, Generation 89, Wendegeneration, Generation X, Generation Y, Generation Z, Generation Ally, Generation MTV, Generation @, Generation Facebook, Generation Smartphone, Null-Bock-Generation, Generation Beziehungsunfähig, Single-Generation, Generation Praktikum, Generation Maybe, Generation Doof, etc …, – such generational labels today serve above all "the middle classes for the descriptive ordering of the social world, for meaningful self-positioning in historical change and as a source of aesthetic experience. An expanding journalistic market, driven by the dynamics of constant differentiation and shortened product cycles, helps people to create catchy generational figures out of the 'primordial soup' of biographical experiences" (Maase 2005, p. 240).
>
> - How would you situate yourself generationally and describe your generation? How do you justify this generational designation? Does the aspect of participation in a "fateful" change play a role here?

Generations, however, are not only relevant from an individual perspective as identificatory self-locations of individuals in history and society, but also from a societal structural perspective as such retrospectively constructed believed communities. "Generational thinking" – according to Jureit – "brings order to modern societies" (2006, p. 125). Matthes attempted to open up this structural, generation-theoretical perspective, which goes beyond an individual self-location function, more than 30 years ago: namely, "to conceive of the generation problem … as one of the cultural regulation of temporality" (1985, p. 367). In this view, generations –

---

[43] Theoretically, the cohort concept, which is methodologically quite easy to handle, exhausts itself in the moment of generational embeddedness (and thus does not represent a further development of the generation concept, as is sometimes claimed – on the contrary: the complexity of Mannheim's generation concept is considerably reduced in Ryder's cohort concept; on the generational-sociological-disciplinary consequences of this loss of complexity, see Fietze 2009, p. 50 ff.).

whether as concrete generational groups or as cultural contents of the generational unit – are indicators of cultural typifications of temporality. The core question in generational sociology is then "how and by whom certain perceptions and experiences are brought to bear on the concept of generation in the historical-social process" (ibid., p. 365). This implies that historical generations feedback and impact on social change, but only indirectly and mediatedly: their formation functions "as a social mechanism through which accelerated social change is brought into the horizon of conscious interpretation and collective self-understanding of society" (Fietze 2009, p. 89). In this respect, studies on historical generations and their formation make it possible "to make chronologically offset patterns of world perception mutually identifiable, to extract them from the self-evidence of their 'conjunctive validity' among simultaneities in their confrontation, to make them attributable and 'negotiable'. It is not a matter of 'generations' as groups that can be shaped and determined in whatever way, but of generational relationships in which the temporality structure of social events is 'polyphonically organized' …, – in which social remembering and forgetting … are regulated, – in short: the reciprocal relation of strangeness that always arises and is produced anew with the lifetime distance of people in constant social simultaneity is made identifiable and copeable" (Matthes 1985, p. 369).[44]

---

[44] See also Weymann's analysis of the correspondence between young Poles who emigrated to the United States and their parents who remained in the homeland, printed in the classic study on "The Polish Peasant in Europe and America" (1995).

Structures of the Life Course

5

This chapter deals with the structures and structuring of individual life courses. The following basic questions arise from the perspective of analyzing the effects of social structural contexts on individual life courses and biographies, which is dominant in life course research: What patterns of life courses have developed in modern societies? How do they differ between socio-historical phases? How do they differ between particular societies? And how within a society between the sexes and between social groups? What are the causes of the social structural positioning of individuals in diverse social contexts over the life course? What are the structuring factors and mechanisms at the micro level of individual biographies, the meso level of organizations, the macro level of societal institutions and structures, and norms. And in the reverse direction of causality, the question is: What effects do changing life courses have on social structural contexts and institutional regulations? These questions will be addressed below on the basis of the tripartite basic structure of the life course (Sect. 5.1), the normative and institutional structuring of life courses (Sect. 5.2) and the "normal life course" as well as the thesis of a de-standardization of the life course (Sect. 5.3).

5.1 The Basic Tripartite Structure of the Life Course

In the chapter on the institutionalization of the life course, the age-related systems of public rights and duties that emerged in the late nineteenth century were already named as central structuring factors of the life course. Fundamental importance is attached to the differentiation of the education and old-age security system as well as to the employment system, which is preceded and followed by these two benefit systems. The establishment of a differentiated education, employment and old-age security system is accompanied by a temporal structuring of the life course: the life courses of individuals are divided by this institutional structure into three life stages with specific social roles of the individuals. The basic institutional differentiation of modern societies into an education, employment and old-age security system thus leads to a tripartite basic structure of the modern life course. Or in other words: the tripartite basic structure of modern life courses reflects the institutional differentiation of modern society, is the "mapping of overall social institutional differentiation onto diachronically ordered segments or life stages" (Mayer and Müller 1989, p. 46).

Historically, the tripartite life course has been formed in the wake of a change in the social organization of work. Since the seventeenth century, and then especially with industrialization, the economic form has changed fundamentally: from a subsistence economy to a (capitalist) gainful employment economy, from a household economy to an industrial economy based on free labor or labor markets.[1] The development of this economic and employment system was accompanied, with a time lag, by the establishment of a preceding education system that prepared people for the increasingly complex demands of work in terms of qualifications, as well as a subsequent old-age security system that served to secure people's livelihoods after they left working life. In this respect, Kohli sees the employment system as the central structuring factor of modern life courses: "In modern societies, the life course is organized around the employment system" (1985, p. 3). Its basic tripartite structure is institutionally determined by the system of dependent gainful employment and the educational and retirement phases that precede and follow it. Over the course of time, especially since the middle of the twentieth century, a close-meshed network of (welfare) state regulation and intervention has been woven over this basic tripartite structure. In view of this increasingly dense network of state regulation spanning all areas of life from the cradle to the grave,

---

[1] In the subsistence economy, as a family- or household-dominated mode of production, the primary concern is to meet one's own needs: production is oriented towards use value; production and consumption form a unit; work ends as soon as needs are met (generated surpluses are demonstratively "squandered" to maintain social networks). In contrast, the industrial-capitalist market economy is primarily concerned with profits: (surplus) production is oriented towards exchange values for the market. In this context, Hareven's socio-historical study on "Family time and industrial time" (1982) is interesting for life course research.

5.1 The Basic Tripartite Structure of the Life Course

the importance of the employment system as a fundamental structuring factor of the modern life course has been criticized with reference to the role of the (welfare) state in structuring life courses (Mayer and Müller 1986; Mayer and Schoepflin 1989). The corresponding discussion, however, represents only a pseudo-controversy: "there is" – as Kohli rightly says in the theoretical perspective of political economy – "indeed space for political regulation but that regulation is confronted by and focuses on a dynamic that is for the most part economic" (2007, p. 260). The basic tripartite structure of the modern life course is structurally anchored in this complex social institutional and political regulatory structure.[2]

The basic tripartite structure of the modern life course, organized around the employment system, has been criticized from the outset as "gender-blind": as a "generalization of a life course configuration that is based unreflectively on the male life course" (Born and Krüger 2001, p. 13). Is this accusation of the unreflective fading out of women's life courses true? The industrial economy, into which this change in the social organization of work finally led, led to a change in the form and significance of the family and thus to a new form and evaluation of the gender-specific division of labor.[3] Until well into the eighteenth century, the family was considered to be the community of all persons living and working together in one house, who were subject to the "pater familias".[4] This common working and living context "under one roof", which was characteristic of the predominant peasant and artisan families, was torn apart with increasing industrialization. In terms of social structure, a private sphere of reproduction was separated from the (public) sphere of production. This separation found its familial equivalent in the bourgeois family model[5] that emerged in this context: the man generates the family income by means of his productive gainful employment in the factory, shop or office – the woman performs reproductive family and domestic work (male breadwinner/

---

[2] This structural anchoring of the modern life course is culturally flanked by an ideology of individualism with its ideas about the individual, the life course and the self (Meyer 1986, 1992), which is deeply rooted and institutionalized in Western culture but will not be discussed further here.

[3] This development can only be outlined here in a few sentences; for more detailed information on the change in form and meaning of the family and the gender-specific division of labor, see Rosenbaum 1978, 1982; Sieder 1987; Gestrich 1999.

[4] It was not until the eighteenth century that the understanding of family that we take for granted today, in the sense of a family based on – emotionally charged – kinship relationships in ascending and descending lines, gradually took hold.

[5] Into which also the proletarian family, which emerged in this context, finally turned in the wake of the increased general level of prosperity in the twentieth century (the bourgeois family model had already served as a normative orientation).

female homemaker model). With this a new form of the gender specific division of labour and role assignment – "naturalized" by the term "Geschlechtscharaktere" (gender character; Hausen 1976) – emerged which not only led to the fact that women's domestic-familial reproductive labour did not count as "true work" compared to male employment but also resulted in women's financial and social dependency from men in the first place.[6] This form of gender-specific division of labor with its family model and concept of a male or female way of life was inscribed in the social institutional and extensive welfare state regulatory structure in many ways. Indicative of this was, for example, §1356, paragraph 1 of the German Civil Code (BGB), which was valid until 1977 and which read: "(1) The woman leads the household on her own responsibility. (2) She is entitled to be gainfully employed insofar as this is compatible with her duties in marriage and family." The pension system may serve as an illustrative socio-political example, which guaranteed the old-age security of the woman – who, as a result of her non- or low gainful employment, could acquire no or only small pension rights – after a widowhood in the form of the survivor's pension and thus via her husband. And to indicate the interlocking of the institutional and welfare state regulatory structure in this respect: with the half-day school system introduced in Germany at the end of the nineteenth century, the necessity of women's non- or at best part-time employment was institutionalized in family terms at the same time.

The three examples illustrate that the concept of the male working life and the dependent female family life as a normality presumption was built into (and consequently perpetuated in) the institutional and welfare state regulatory structure in many ways. Because the many and diverse regulatory elements of this structure did not stand unconnected next to each other, but rather related to and interlocked with each other, a "holistic" life course regime was formed as an expression of precisely this coherent social institutional and welfare state regulatory system (see the following subchapter). This life course regime with its structurally, normatively and legally anchored normality presumption experienced its heyday in the second half of the twentieth century until towards the end of the 1970s. In these decades, the institutionalized model of the tripartite life course organized around the employment system (or "male" gainful employment) (in which a functionally necessary complementary role of reproductive family and domestic work for women is implicitly conceived) was social reality: was – as Kohli only briefly notes[7] – the woman

---

[6] This also applies to the modernized bourgeois family in the form of the "additional earner model", in which the woman works part-time but ultimately retains her homemaker role.

[7] Looking back, Kohli explains that "my argument described the logic of the male breadwinner model instituted in the Fordist regime without intending to explain neither its evolution nor its emerging transformation" (2007, p. 261).

5.1 The Basic Tripartite Structure of the Life Course

"socialized through her husband" (1985, p. 24). His thesis of the tripartite basic structure of the modern life course organized around the employment system refers to the life course regime of the 1950s, 1960s and 1970s, that is, to a historical phase in which gender relations were institutionalized in the specific form of the male breadwinner/female homemaker model. This accusation of an unreflective, "gender-blind" generalization of the male life course model is misguided insofar as the thesis of the three-part basic structure of the modern life course organized around the employment system is "not so much a male argument as an argument appropriate for a male-dominated and work-dominated society" (Kohli 1986b, p. 297).[8] The fact that this thesis ignores neither the empirically ascertainable diversity of female (and, incidentally, also male) life courses nor the discrimination of women that goes hand in hand with the life course regime on which it is based should not really need to be emphasized – in order to conclude the comments on the accusation of a conceptual gender bias (Krüger and Levy 2000; Krüger 2001, 2003).

Riley and Riley formulate a truly radical critique of the tripartite basic structure of the modern life course with their thesis that in today's industrial societies "changes in age structures lay behind changes in lives" (1994, p. 16) and that, as a result, the age structures and criteria built into the social institutional and welfare state regulatory structure would be dysfunctional both individually and socially. Based on Riley's age stratification model (see Sect. 2.1), they argue that asynchronies inevitably occur between the two dynamics of individual ageing and social structural change, because ageing is a continuous process, whereas social structural change is a discontinuous process. These inevitable asynchronies produce "a recurring mismatch" (ibid., p. 24). For example, new work technologies can lead to "people's lives lag behind structural change … More critical in modern society than this 'people lag,' however, is the converse problem of the lag of structures behind lives" (ibid.). This structural lag results from the profound changes in people's lives in the course of the twentieth century, whereby the considerable increase in life expectancy is of particular relevance. For if an ever-increasing number of people have to spend a considerable part of their lives in the "roleless role" (ibid.) of retirement, this creates increasing structural pressure for change. What form might the structural change necessary to eliminate the current mismatch or structural lag take?

The Rileys want to answer this question by means of a heuristic contrast between the two ideal types of age-differentiated and age-integrated social structures,

---

[8] Thus, in the conclusion to her and Krüger's extensive empirical project, Born must also concede that Kohli's "statement regarding the market-centeredness of the life course … also proves to be astonishingly true for the life courses of women (of different cohorts and independent of their family status)" (2001, p. 45).

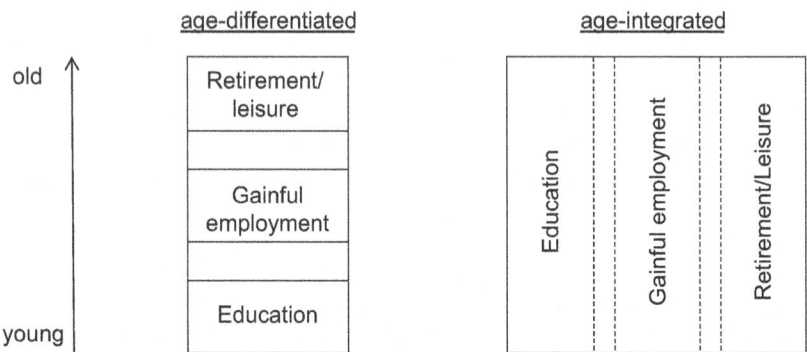

Fig. 5.1 Age-differentiated and age-integrated (life course) structures. (Based on Riley and Riley 1994, p. 26)

whereby – according to their socio-political demand – the former would have to be changed in the direction of the latter (Fig. 5.1). Their normative argument focuses on the area of (gainful) employment and the family. The prevailing age-differentiated family structure is characterized by age- and generation-related family and kinship roles. In an age-integrated ("family") structure "the constraints imposed by age and generation have been submerged. Here we imagine a boundless network of kin and kinlike relationships, in which people of any age … are free to choose (or to earn the right) to support, love or confide in one another" (ibid., p. 28).

> Give examples of what age-integrated structures might look like. In relation to this, consider what advantages the ideal of age-integrated kinship/relationship structures has? What disadvantages or problems do you see in this respect? How (un)realistic do you think the emergence or spread of age-integrated structures (such as multi-generational homes) is?

The Rileys' explanations are somewhat less vague with regard to the area of (gainful) employment. The basic institutional differentiation of modern society into an education, employment and old-age security system divides the life courses of individuals into three phases of life with specific social roles, activities and scope for action. While "young and middle-aged adults, especially women, are deprived of free time by the doubly demanding roles of work and family, many older people tend to be surfeited with it. Yet there are few normative expectations to give meaning to this time" (ibid., p. 16). In contrast to older people who have left the labor market, dealing with socially unstructured time without institutionalized behavioral expectations is unlikely to be a problem for younger people absorbed in the education system. Rather, the problem for younger people in education and training is that they "are offered few clear role opportunities for being, or feeling, useful" (ibid.). For the Rileys, this linking of certain roles and options to certain phases in the life course represents a dysfunctional structural limitation of individuals, or is a socially dysfunctional (age) structure. In contrast, age-integrated (life course) structures, in which the "age barriers are removed, so that role opportunities in all structures – education, work, and leisure – are open to people at every age", would be appropriate to the interests and needs of individuals and thus also socially functional (ibid., p. 27). (ibid., p. 27). What the Rileys are imagining here is an age-independent option space of flexible (multiple) changes between education, gainful employment and retirement/leisure over the entire life span.

How are these Riley reflections on an age-integrated society and flexibilisation of the life course to be evaluated? Do they only formulate a utopia or can they refer to empirically ascertainable undermining of the current age-differentiated (life course) structures? And do their socio-political demands for the transformation of age-differentiated structures into age-integrated structures and an accompanying flexibilisation of the life course[9] meet with broad approval among the population? The latter – to begin with – is less self-evident than it might seem at first glance. For example, a recent empirical study of older workers' preferences regarding retirement, based on data from the European Social Survey (ESS), shows that "individual retirement plans still continue to be oriented at the idea of withdrawing from employment before mandatory eligibility ages" (Hofäcker 2015, p. 1552). It is well known that people often feel they are "falling into a hole" when they leave the workforce and have problems filling their new "roleless role" in a meaningful way. However, individuals also often perceive the transition to retirement as a release from the constraints of working life, allowing them to try new things or have time for previously neglected interests. These two views, which tend to be exaggerated in the public debate, also exist in the academic discussion – and empirical evidence can be found for both. In this respect, it may be useful to consider what demands age-integrated social structures and a flexibilisation of the life course place on individuals. This is precisely what Settersten has done – who is very much in favor of the socio-political programme of the Rileys – who has shown that their realization on the part of individuals presupposes personality traits or competences such as a self-determined, planned way of life, strong self-motivation, high problem-solving ability and willingness to take risks, as well as the availability of time and financial resources, the existence of family support networks, relatively secure employment

---

[9] Programmatically formulated early on as a book title by Best: "Flexible life scheduling. Breaking the education-work-retirement lockstep" (1980).

and a good professional position (1999, p. 58 ff., 2003a). In this respect, the vision of an age-integrated society and flexibilisation of the life course "turns out to be a very presuppositional programme that appears to be more attractive and feasible for materially and socially better-off people with a higher educational and occupational status" (Amrhein 2004, p. 155) – and tends to be limited to this group of people.

With regard not to individual but to socio-structural preconditions for the realization of age-integrated, flexible (life course) structures, it should be noted that a strong, stable economy and the accompanying high level of employment security are of central importance. During the two decades preceding the first calls for age-integrated, flexible (life course) structures and policies towards the end of the 1970s, these structural conditions were in place. But already when those demands arose, as Lutz (1984) aptly put it in a book title, "The short dream of perpetual prosperity" was in fact already over. In view of the economic development since then, a good decade later Best, a prominent advocate of the flexibilisation of the life course, already asked rather sceptically: "Does flexible life scheduling have a future?" (1990) and conceded: "major initiatives concerning life scheduling flexibility are not likely to occur within American society for some time" (ibid., p. 235) – a prognosis that proved to be accurate for the Western industrial nations as a whole.

> Discuss the positions and considerations presented in this paragraph. Try to provide empirical support for your arguments or consider how sociology might produce empirical evidence.

So are the Rileys only propagating a normative vision or is their utopia based on empirically ascertainable underminings of age-differentiated (life course) structures or even a tendency towards their transformation into age-integrated (life course) structures? Quite obviously, education, gainful employment and retirement/leisure time are not so rigidly separated from each other as the ideal type of an age-differentiated (life course) structure suggests. For example, schoolchildren and students work part-time or during holidays or lecture-free periods; employed persons take part in continuing vocational training measures, go on parental leave or voluntarily decide to work part-time; some employed persons take a sabbatical year; retired persons attend senior studies or work in marginal employment (mini-job). Employed persons have a legal right to educational leave; vocational training in the dual system institutionally links the areas of education and employment; something similar applies to the Partial Retirement Act with regard to the transition to retirement. The question is how these empirical facts are to be evaluated.

5.1 The Basic Tripartite Structure of the Life Course

With the heuristic contrasting of two ideal types, the Rileys draw a continuum between the two poles of age-differentiated and age-integrated (life course) structures and thus constitute an interpretive framework that suggests understanding those empirical facts as deviations or departures from the age-differentiated pole and indications of a movement towards the age-integrated pole: as a real tendency of a transformation of age-differentiated into age-integrated (life course) structures. And consequently they conclude or postulate that the tripartite basic shape of the modern life course and its "age-based structures and cultural norms can be seen as outdated vestigial remains of an earlier era" (1994, p. 27). A visionary view may see it that way. In fact, however, there is still no question of the age-differentiated tripartite basic structure of the life course being outdated. This is because it results from the functional differentiation of a system of employment, education and old-age provision – and functional differentiation is the fundamental socio-structural organizational principle of modernity and as such an evolutionary achievement and stage of development that cannot simply be abolished, i.e. without considerable costs and side-effects. But this is precisely what age-integrated (life course) structures ultimately presuppose: that functional differentiation as the fundamental structuring principle of modern society would be suspended and the resulting structure, i.e. those three differentiated systems, would be abolished, dissolved.[10]

From a less visionary than realistic point of view, these empirical facts can be interpreted differently (which, however, the Rileys have conceptually obstructed with their heuristics): namely as an expression of a grown flexibilisation of the life course not beyond – i.e. through dissolution – but within the functionally differentiated systems of education, gainful employment and old-age provision and the thus institutionalized sequence logic of life. Neither jobbing pupils, students and pensioners nor employees on educational leave or further vocational training abolish the boundary between the employment and education systems. Neither partial retirement nor other part-time work, neither parental leave nor sabbaticals dissolve the boundary between the employment system and the retirement/leisure system.

---

[10] What is quite possible in terms of social evolution. It is not a question here of elevating the principle of functional differentiation to an iron law. Even in the functionally differentiated modern society there are (in addition to further, but secondary forms of differentiation) processes of de-differentiation everywhere, which are not to be demonized without hesitation as a social-evolutionary step backwards (there are also such), but can also be understood as a reaction to problems resulting from the (exaggerated) functional differentiation. Here it is only a matter of becoming aware that a de-differentiation (or a switch to another form of differentiation as the primary structuring principle of society) is not a silver bullet to the solution of current social problems, but would itself result in serious consequential costs.

Neither senior studies nor other forms of (non-vocational) lifelong learning abolish the boundary between the education system and the retirement/leisure sector. Such empirical facts are not evidence of the emergence of age-integrated (life course) structures, but mere "interspersions" from other differentiated areas or "secondary roles" – often limited in time – within the functionally differentiated education or employment or old-age security system or the respective phase of life.[11] The basic institutional structure of modern societies with a system of employment, education and old-age provision and thus also the (procedural) logic and tripartite basic shape of the institutionalized life course still exist today and are likely to remain in place as an age-differentiated supporting structure for the foreseeable future.

> The Rileys consider age-differentiated (life course) structures and the basic tripartite structure of the modern life course to be socially and individually dysfunctional. Given the persistence of these structures (after all, "age integrationists" have been propagating their dissolution for almost four decades now), it would be more reasonable to assume that they are functional. Consider and discuss whether and to what extent age-differentiated (life course) structures or the basic tripartite structure of the modern life course are functional for the individual, for organizations and for society as a whole.

5.2 Social Structuring Factors of the Life Course

The basic structure of the modern life course consists in its tripartite nature, which is determined by the structure of society and institutions. This basic tripartite structure does not describe modern life courses in their factual complexity and diversity,

---

[11] Similarly, Amrhein distinguishes between the primary socialization of individuals, which continues to take place via the institutionalized sequence "education – gainful employment – retirement/leisure time", and areas of secondary socialization, which are, however, subordinate to the logic of the institutionalized life course, "since with them the biographical transitions between education, work and retirement are not dissolved, but only stabilized and 'liquefied'" (2004, p. 161).

5.2 Social Structuring Factors of the Life Course

but abstracts from it precisely in order to make their fundamental structural framework clear. But even at the level of real individual life courses and their empirical diversity, life course patterns can be identified with regard to the temporal location of events, positions, roles and status changes. What do these life course structures look like and, above all, how do they come about? What gives modern life courses their structure?

An individual life course is the (contingent) result of a complex structure-agency interplay over time.[12] In this context, "non-social" factors such as a genetically determined illness or a (recurring) natural event that destroys the material basis of existence of a person or a social collective can also imprint a structure on the life courses of the individuals concerned. Here, however – entirely in the perspective of the life course as a social construction that is to be described and explained by means of social factors – the social structuring factors of life courses are addressed. This social structuring of the life course can be normative (5.2.1) or socially structural and, in particular, institutionally determined (5.2.2).

5.2.1 "Act Your Age!" – Age-Appropriateness-Ideas and Timetables

Just as all cultures know a division of the lifespan into a sequence of definable age phases, there are also culturally shared ideas in every society about what behavior is age-appropriate and whether life events and status changes occur at "the right age". And just like those age-phase divisions, these notions of age appropriateness vary cross-culturally and historically. This can be easily illustrated by the example of the topic of "child marriage", which has recently been placed on the agenda of public and political discussion in Germany.[13] In the Federal Republic of Germany, the so-called age of consent is legally linked to the age of majority, with one exception: anyone who is at least 16 years old may marry, provided that the competent

---

[12] The possible combinations of factors that are conceivable as relevant on the part of the social structural context and on the part of biographical action in the course of a life, which can be of quite different kinds, constitute an almost unlimited spectrum of individual life courses – and ultimately make the life course of an individual unique.

[13] In the vast majority of cases, child marriages involve the marriage of underage girls. Nearly half of all child brides worldwide live in South Asia (42%); a quarter resp. 56%, of women aged 20–49 there were "married or in union before ages 15 and 18" (United Nations Children's Fund 2014, p. 2; for West and Central Africa, the figures are nearly a fifth and 46%, respectively).

family court suspends the age of consent requirement and the partner is of marriageable age. Nevertheless, in 2016, a total of 1475 minors were registered as married in Germany – including as many as 361 foreign children under the age of 14 – almost half of whom came from Syria (664); other countries of origin were Afghanistan (157), Iraq (100), Bulgaria (65), Poland (41), Romania (33) and Greece (32). In Europe, child marriages with under-16 s occur mainly in the Balkans among the Roma. In the Federal Republic of Germany, marriage for under 16 year olds is legally prohibited in principle,[14] although such child marriages were not at all unusual here, i.e. in the corresponding region or cultural area, and were still to be found in the nineteenth century. It should also be noted that the legal regulation of the age of marriage in a society and its culturally shared ideas about what age of marriage is inappropriate, "too early" and therefore deviant, can differ: for example, in India child marriage is prohibited, but a quarter of Indian women are already married or living in a partnership at the age of under 15 (United Nations Children's Fund 2014, p. 2).[15]

- Give and discuss other examples of cross-culturally and/or historically varying age appropriateness assumptions in relation to life events and social status throughout the life course.
- Discuss the following pictures with regard to culturally shared ideas of the age-appropriateness of behaviour:

---

[14] http://www.spiegel.de/panorama/gesellschaft/kinderehen-1475-minderjaehrige-in-deutschland-sind-verheiratet-a-1111624.html (a considerably higher number of unreported cases can be assumed).

[15] Whereas in Andorra, for example, one may marry at the age of 16 and, with a court order, even at the age of 14 – but there are virtually no child marriages there.

5.2 Social Structuring Factors of the Life Course

Foto: Kiana Bosman (unsplash.com)

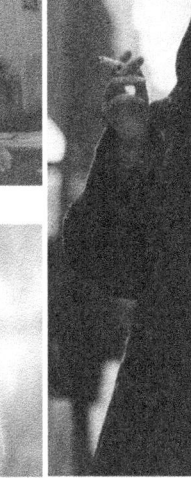

Foto: shutterstock_1018119094

Foto: Mikail Duran (unsplashcom)

Foto: shutterstock_37174705   Foto: asierromero (freepik.com)

Foto: shutterstock_170262146
Foto: shutterstock_42485560
Foto: shutterstock_120984757
Foto: shutterstock_49096135

Do such ideas of age appropriateness that exist in a society give life courses their structure by prescribing the "right" time or space with regard to important life events and status changes? Neugarten developed a corresponding approach at the end of the 1950s that was committed to the structural-functionalist perspective of the time. According to this approach, culturally shared ideas of age appropriateness function as "an elaborated and pervasive system of norms governing behavior and interaction … There exists what might be called a prescriptive timetable for the ordering of major life-events: a time … when men and women are expected to marry, a time to raise children, a time to retire. This normative pattern is adhered to, more or less consistently, by most persons in the society" (Neugarten et al. 1965, p. 711) – this is the basic idea of Neugarten's age norms approach. It is obvious that formal age norms, i.e. age-related legal regulations, structure life courses (one only has to think of, for example, school enrolment and full-time compulsory schooling, the transition to retirement, or age limits with regard to the age of majority, the age of marriage, the age of criminal responsibility, and juvenile criminal law). In Neugarten's age-norm-timetables (and in what follows), however, the focus is not on such formal age norms in the form of legal regulations, but on the broad field of informal age norms.

5.2 Social Structuring Factors of the Life Course 117

Neugarten empirically demonstrated for the USA, on the basis of a representative sample of members of the middle class, a large consensus on the "correct" life-time location of events, positions and status changes and with regard to what is considered age-appropriate behavior.[16] The questionnaire not only collected respondents' personal opinions; they were also asked about how they thought "'most people' would respond" (ibid., p. 714). In both sets of data, men's views were more restrictive – albeit only slightly – than women's (the exception being young women), i.e. men perceived and held age norms themselves to be somewhat stricter. Both men and women considered the age norms imputed to "most people" (generalized others) to be significantly more rigid than their own age appropriateness perceptions. While the rigidity of age constraints attributed to the generalized other was perceived to decrease slightly over the life course, there was a substantial "increase in the extent to which respondents ascribe importance to age norms and place constraints upon ... behavior in terms of age appropriateness" (ibid., p. 715; in the 65+ respondent group, there was little difference between own opinions of age constraints and age norm rigidity attributed to the generalized other). Neugarten emphasizes that in all behavior-related questions over 80% of respondents "made age discriminations when asked for 'most people's opinions'" (ibid., p. 716) and sees this as empirical evidence for the existence of behavior-guiding age norms: "findings support ... that age norms are salient over a wide variety of adult behaviors" (ibid., p. 717).

Studies in the tradition of Neugarten's classic work show that although the age considered "right" for certain events and status transitions has shifted since then, there is still a remarkable consensus on the age or age range at which such events and status transitions should take place (although, of course, a differentiation must be made between age appropriateness ideas of, for example, men and women or different social milieus). A study from the 1990s in the USA, for example, shows that 85% of men and 82% of women drew or assumed an upper age limit with regard to (first) marriage, and 74% and 67% respectively thought that the years between 25 and 30 were the best age to marry (Settersten 2003b, p. 68). According to the 2006 European Social Survey (ESS) "Timing of Life" module, German men and women consider an age of 26.6 and 24.7 respectively as the ideal age of first

---

[16] Questions were asked, for example, about the ideal age for men and women to marry, when a man's professional career should be consolidated, or at what age a woman has the most responsibilities. In terms of age-appropriate behavior, questions were asked, for example, about accepting or rejecting the view that an 18 or 30 or 45 year old woman might wear a bikini on the beach or about agreeing or disagreeing with regard to a 20 or 30 or 55 year old couple who like to twist dance.

marriage – however, the average age of marriage for single men in Germany in that year was actually 32.6 and that for single women 29.6 years (the average age of first marriage for men and women in Germany corresponded to this idea of the ideal age of marriage for the last time in 1985 and 1987, respectively, and has risen continuously since then to 33.8 and 31.2 years in 2015).[17] Is such a deviation still within the age norm for first marriages, or does it indicate that the ideal age for marriage – and ideas of age appropriateness in general – are not behaviorally relevant norms at all?

In order to be able to answer this question, it is first necessary to clarify or recall what is meant by a norm in sociological terms. A social norm specifies in the form of an (explicit or unspoken) commandment or prohibition which behavior is appropriate in recurring situations. Social norms are widely applicable rules and expectations in a society, internalized by its members, which guide the behavior of individuals and which are sanctioned. The moments of widespread validity, practical relevance to action, and (positive or negative) sanction are essential to the sociological understanding of norms. This means: in order to prove the existence of age norms (and thus uno actu a structuring of the life course by age norms), it is not sufficient to establish a broad consensus with regard to age-appropriate behavior – the behavioral relevance as well as the sanctioning moment must also be empirically proven. Whether there really are age norms that function as structuring factors of the life course will be briefly discussed using the example of the status passage into adulthood. The well-researched transition to adulthood, often analyzed in the sociology of the life course (Hogan and Astone 1986; Blossfeld et al. 2005; Billari and Liefbroer 2010; Konietzka 2010; Buchmann and Kriesi 2011), is temporally determined by the occurrence of a series of life course events and status or role changes. The most important of these are the end of (school) education, the start of (full-time) employment, moving out of the parental home, marriage or the establishment of a common-law marriage, and parenthood. These markers of adulthood are mostly examined at the behavioral level, i.e. as real events and status changes, less frequently at the perceptual level.

---

[17] Sources: ESS3 2006: own calculation; Federal Institute for Population Research 2016 (*www.bib-demografie.de/SharedDocs/Publikationen/DE/Download/Abbildungen/04/xls/a_04_14/*); Federal Statistical Office (de.statista.com/statistics/data/study/1329/survey/marriage-age-of-married-men/women)

5.2 Social Structuring Factors of the Life Course

> In this context, "markers of adulthood" are usually only mentioned in relation to leaving the parental home, marriage or partnership and parenthood, while age norms do not play a role as explanatory factors with regard to the end of (school) education and taking up (full-time) employment. Consider and discuss possible reasons for this.

To start with the level of perception: it is quite undisputed that – as with marriage – there is a broad consensus on the beginning of adult life in general. Indeed, the data from the Timing of Life module show that "views of the age of reaching adulthood are rather uniform across Europe" (Spéder et al. 2013, p. 882). According to this common European idea, the adult phase starts at 18–20 for women and 20–22 for men (ibid., p. 890). At the same time, it should be noted that the relevance of those markers of adulthood not only varies greatly across countries, but is relatively low overall: the proportion of those who attach importance to these markers is mostly well below 50% (on average across all markers: approx. two-fifths of men, one-third of women); the lowest relevance value, at only 5.7% for the partnership marker, is shown by women in Sweden; in Germany, the values vary between 47.6% for the employment marker among men and 26.4% for the partnership marker among women (ibid, S. 884). It remains to be seen whether the empirical evidence of this study is convincing or rather weak with regard to the moment of far-reaching validity – what is at stake here is a fundamental conceptual-methodological problem of such perception studies. In the summary discussion of the results, the authors of the study point out that it is based on "perceptions of the age and markers of adulthood. Lives as they are actually lived may certainly differ from these perceptions" (ibid., p. 894).[18] In plain language, this means that studies on age perceptions cannot, in principle, provide evidence of the behavioral relevance that is essential for the concept of norms, because they ignore the behavioral level.

Studies conducted at the behavioral level logically do not have this problem, but neither can they prove the existence of life-course structuring age norms, because studies of the factual transition to adulthood also have a fundamental conceptual-methodological problem. For example, if a study shows that a large proportion of individuals in a (sub)population move out of the parental home at a certain age or

---

[18] This discrepancy between perception and factual behavior illustrates the difference between ideal and factual age at first marriage already mentioned. Such differences show empirically that it is quite problematic to understand perceptions of age appropriateness in terms of age norms: such differences should not occur if these perceptions of age-appropriate behavior were to function as (action-relevant) age norms.

complete those markers of adulthood in the same order, this does not prove the existence of corresponding age norms, but "simply a regularity in behavior, represented by a statistical average or typical value" (Marini 1984, p. 232). An empirically established regularity in behavior could, for example, also be institutionally conditioned[19] or come about because individuals orient their actions to the behavior of significant others, such as their peer group, whereby the social pressure to do or not to do something, which is essential to a norm, plays no role at all. However, in order to be able to attribute behavioral regularities such as moving out of the parental home at a certain age or passing through the markers of adulthood in a certain sequence to corresponding age norms, it must be shown that the individuals also felt a social pressure to move out at precisely this age or to become adults in precisely this markers of adulthood sequence. Anyone who thinks that "behavior which is statistically modal is socially normative for all individuals" (ibid., p. 237), that is, who equates behavioral regularities with social (age) norms, is simply committing a logical fallacy, as did Hogan (1978, 1980), for example. Studies on the behavioral level have the conceptual-methodological problem of not being able to prove in principle that individuals felt a normative pressure to behave as they did in fact, i.e. they cannot prove the existence of age norms.

The existence of age norms would only be empirically convincing if studies using suitable (longitudinal) data sets showed that individuals feel a social pressure to act in a certain way (perception level) and also act accordingly (behavioral level). However, this remains a task "for future research, should longitudinal data on both perceptions and behavior be gathered" (Spéder et al. 2013, p. 895). In addition to the proof of far-reaching validity and behavioral relevance, the third moment essential for a norm would also have to be proven: that of sanctioning. With regard to age norms, it must therefore be empirically proven that behavior that deviates from them over time is socially sanctioned in a negative way. This is easy in the case of formal age norms in the form of age-related legal regulations, but not in the case of informal age norms. In this respect, firstly, there is a lack of data sets that plausibly document sanctions as a reaction to temporally deviating behavior from an age norm.[20] More-

---

[19] "Just as it is often asserted that individuals tend to marry within a certain range of ages because social norms govern marital timing, it might be asserted that individuals tend to obtain between ten and 20 years of formal schooling and do so at certain ages because social norms govern the amount and timing of education" – Marini (1984, p. 235) ironically states.

[20] At the level of perception, the social pressure emanating from age norms should be empirically reflected in anticipated sanctions, i.e. in fears of sanctions. Biographically anticipated sanctions, however, remain merely potential sanctions, i.e. here again – as with the moment of behavioral relevance – the aforementioned fundamental problem of perception studies

over, second, unlike violations of formal age norms, it is theoretically completely unclear what kind of sanctioning might be associated with violating an informal age norm in the first place. For example, how is a person sanctioned who does not move out of the parental home until the age of 30? What sanctions does a couple experience who do not marry until they are over 40? And who sanctions in the first place? What sanctions does a man face who violates the normative sequence of not becoming a father until after he has completed his education and taken up gainful employment? What sanctions does a girl face who becomes a mother at the age of 16? And are the problems and disadvantages resulting from such early motherhood in the further course of life really to be understood as sanctions?

> For a long time, the transition to adulthood was only considered complete when all markers of adulthood – i.e.: the end of (school) education, taking up (full-time) employment, moving out of the parental home, marriage or the establishment of a common-law marriage, and parenthood – were in place. Social change since the mid-1960s has made this view problematic (Klein 1990a, b; Bynner 2005). According to Arnett, a new phase of life course and developmental psychology, which he calls "emerging adulthood" (2000), has since emerged and must be taken into account.
>
> - How do you feel about the notion that someone is not an "adult" until he has "graduated" from all those markers of adulthood?
> - Do you have "adult" status as a student, i.e. are you treated as an "adult" socially and by others? Would you claim "adult" status for yourself without qualification or would you rather see yourself in the state of "emerging adulthood"? On what do you base the status of "adult"?

Fom a sociological perspective, the existence of informal age norms that function as structuring factors of life courses has not been convincingly demonstrated empirically. In the strict sociological understanding of the term, ideas of age appropriateness are not (informal) age norms. From a sociological point of view, informal age norms usually represent a mere epiphenomenon of socio-structural condi-

---

applies. In this respect, evaluative ex post surveys of actual sanction experiences are more meaningful – but only on the condition that the sanctions actually experienced by an individual were also anticipated by that individual: feared ex ante, because otherwise they could not have had any behavioral relevance.

tions as the ultimately decisive structuring factors of life courses.[21] They are usually rooted in and result from socio-structural and institutional conditioning factors and mediate these, but may occasionally also be independent structuring factors of individual life courses that cannot be derived from socio-structural conditions (Mayer and Diewald 2007, p. 524). Although ideas of age appropriateness cannot be equated with age norms, they can nevertheless (normatively) structure life courses. Developmental psychological considerations attempt to describe how this works (Heckhausen 1999; Rothermund and Wentura 2007).

For developmental psychology, Neugarten's age-normative timetables represent the socially prevailing ideas about "normal" developmental courses. Such timetables, in which age norms are integrated into a comprehensive life-time system, represent an orientation and evaluation framework for individual developmental trajectories: these can be compared with the temporal and age specifications of the "normal course" and assessed as to whether they correspond to it or deviate from it, are on-time or off-time. Whether such evaluations are carried out by the individual himself or by other persons or organizations (whether factually or only supposedly) – socio-culturally shared ideas of age appropriateness and corresponding timetables are biographically momentous for the self-concept of the individual, because they "as such (establish) age-graded levels of aspiration and goals for the individual, which failure to meet entails negative self-assessments" (Heckhausen 1990, p. 354).[22] If an individual's development deviates from the "normal course", the individual himself is almost always held responsible for this by his social environment and, because of this (factual or supposed) determination of his failure to meet those standards of normality, comes under pressure to justify his "nonnormal" course of development – which is why being off-time is also usually experienced and seen negatively by the individuals concerned themselves. In order to avoid such negative consequences for the self-concept, individuals normally orient their biographical actions to those temporal and age-related normality specifications, i.e. individuals normally strive to be on-time and attempt to correct off-time developments that have already occurred.

---

[21] Age gradings are "in the most frequent cases primarily not directly normed facts, but empirically subordinated consequences" (Mayer 1996, p. 48, 1986; on the empirical example of the status passage into adulthood, see Mortimer et al. 2005).

[22] Havighurst argued similarly almost 70 years ago with his concept of "developmental tasks" to be completed by the individual (1948).

5.2 Social Structuring Factors of the Life Course

> - Consider examples where being off-time is not viewed negatively or even positively from a societal or individual perspective.
> - How does an individual react when an *off-time development* can no longer be corrected, i.e. when, in the course of his self-evaluation, he finds that he has definitively missed a time or age target of the "normal course"? Consider and discuss possible coping strategies.

Of central importance here is that the individuals have internalized those temporal and age specifications of the "normal course", i.e. see them as their own personal objectives, orient themselves biographically to them, and adapt their behavior ex ante to these age-related notions of normality. In analogy to the civilizing process of the replacement of external coercion by self-coercion described by Elias in his classic study (1992b), Heckhausen sees the age-appropriateness concepts integrated into timetables as having the "function of guiding principles regulating action, the binding nature of which results precisely from the fact that they are not imposed by external institutional coercion, but are internalized as a standard reference" (1990, p. 353). According to these considerations of developmental psychology, the empirical proof – essential for the sociological understanding of norms, but problematic – of the social sanctioning of an individual in the case of deviant behavior is superfluous. The social sanctioning is reinterpreted as a kind of self-sanctioning, which can only be determined on the level of perception. Sanctions consequently consist of nothing more than a negative self-evaluation of the individual or a negative evaluation (factual or supposed) perceived by the individual by his social environment: "the 'punishment', so to speak, is that you cannot respond to age norms" (Rothermund and Wentura 2007, p. 544). Although this developmental-psychological argumentation cannot convincingly justify age norms in a strictly sociological understanding of the term, it can make it understandable that and how ideas of age appropriateness function as a kind of informal age norm and can have life-course-structuring significance.

Age-normative timetables, in which ideas of age appropriateness are integrated into a comprehensive life-time system, indicate socially expected, "normal" life courses and have an orientational and regulative function. The empirically repeatedly observed fact that there is a large consensus regarding age-appropriate behavior and the "correct" timing of events and positions, but that individual life courses more or less deviate from these specifications, points to the fact that such timetables are not immediately relevant to action, quasi one-to-one, but "regulate behavior

... comparatively indirectly" (ibid.). Thus, for example, an individual considers the socially considered appropriate ("ideal") moving-out age of early 20s to be the "right" time to leave the parental home – but in fact does not move out until the age of 30. It seems reasonable to assume that individuals biographically specify age-normative timetables and adapt them to their personal life situation and planning. Nydegger already showed empirically at the beginning of the 1980s that chronological age is not the decisive aspect – let alone the only relevant one. Her analyses certainly show a behaviorally relevant norm system at work – "but it is not in years. Aside from the proscriptive lower-age limit, age is weakly involved in this system (…) The norm system specifies maturity and a desirable synchrony among social roles – a system of prerequisites and orderings. Age is almost irrelevant" (1986, p. 723). In general terms, this means that behaviorally relevant for individuals are not age-normative timetables, but their biographical specification, in which age is only one factor among others – and often of secondary importance. At least as important are an individual's currently available and expected future economic, social and cultural capital, his assessment of his psychological, emotional and health developmental status, the – possibly conflicting – role requirements with which he is confronted and, last but not least, his personal life goals and plans. To take up the example of the "late" (off-time) departure from the parental home at the age of 30 again: the financial situation of the person in question could be responsible for this, for example, or a particular psychological strain due to a dual course of study including entering a "stressful" company career start phase. In this respect, Nydegger rightly emphasizes that any biographical specification of age-normative timetables "involves an intricate meshing of many elements (…) The preferred timetable for an entrepreneur bears only slight resemblance to that of a civil servant" (ibid., p. 727).

Age-appropriateness concepts – whether as individual ones or bundled in the form of life-time timetables – do not structure life courses directly, but indirectly and mediated: they are biographically specified by the individual, i.e. adapted to personal life circumstances and plans. Direct and deterministic life course control would contradict the basic assumption of life course research that individual life courses represent the respective results of a complex structure-agency interplay over time. This basic assumption of life course theory and the individual agency moment also applies with regard to the institutional structuring factors discussed in the following subchapter: just as individuals are not mere "agents of execution" of socially prevailing age norms, they are not institutionally directed through their lives as quasi-passive objects.

5.2.2 Institutional Life Course Structures

An institutional structuring of individual life courses takes place both within the socially differentiated systems of education, gainful employment and old-age provision and between these areas, i.e. in the transition from education to employment and in the transition from the labor market to retirement. Even the institution of the "family", which does not follow the tripartite "life course logic", but lies across the fields of education, gainful employment and retirement, is subject to institutional structuring. Institutional structuring of individual life courses can be direct effects of the structure and organization of the education, employment and old-age security system and its institutions (e.g. school, vocational training, company, early retirement). Frequently, however, institutional structuring also results from the socially given system of welfare state regulations, interventions and benefits (e.g. entitlement to daycare, parental leave, unemployment benefit, taking into care, care allowance). Welfare state regulations[23] show a strong expansion tendency in the historical framework of the emergence and development of the interest of the nation state in its citizens (Thomas et al. 1987). Welfare state regulations extend across the entire lifespan, from prenatal care to hospice care for the dying, and encompass all spheres of life, right into the "private" sphere of marriage, partnership and family. "The welfare state has a tendency to become universal. Programs started for small and restricted groups at risk are gradually generalized to the whole population … Moreover, there is no limit to the kinds of problems that might be taken up for social policy intervention" (Mayer and Schoepflin 1989, p. 193).[24] However, international comparisons reveal considerable differences between societies with regard to the scope and quality (or intensity) of their welfare state regulatory network. Germany, for example, is a highly developed welfare state with a tightly meshed social policy regulatory network, while the USA is regarded as a residual welfare state (as the discussion on statutory health insurance for all citi-

---

[23] The (welfare) state's grip on individual life histories is particularly pronounced and direct in authoritarian regimes: in the "Great Proletarian Cultural Revolution" in China, for example, since 1967 there has been the forced resettlement of around 17 million urban youths in peasant villages for up to ten years and their (labor) re-education there (Zhou and Hou 1999).

[24] Although there has been talk since the 1980s of a crisis of the welfare state and a welfare retrenchment (OECD 1981; Levy 2010), it remains to be seen whether the quoted statement needs to be revised in the light of these discussions.

zens shows).[25] The different role and relevance of welfare state policy in Germany and Europe on the one hand and in the USA on the other is an important reason for the difference already mentioned (see Sect. 2.2) between German and European and US life course research. The latter focuses primarily on the individual with his agency within the framework of the primary everyday worlds of family, school, work and circle of friends. In contrast, European, and especially German, life course research focuses primarily on the institutional "pre-programming" of life courses, i.e. on the structuring specifications of the social institutional and welfare state regulatory system as the basis and frame of reference for the biographical life course constructions of individuals.

In the following, a few examples of institutional structuring of life courses by the education system are highlighted. The most serious structuring of life courses results from compulsory schooling, which begins at the age of six and lasts for at least 12 years (nine or ten years of full-time compulsory schooling in primary and lower secondary education, followed by three or two years of general upper secondary schooling, full-time vocational schooling or, as a rule, three years of part-time compulsory vocational schooling).[26] Between the ages of six and 18 – i.e. over 12 particularly developmentally relevant years – individuals spend a large part of the day in educational institutions, which also extend into their extracurricular everyday life (e.g. through homework, annual work or preparation for achievement tests). Even for pre-school education, life-course structuring effects can be identified. For example, children who do not attend a day care center (Kita) are much less likely to go on to secondary school than children who do (Becker and Lauterbach 2004). Although the longer-term effects of preschool educational institutions have not yet been adequately researched, empirical studies indicate that preschool education in daycare centers can be a suitable means of compensating for educational inequality (Stamm 2010; Becker 2016).[27]

---

[25] This residual meaning "reflects an individualistic culture and a preference by most citizens for a smaller role of government in directing their lives than is customary in Europe" (Leisering 2003, p. 206), whereas "in the German case all key institutions ... add up to a tight regulatory framework for social life. The underlying idea is a wide-ranging responsibility of government for the well-being of its citizens" (Leisering and Schumann 2003, p. 200).

[26] Unlike in Germany, in most European countries and also in the USA there is no compulsory schooling, but compulsory teaching or education, i.e. there is no compulsory school attendance imposed by the state.

[27] However: the educational or structuring effect of "preschool education and elementary education (is) relativized when socioeconomic and educational resources of the parental home are controlled" (Becker 2016, p. 174). It becomes clear that the educational disadvantages of children of unskilled and semi-skilled workers as well as children with a migration background "are obviously hardly compensated by current programs of preschool care" (ibid.).

5.2 Social Structuring Factors of the Life Course

All modern, performance-differentiating education systems "sort" their pupils, i.e. assign them different positions. In most countries, this differentiation takes place within schools in the form of temporary performance or interest groups, while the German education system differentiates between schools, i.e. assigns pupils to different types of school. Both forms of differentiation condition and reproduce – alongside and with other factors – educational inequalities (Gamoran and Mare 1989; Lucas 1999, 2001; Maatz et al. 2009). However, in educational systems structured according to school types, social inequalities due to origin are more pronounced and less compensated for than in systems with differentiation within schools (Shavit and Blossfeld 1993; Baumert et al. 2001; Pfeffer 2008; Müller and Pollack 2016). In Germany in particular, educational opportunities and success depend more on social background than in other countries. This is not only true for the decades of the "purely" tripartite German school system with Hauptschule, Realschule, and Gymnasium[28] but also still (as the PISA shock in 2001 showed) after the introduction of different types of comprehensive schools and further school types with different educational tracks, which are called differently in the federal states. As Geißler aptly titled: "The illusion of equal opportunities in the education system – disturbed by PISA" (2004a, b).

Visualize the structure of the German education system using a schematic representation (e.g.: www.kmk.org/fileadmin/Dateien/pdf/Dokumentation/dt-2015.pdf/). Also get schematic representations of the educational systems of Finland and other European countries as well as the USA.

- Compare them with each other: what are the advantages and disadvantages of each institutional structure.
- Discuss the question of whether the highly differentiated German education system, due to its institutionalization of comparatively homogeneous learning levels in the various types of school, is not better able to do justice to the individual educational level and potential of each pupil than joint schooling in integrated systems?
- In your opinion, what should the institutional structure of an education system that provides opportunities and is fair in terms of performance look like? Describe this "ideal" education system schematically.

---

[28] This is about mainstream schools; no reference is made to the special school (today: Förderschule) for pupils with special socio-educational needs.

The performance-related "sorting" of pupils takes place in education systems differentiating between school types (such as the German system) at the transition from primary school to lower secondary level, whereas the integrative systems differentiating within schools teach their pupils together – essentially – up to upper secondary level. Whereas in these systems institutional differentiation of pupils does not take place until the age of 16, in Germany pupils are assigned to the various types of school as early as the age of 12 (before the introduction of the two-year Orientierungsstufe even at the age of 10). From the point of view of developmental psychology, this early channeling of pupils into different types of school or school careers is problematic because it is premature. This institutional differentiation would be less problematic if the system were sensitive and open to developmental or performance-based revisions of such early assignments. What about such permeability of the German school system? It is indeed permeable – but primarily in the sense of a "downward relegation", as Bellenberg shows in her study on changes of school types:[29] "the vast majority of school form changers (change) from a more demanding to a less demanding school form" (2012, p. 9). Overall, her study confirms "once again ... that the number of descents in Germany clearly exceeds the number of ascents" (ibid.).[30]

The structuring consequences of different school types are likely to extend as a "Matthew effect" into the quaternary area of general, vocational and in-company continuing education (although strict proof of causality is difficult): lifelong learning, which has been propagated internationally since the 1970s, is extremely selective in terms of access, i.e. is practiced primarily by well-qualified individuals with an affinity for education – which is why educational disparities in the (structurally very heterogeneous) continuing education sector are not compensated for but rather reproduced or even increased (BMBF 2015; Offerhaus et al. 2016).

The institutional structure of the German education system, which sorts pupils into different types of school already in the general lower secondary level, also shapes their distribution between the general upper secondary level (Gymnasium) on

---

[29] These can be "a sign of the permeability of a school system if they enable pupils to progress to more demanding school forms and thus open up educational opportunities. But they can also be an indicator of the long-lived pedagogical tradition of selection in Germany's segregated school systems, when many young people experience relegation" (Bellenberg 2012, p. 9).

[30] Whereby – as Bellenberg's state-specific descriptions show – there are considerable differences between the federal states (see also Schümer et al. 2002, p. 209 f.).

5.2 Social Structuring Factors of the Life Course

the one hand and vocational training institutions on the other in the upper secondary level. Although those who have obtained the Abitur can also start vocational training – and this is increasingly happening (Steinmann 2000) – by far the majority of Abitur holders take up university studies or attend a university of applied sciences (Fachhochschule). The Hauptschule or Realschule certificate, on the other hand, usually leads to vocational training.[31] Vocational education and training in Germany takes place predominantly within the framework of the dual system, which combines vocational school and (work in) a company; in addition, there is full-time school-based training at full-time vocational schools.[32] The dual system of vocational education and training is an institutional characteristic of the German education system, whereas in most industrialized countries vocational education and training is provided in purely school-based form or only on the job. In the dual system, young people acquire specific vocational qualifications which are also standardized, i.e. not company-specific, and are thus generally usable in the relevant vocational segment of the labor market. Because young people are not only trained at vocational schools but also gain practical work experience in companies, they are already familiar with the (company) world of work during their training; the companies that decide on the allocation of training places are in turn familiar with the qualifications and personalities of the young people they themselves have trained. In this respect, misallocations with regard to regular employment relationships after the end of training tend to be avoided from the point of view of both young people and companies. By imparting specific vocational qualifications that are standardized throughout Germany and by linking (vocational) school and in-company forms of training, the dual system of vocational education and training has an important effect on the structuring of people's lives: For the majority of graduates, the transition to employment is relatively free of friction, i.e. without a lengthy period of search unemployment, and it is appropriate to their qualifications. This institutional effect of a relatively low youth unemployment rate as well as a change of occupation or company during the first years of employment has been repeatedly confirmed empirically by international comparative studies

---

[31] Theoretically, lower secondary school and intermediate secondary school graduates can, of course, also acquire a higher education entrance qualification – then usually subject-linked – through further qualifications (e.g. the intermediate secondary school certificate enables attendance at the two-year specialized upper secondary school, which leads to the advanced technical college entrance qualification – and in the case of a possible grade 13 even to the general higher education entrance qualification.

[32] And meanwhile there is a large number of measures that are intended to prepare young people for taking up vocational training ("transition system"; Lex and Geier 2010).

(Büchtemann et al. 1993; Shavit and Müller 1998; Sackmann 2001; Kerckhoff 2003; Müller and Gangl 2003; Scherer 2005; Konietzka 2016).[33]

Since the end of the nineteenth century, a roughly simplified "male" and a "female" vocational training system has been established in Germany: while the dual system trains for ("male") occupations in industry and crafts, qualification for "female" occupations in the sense of household-related and family-like service activities takes place in the form of full-time school-based training. This institutional division of the vocational training system – motivated by gender ideology (Mayer 1992) – produces or consolidates a gender-specific occupational and labor market segregation with considerable consequences for the positioning of women when entering employment and their further course of employment in the employment system – and thus also their life course as a whole (Gottschall 2000). Compared to "men's jobs", typical "women's jobs" are usually lower paid, lower prestige and offer significantly fewer opportunities for advancement (Krüger 1996; Solga and Konietzka 2000; Feller 2002; Falk 2005; Trappe 2006). The "'doing gender' of institutions, the production of gendered life paths, thus runs through structural and cultural levels that transform horizontal into vertical processes of differentiation" (Krüger 1995, p. 141). In the wake of the economic shifts from the industrial to the service sector, however, full-time school-based vocational training at the various vocational schools has recently gained in importance, and not only in quantitative terms (Dobischat 2010; Hall 2012).

These are just a few examples of the institutional structuring of individual life courses in the education system and with regard to the transition from education to employment. A wide variety of examples of institutional life course structuring can also easily be shown for the employment and old-age security system and for the institution "family", which lies across the basic tripartite structure of the life course, as well as with regard to transitions and connections between these areas. With regard to the employment system, one might think of differences in job and life planning security between employment in a private company or in the public sector; or of internal career paths that exist in larger but not in smaller companies. With regard to the transition to the old-age security system, one could think of early retirement and – if this possibility exists – its institutional design; in the old-age security system, one could think of the different public-private mix of national pen-

---

[33] In terms of life course theory, the structural linking of vocational school and (work in) the company in the institution of dual vocational training can be understood at the microsociological level as a "bridge sequence" or a combined state of the individual that links education and employment or the education and employment system with one another (Sackmann and Wingens 2003).

5.2 Social Structuring Factors of the Life Course

sion systems. With regard to the family sphere, one could think of different legal regulations on divorce or also of tax law (keyword: spousal splitting). And with regard to links between the institution of the "family" and the employment and education system, reference could be made, for example, to internationally differing regulations on (the possibility of) parental leave or on the design of childcare facilities (half-day vs. full-time). In addition, there is the institutional structuring of the life course through welfare state risk management in the narrower sense: here, for example, the duration of unemployment benefits, state measures for reintegration or the regulations on reduced earning capacity pensions due to illness or disability should be considered.[34]

- Specify what effects the institutional structuring factors just mentioned (can) have on individual life courses.
- Consider other examples of institutional life course structuring.
- Find and discuss empirical studies or evidence on the examples given as well as your own.
- If you cannot find empirical evidence or studies for an institutional life course structuring you suspect: develop a research design that could be used to obtain empirical evidence for the suspected effect.

Institutional structuring factors can have very far-reaching effects on individual life courses. This applies both in a temporal sense, i.e. that a structuring effect can have an impact on the entire further life span and can even increase over the life course, and in the sense that an institutional structuring effect, e.g. of the education system, can also reach into other areas of life and social fields of action. Six decades ago, Schelsky (1957) already pointed out the (potential) enormous scope of the consequences of institutional structuring factors with regard to the education system: its institutional "shifting the switches" not only channel students into specific school careers, but also – and much more far-reachingly – into entire "life careers" with their respective different occupational statuses, social risks and general life chances as a result of the connection options that are possible or probable in each case. The far-reaching consequences of an institutional structuring of life courses in this dou-

---

[34] Social policy regulations and interventions of the welfare state aim directly at changing the life situation of individuals and thus intervene in their life courses (Kaufmann 2002; Leisering 2003; Settersten 2003a; for a general understanding of life course policy that goes beyond the field of social policy see Weymann 2003).

ble sense can easily be illustrated: if, for instance if a female pupil – for whatever reason – decides to undergo vocational training at a vocational college leading to a typical "female occupation", this results in a (gender-)relatively unfavorable labor market position and employment prospects; if the young woman marries after a few years of gainful employment, it would be rational – at least economically speaking – in the event of the birth of a child or the need for care of the (in-)parents, if the woman (and not her husband) were to interrupt gainful employment; these interruptions in gainful employment, which often last several years, often lead to the woman only working part-time when she later resumes employment (or even to her not taking up gainful employment permanently); this in turn leads to a considerable reduction in the level of the woman's old-age security and has biographical consequences with regard to the woman's economic (in)dependence on her husband.

This (admittedly woodcut-like) example – it should be emphasized once again in conclusion – must not be misunderstood in the sense of a determinism of institutional structuring factors. Just as age norms do not determine the life courses of individuals (but are rather individually specified by them biographically), institutional structuring factors do not determine the life course of the individual. Individual life courses are – this is the basic thesis of life course theory – the results of complex structure-agency interactions over time. If the role of biographical agency has been omitted here, it is only in order to make the institutional formations of individual life courses and the serious life course effects of institutional structuring factors particularly clear. However, the focus solely on the moment of institutional structuring or structure should in no way be misunderstood as a determination of individual action by institutions or structures. The fact that such a one-sided – and thus deterministic – focus on structure alone is problematic can be easily illustrated with an example from the field of education: the fact that in recent times a growing number of individuals are completing a second education or multiple courses of training (Hillmert and Jacob 2003; Jacob 2004) cannot be explained by means of institutional structuring factors – there are no institutional structural specifications for this in the education system.

Find further examples which – in the education system as well as in the other fields of society and life – show the importance of biographical agency against the background of the institutional preformations and structuring factors of life courses.

5.2 Social Structuring Factors of the Life Course

The (in this double sense) far-reaching life course effects of institutional structuring factors suggest the question whether the many and diverse institutional preformations and welfare state regulations represent a mere accumulation of institutional and socio-political individual factors – then a mere conglomerate of diverse life course effects would result from these heterogeneous structuring factors. Or whether the institutional and socio-political structuring factors do not rather tend to follow a general social (regulatory) logic in the sense of institutional complementarities – then these structuring factors would generate, holistically so to speak, a relatively coherent, overarching life course regime. This question has long been controversial, but is now considered "positively resolved. There is wide agreement … to conceptualize the specific institutions as parts of an overarching pattern with a higher or lesser degree of complementarity among them" (Kohli 2007, p. 259). But even if it is hardly disputed any more that the institutional and regulatory structure of a society has a tendency towards holistic structuring logic, determining the content of the resulting life course regime remains a difficult undertaking.

The macro-structural determinants of life course regimes (as the "dependent variable") are essentially the constitution and regulation of the political economy and the welfare state of a society. However, life course regimes cannot simply be derived from the well-known varieties-of-capitalism typology (liberal vs. coordinated market economy; Hall and Soscike 2001) nor from the widespread welfare state typology (liberal, conservative, social democratic welfare regime; Esping-Anderson 1990) nor from any of the various modifications and extensions of these societal typologies. The level of aggregation of such typologies, which group nation-states with similar political-economic or welfare-state structures into a kind of "family of countries", is simply too high for this. The USA and Great Britain, for example, represent the type of liberal market economies and welfare states, while Germany is assigned to the type of a coordinated economy or a conservative welfare state. If, however, one looks beyond (or better: this side of) such general classifications to specific institutional structures and their life course effects, i.e. focuses, for example, on socio-political assistance, these classifications no longer hold: Germany would then be "close to Britain as a 'welfare state with integrated safety nets', which promotes a continuous life course; whereas the United States belongs to a different type, which offers little security and continuity" (Leisering 2003, p. 216). The same applies, for example, with regard to the scope and level of benefits of the German, US and British (state) health care systems. To give a third example: although both Germany and France are classified as conservative welfare regimes, the proportion of full-time working mothers in France is almost twice as high (56% vs. 30%) and that of part-time working mothers not even half as high (16% vs. 39%) as in Germany.[35]

> The different life course patterns of French and German women (indicated by the above data) cannot be understood as structuring effects of the conservative welfare regime, since both countries belong to the conservative welfare state type. But how can these different life course patterns be explained? Which institutional structuring factors are relevant?

As the examples show, life course effects and patterns can vary widely across countries subsumed under the same type of society. References to political-economic or welfare-state types of society thus tell us little about the life course regimes of the countries subsumed under a type.[36] What is more, such references cannot explain empirically ascertainable life course patterns – the factors and mechanisms responsible for their emergence cannot be identified at the level of those highly aggregated types or typologies of society (which are often invoked). In their aggregation, these imply "ambiguities that undermine the uses of such schemata in developing causal hypotheses about life course outcomes" (Mayer 2005, p. 35). Therefore, they can at best serve as interpretative initial heuristics. Life course research that really wants to explain life course effects and patterns has "no alternative than to resort to the level of particular countries and particular institutions" (ibid., p. 36). However, even at the level of individual countries, it should be noted that the institutional and regulatory system of a society as a whole is not cast from a single mould, but represents a historically evolved, highly complex and heterogeneous (sometimes even contradictory) social construct. There is no simple logic of derivation between the institutional and regulatory structure of a society and its life course regime; instead, there is only a loose and often fractured relationship of correspondence. In this respect, Mayer rightly emphasizes that life course research interested in explanations must ultimately refer to specific institutional configurations (particular institutions). Accordingly, he has compiled an overview of the institutional configurations that have a particular structuring relevance for the life courses of individuals for the USA, Germany and Sweden (Fig. 5.2).

---

[35] The data are taken from the OECD Family Database and refer to 2013 for France and 2014 for Germany. In the example, it should still be noted that the fertility rate in France is still higher than that of Germany (in 2015: 1.9 vs. 1.5 children per woman; 1970:2.5 vs. 2.0; 1995:1.7 vs. 1.2).

[36] What Mayer (1997, 2001, 2004, 2005) has convincingly and informatively argued (using concrete examples).

5.2 Social Structuring Factors of the Life Course

Life course institutions	United States	Germany	Sweden
schooling	low stratification, low standardization, general education	highly stratified, high standardization	low stratification, high standardization
vocational training	marginalized vocational school, on the-job training	apprentice/vocational school, dual system, highly standardized, employer/union coordinated	vocational school (upper secondary), unstandardized, uncoordinated
school-to-work linkages	loose linkages, personal networks	tight linkages, apprenticeships, employment offices	loose linkages, labor exchange
production systems	low skill, mass products, high external flexibility, service based economy	high skill, export-oriented, high-quality niche, high internal flexibility	high skill, export oriented
labor relations systems	decentralized bargaining, low union density, contentious relations	coordinated (sectoral) bargaining encompassing employer association, medium union density, cooperative relations	coordinated (sectoral) bargaining encompassing employer association, high union density
firm-based institutions	weak internal labor markets, high occupational welfare	strong internal labor markets, medium occupational welfare	weak internal labor markets, low occupational welfare
welfare state (general)	low decommodification, means-tested benefits, mixed services, flat benefits	medium decommodification, employment-related benefits, transfer payments, contribution related	high decommodification, universal benefits, public services, redistributional
public sector	low	medium	high
active labor market policy	low	(medium) training employment subsidies	high vocational (re)training, low skil public employment
labor market regulation	deregulated, weak job protection	highly regulated, work conditions and benefits, strong job protection	medium regulation, work conditions and benefits, weak job protection
retirement/pensions	flat social security, partial firm pensions, pre-tax pension savings	dual system: earnings-related pensions, high level company-based supplement	two-tiered: flat universal and supplemental earnings related, early exit schemes, long-term unemployment/disability
system of taxation	low level of taxation, unit = individual (dual earner model)	moderate level of taxation, unit = household (male-abreadwinner model)	high levels of taxation, unit = individual (dual earner model)
family policies: family allowance, childcare, parental leave	no family allowance, privatized child care, short, job protection, zero income replacement	direct cash transfer – entitled to household head, low public child care, half-day schooling, short income replacement, long job protection	direct cash transfer to child, strong public provision of child care, long/generous income replacement and job protection

Quelle: Mayer 2005:38f

Fig. 5.2 Life course-relevant institutional configurations of US, German and Swedish society. (Source: Mayer 2005, p. 38 f)

First of all, it should be pointed out that although the institutional and regulatory structure of a society exhibits great stability and reformative path dependency, it can nevertheless change as a result of ongoing social change (not to mention revolutionary upheavals). In this respect, each determination of the life-course-relevant institutional configurations of a society refers to a specific socio-historical phase and is to be explicitly located in time. Mayer's overview of the life-course-relevant institutional configurations of the USA, Germany (more precisely: West Germany) and Sweden refers to the second half of the twentieth century (on the change of life-course-relevant institutional configurations and corresponding life-course regimes see the following subchapter).

The table shows that the life-course-relevant institutional configurations of the USA, (West) Germany and Sweden differ both in and between the basic, socially differentiated systems of education, gainful employment and old-age provision and also with regard to the institution of the "family" and the welfare state social policy sphere, which temporally cut across them. The fact that these different institutional configurations give rise to specific life course effects and patterns will be outlined using the example of the institutional structuring of the education system, or more precisely the school system, and the transition to the employment system for the USA and Germany. For international comparisons, education and school systems are characterized in terms of their standardization and stratification. The degree of standardization indicates the extent to which curricula, examinations, grading, certificates, etc. are subject to uniform national standards. The degree of vertical stratification indicates the extent to which there is internal differentiation into different types of educational pathways with different levels; horizontal stratification refers to the separation of general and vocational education (Allmendinger 1989; Shavit and Müller 1998). As the table shows, the German school system is standardized and highly stratified; there is a separate VET sector – also standardized – which provides specific vocational qualifications; VET is structurally closely linked to the paid labor system through the dual system (this has already been illustrated above). In contrast, the degree of standardization and stratification in the US school system is low; vocational education and training exists in a rudimentary form at best; the school and employment systems are not structurally linked.

Mayer describes the life course structuring resulting from these different institutional configurations as follows: "In the United States, universal and comprehensive schooling without institutionalized apprenticeships make for a fairly standardized age at leaving secondary school around 17 (with a non-negligible rate of high school dropouts). Labor market entry comes early even for college graduates, but

5.2 Social Structuring Factors of the Life Course

the transition between education and full labor market integration is often marked by a sequence of stop-gap jobs ... Low-paid and marginal employment as well as unemployment is widespread among young workers. Moreover, even starting in high school and continuing through college, full-time education and work are frequently combined. Educational certificates are of minor importance, occupational identities are weak, and therefore work lives are primarily structured by individual attempts to make good earnings. Commitment to given firms is low, and job shifts between firms are frequent. Deregulated labor markets foster employment, but depress and polarize wages. Mean income trajectories are fairly flat across working lives because efficiency wages and seniority premiums are weak, and effects of the business cycle are stronger than age effects" (2005, p. 36). The corresponding institutional configurations in Germany, on the other hand, cause other life course effects and patterns (as already described in part above): "(West)Germany stratifies school and training tracks and thus induces a higher variance at the ages at which young adults leave the formative period. A prolonged educational period also pushes the age of entry into the labor market upwards. Because training is dominantly organized in the dual system, transitions to employment are smoother and integrated along the lines of occupational tracks. Training investments by both firms and young people are high, and therefore the attainment and the later use of certified skills play a large role in young people's lives. About 40 percent add an additional training period after the first concluded training, but most of that is an orderly progression in the same occupational domain ... Job shifts between firms are rare (but increasing for men), and changes between fields of occupational activities are even rarer ... For those who successfully manage their labor market entry, mean income trajectories are progressive" (ibid., p. 37).

Mayer's statements indicate that the different life course patterns and occupational and employment biographical orientations of young adults in the USA and Germany are not solely due to the different institutional configurations of the two societies in the school system and transition to employment. The institutional configurations of the employment system (mass vs. quality production; conflict vs. cooperation-oriented industrial relations; absence vs. existence of an occupational labor market segment; weak vs. distinct internal labor markets; deregulated vs. coordinated labor market) also have a complementary and reinforcing effect. This means that life course patterns are not conditioned by one institutional configuration alone, but rather result from an ensemble of institutional configurations or even the societal institutional and regulatory structure as a whole. The relatively frictionless school-to-work transition of young people in Germany can certainly be seen primarily as an effect of the dual system of vocational training. But what single institutional configuration could explain, for example, the lower proportion of working women in Germany than in the USA or Sweden (or France), and in particular the lower proportion of full-time working mothers? Mayer has attempted to illustrate the loose correspondence between the institutional and regulatory structure of a society and the corresponding life course regime with the help of a further general overview of life course effects and patterns in the USA, Germany and Sweden that goes beyond the example outlined. This second overview table contains the current state of knowledge about "life course outcomes" (ibid., p. 36) in these societies (Fig. 5.3). At first glance, the separate presentation in the form of

	United States	Germany	Sweden
leaving home	early, high variance	medium, high variance	early, low variance
age leaving school / training	early, unstratified	late, highly stratified	medium, unstratified
labor market entry	early, loosely coordinated stop-gap, general skills	late, highly coordinated, industry-specific skills	medium, moderately coordinated, general skills
economic self-sufficiency	early, earnings	late	early, earnings + study grants / welfare transfers
family formation	early entry into marriage / parenthood	cohabitation before marriage, delayed entry into marriage / parenthood	high permanent cohabitation, delayed entry into marriage / parenthood
job shifts	high intrafirm mobility, high interfirm mobility	moderate intrafirm mobility, low interfirm mobility	high intrafirm mobility, high interfirm mobility
worklife class mobility	high, upward and downward	low, upward	intermediate, upward
employment / unemployment	high employment, continuous / frictional unemployment, early entry / late exit	low employment, low youth unemployment, prolonged unemployment, late entry / early exit	high employment, continuous / frictional unemployment, high youth unemployment, late entry / late exit
careers of women	high participation, high qualifications variance, mostly full time, continuous	medium participation, medium homogeneous qualifications, mostly part time, interrupted	high participation, low + high qualifications, full time / part time, continuous
family life course	unstable, high single mothers, medium fertility	stable, low single / nonmarital parenthood, low fertility	moderately stable, high (single) / nonmarital parenthood, medium / declining fertility
income trajectories	flat, high variance, high poverty	progressive, low variance, (low) poverty	flat, low variance, low poverty
retirement	late exit, high variance, low replacement, high inequality in old age	early exit, low variance, high replacement, medium income inequality	gradual late exit, medium variance, high replacement, low income inequality

Quelle: Mayer 2005:40f

Fig. 5.3 Life course outcomes in the USA, Germany and Sweden. (Source: Mayer 2005, p. 40 f)

5.2 Social Structuring Factors of the Life Course

two tables is irritating – relations are normally presented in one figure or table. However, the fact that Mayer presents and requires two tables results – as a technical consequence, so to speak – from the aforementioned fact that there is only a loose coupling and not a one-to-one correspondence between the institutional and regulatory structure of a society (or the institutional configurations) and its life course regime (or its life course outcomes).

Even the two overviews with which Mayer attempts to grasp the loose correspondence between the institutional and regulatory structure of a society and its life course regime are not themselves an explanation of the institutional conditionality and structuring of life course outcomes. In contrast to those highly aggregated societal typologies, however, they are a productive starting point for the formulation of causal assumptions and substantial hypotheses, through whose empirical testing the concrete institutional conditioning factors and causal mechanisms of life course outcomes can be identified. And this is what life course research is all about: Not only to describe life course effects and patterns, but also to explain their occurrence, i.e. to work out the causal institutional structuring.[37]

---

[37] The interest in a causal explanation of life course patterns also prohibits abandoning the institutional-macrostructural perspective and instead pursuing a micro-sociological approach that constructs life course regimes empirically on the basis of data on individual life courses. The approach of a purely micro-sociological foundation is followed, for example, by Möhring, who uses data from the Survey of Health, Ageing and Retirement in Europe (SHARE; third wave: SHARELIFE) to construct life course regimes focused on employment biographies. As Möhring shows, these result from "long-term economic and political developments" (2016, p. 135) in the 14 countries studied "rather than being consistent with common welfare state typologies" (ibid.). That such highly aggregated societal typologies are not explanatory is (as said) true. However, there are also serious (explanatory) problems associated with the micro-sociological approach. Firstly, there is a lack of "holistic" data sets, i.e. data sets that provide relevant information both over (as far as possible) the entire life span and over (as far as possible) all areas of life – and not just, as in Möhring's case, e.g. employment biography. Secondly, with regard to "holistic" methods, quantitative social research has developed innovative analytical instruments – but optimal matching or sequence pattern analyses are not causal-analytical but descriptive-explorative procedures, i.e. they cannot explain life course regimes. And theoretically, it would have to be asked whether, at the micro level of the individual life course, a formative (trigger) event that gives a life course its factual structure – and indeed across the entire life span and diverse life domains – can exist at all (see also the criticism of the assumption of a "formative phase" in the cohort and generation approach in Chap. 4).

> - Relate the two overview tables to each other, i.e. illustrate the loose coupling between the institutional and regulatory structure of a society and its life course regime using concrete examples. First, become aware of the different institutional configurations in the USA, Germany and Sweden – for example, with regard to employment security, unemployment and re-entry opportunities or with regard to women's employment histories or with regard to (the transition to) retirement. Then consider which different life course effects and patterns can be caused by or attributed to this.
> - Read and discuss DiPrete's study on "Life Course Risks, Mobility Regimes, and Mobility Consequences: A Comparison of Sweden, Germany, and the United States" (2002).
> - Find further empirical studies on the examples of institutionally determined life course effects and patterns you initially named. Are your considerations supported or rather challenged by these empirical studies?

5.3 "Normal Life Course" and De-Standardization of the Life Course

5.3.1 The Chronologically Standardized "Normal Life Course"

The institutionalized life course represents – as explained in Chap. 3 – a system of rules for the temporal dimension of life (life course as institution). The institutionalization of the life course means the process of the formation of the life course as an institution: in other words, it denotes the process of the formation of an increasingly chronologically standardized "normal life course" in the sense of socially and individually normally expectable event and position sequences and configurations ("external" institutionalization). As a life-time process model, this socially structurally anchored, and in particular institutionally pre-programmed standard life course represents a culturally provided scheme to which individuals orient their biographical planning and life plans, conforming to or deviating from it ("inner" institutionalization). According to Kohli, this institutionalization of the life course, or the formation of the life course as an institution, was part as well as the result of the social structural change of the last 250 years. The beginning of this development could therefore be dated to the eighteenth century. In the eighteenth century and well into the nineteenth century, however, there was no question of an institu-

5.3 "Normal Life Course" and De-Standardization of the Life Course

tionalized life course in the sense of chronological standardization: life events often occurred as fate, i.e. not yet chronologically standardized and expectable (which is why the life course could not be planned). But when had the process of institutionalization of the life course progressed so far that one could, empirically justified, speak of a chronological standardization of the life course? And when did the institutionalized life course as a chronologically standardized "normal life course" reach its strongest expression and heyday?

Neither of these questions can be answered in the sense of specifying a particular date; there are no concrete starting points that can be precisely dated in this respect. However, the phase of early industrial society can be named as the initial period. The fateful, "coincidental" occurrence of life events, which was characteristic of traditional life courses in terms of time, gradually gave way from the last third of the nineteenth century onwards to an increasing chronological expectability and thus also predictability of life courses. Of particular relevance was the introduction of public rights and obligations based on age, above all the school and old-age insurance system (1871: compulsory schooling; 1889: workers' pension insurance). The lives of the growing number of people who worked in the industrial and craft sectors were shaped by the long – one could almost say lifelong – phase of physically strenuous gainful employment, which began at around 14 years of age and lasted until retirement, initially at the age of 70 or as a result of invalidity. In addition, recurring (or threatening) periods of unemployment and health risks shaped the course of life. Until marriage, women were also gainfully employed; after marriage, the birth of the first child soon followed. This life course pattern, which was widespread in the early phase of industrial society and which Rowntree (1901) appropriately characterizes as a "cycle of poverty",[38] showed a certain rudimentary chronological standardization, but was still essentially determined by discontinuities in terms of time.

This discontinuity gradually gave way to a chronological standardization of life events from the late nineteenth century onwards. Of decisive importance here was the progressive establishment and expansion of an age-related socio-political regulatory network, or more precisely: a certain – quantitative and qualitative – level of welfare state regulation. As the history of social policy and the welfare state shows, Germany can only be said to have had a developed welfare state as a socio-structural

---

[38] Rowntree's "cycle of poverty" consists of five phases: first, one grows up in poverty as a child; if one is employed and earns money, one can temporarily escape poverty; but with marriage and the birth of children, one is caught up in poverty again; later, the children work themselves and move out, one can again leave poverty behind for a while; one then spends one's old age in poverty again.

characteristic since about the mid-1950s.[39] In 1953, Adenauer had announced a comprehensive social reform in his government declaration; in fact, this was limited to the pension reform of 1957 – however, this marked the beginning of a welfare state version of the "social market economy". With the first Grand Coalition (1966–1969) and especially under the subsequent first Social Liberal Coalition (1969–1972) there was then an "unprecedented expansion of the welfare state" (Schmidt 1998, p. 78). Taking into account the central role of a developed welfare state in the formation of a chronologically standardized "normal life course", its beginnings can be dated to the period towards the middle of the 1950s. Or to put it another way: the heyday of the institutionalized life course began around the mid-1950s.

Does this heyday continue to this day? Or has the institutionalized life course now passed its zenith? Are we even experiencing a regressive process of "de-institutionalization" of the life course? In the last part of his fundamental work on the institutionalization of the life course, Kohli himself already points to empirical indications of an end, possibly even a reversal, of the process of chronological standardization of life courses and raises the question – with the due restraint often lacking in contributions on this topic – whether these facts "represent signs of a new structural change?" (1985, p. 22). The question of whether these empirical indications are to be understood as signs of a "de-institutionalization process" will be addressed later, but will be left aside here for the moment. For the time being, the point here is simply to note that there are empirical findings that suggest that the chronological standardization of life events began to erode towards the end of the 1970s. In terms of the question of the heyday of the institutionalized life course, this means that it began around the mid-1950s and extended into the early 1980s. For this period of 25 or 30 years one can "reasonably talk about a 'normal' life cycle that most people's experience followed quite closely. Most people indeed ... planned their lives on the assumption that they would follow the 'normal' pattern at about the 'normal' age" (Anderson 1985, p. 69 f.).

Before describing the institutionalized life course in its zenith, during its heyday as a chronologically standardized "normal life course", a conceptual clarification is in order. Individual life courses are formed over time as contingent results of complex structure-agency interactions. As a result of the multitude and diversity of socio-structural contexts and subjective-biographical factors, there are almost infinite possible combinations that ultimately make the real life course of an individual

---

[39] And this despite the fact that Germany had a pioneering role in terms of state social policy.

unique.[40] The term "normal life course" is therefore not to be understood empirically, i.e. it does not refer to a real life course. Rather, the term "normal life course" refers to a basic pattern or model that varies in the real life courses of individuals, but is not abandoned. As such a pattern or model, the "normal life course" is "normal" in a double sense: in a statistical and in a normative sense. Statistically, it means the prevalence of this pattern in a population, that is, that it underlies the life courses of the vast majority of individuals in the population in question. In the normative sense, the orientation function of this model is meant: that the "normal life course" functions as a pattern of expectations and an evaluation framework with regard to the occurrence of life events and circumstances.

It is obvious that its model character makes the "normal life course" biographically relevant: an individual life course – in its moments, sequences and longer phases – is perceived both by the individual concerned and by other persons or organizations against the background and in the frame of reference of the life course model that is socially regarded as "normal". The concept of the "normal life course" provides a benchmark for the assessment of individual life courses as corresponding to this or deviating from it (on/off-time). The biographical significance of the "normal life course" has already been discussed in the context of the comments on ideas of age appropriateness and timetables (see Sect. 5.2.1), which are inherent in the concept of the "normal life course". In this respect, the "normal life course" can be pointedly described as a yardstick for "(dis)orderly" and thus for biographically or socially "unsuccessful" or "successful" life courses. However, the concept of "normal life course" is not only relevant biographically, but also organizationally and on the macro level of society. The assumption of a social normality and thus also of a "normal life course" is built into the constitution and functioning of organizations, welfare state institutions and social systems. If, for example, a company prefers men to women in internal career paths, this personnel policy is based not least on the assumption that child-related absences are "normally" more likely and more extensive among women than among men. This organizational action, which does not do justice to a concrete individual case (nor is it irrational discrimination against women), is based on a generalization of the company's "previous statistical experience" (Phelps 1972, p. 659) with regard to absen-

---

[40] Even if one were to exclude the agency dimension, "in any given society, social forces create patterns in biographies but a multitude of contexts and consequent contingencies nevertheless render each life different" (Shanahan and Macmillan 2008, p. XIII).

teeism among women or men (statistical discrimination).[41] As an example at the macro level, consider the statutory pension insurance system, which was fundamentally constructed as a pay-as-you-go system financed by contributions. A central assumption of this construction logic is that the vast majority of (male) workers will work continuously after their education, i.e. without periods of unemployment or other interruptions in employment, and that they will work full-time until they reach retirement age. To the extent that this assumption becomes problematic, i.e. the assumed "normal" employment pattern is no longer reality for a growing part of the population due to demographic or economic developments, financing problems arise for the statutory pension insurance (which are then countered, among other things, by raising the standard retirement age: in 2006, the Bundestag adopted a gradual increase in retirement at 65 to a standard retirement age of 67, and a further increase in working life cannot be ruled out due to further increases in life expectancy).

For the following task, first visualize important political, economic, cultural and social aspects of German history in the 20th century (the timeline at "www.bpb.de/shop/lernen/falter/137101/zeitleiste-1914-1990-und-methoden" and the website "www.was-war-wann.de/1900/" can be helpful here). Against this background, sketch – probable – biographies:

- Start with Peter, born in late 1945 in a small town in southern Germany; his father is a pharmacist, his mother a housewife; Peter has a sister one and a half years younger than him.
- What will Peter's life be like (locate important life events on a timeline)? Compare your ideas about Peter's life with each other: what similarities are there? At what points are there divergent ideas? Discuss these differences. Consider why your drafts of Peter's life diverge on certain aspects and agree on certain other points.

---

[41] Phelps emphasizes at the end of his short article that "discrimination is no less damaging to its victims for being statistical. And it is no less important for social policy to counter" (1972, p. 661). Insofar as this organizational action is statistical discrimination, social policy can, for example, change the "statistical experience" of companies and thus their gender-specific expectations with regard to child-related absenteeism by expanding childcare facilities – which has a lasting effect on personnel policy discrimination against women in companies.

5.3 "Normal Life Course" and De-Standardization of the Life Course

> - Take a Petra instead of Peter (the familial frame data remains the same).
> - Vary the framework data: Would Peter's or Petra's life have been different if the father were a bricklayer? Or if the family lived in a village in the Hunsrück? Or in Berlin? How would Peter's or Petra's life have turned out if he or she had a brother one and a half years younger? Or an older brother? Etc. etc.
> - What would Peter's or Petra's life have been like if he or she had been born in 1900 or 1915 or 1930? And what if he or she had been born in 1960 or 1975?

What did the institutionalized life course look like during its heyday from the mid-1950s to the late 1970s in (West) Germany? In contrast to the pattern of life courses in early industrial society and up to the 1930s (the end of the Great Depression), which was characterized by only rudimentary chronological standardization and discontinuities, i.e. uncertainties, risks and imponderables, life courses in these heyday years were characterized by pronounced chronological standardization as well as continuity, security and predictability.[42] The basic tripartite structure of the modern life course, with its distinct phases of education, gainful employment and retirement, was clearly formed and established for men, while women assumed the homemaker role after the birth of their first child.

In the course of the institutional reform and expansion of the education system, especially higher and vocational education, and changed educational concepts, a "differentiated pattern of educational trajectories established itself for the first time historically – also for women" (Mayer 1998, p. 442). Previously, the vast majority of students had attended elementary school (Volksschule, since 1964: Hauptschule), then completed a vocational apprenticeship. In the wake of those educational reforms, a majority of pupils gradually moved on from the four-year primary school to a higher secondary school: either to the Realschule (until 1964:

---

[42] Life courses during National Socialism, the Second World War and the immediate post-war period up to the 1950s are not discussed here. According to Mayer, life courses in immediate postwar Germany were characterized by "disorder without norm change" (1998, p. 441). The fact that life courses in these years were "disorderly" (and did not follow traditional paths) is understandable in view of the consequences of the war and the destruction in all areas of society and life, and to be seen as of necessity; however, this "did not lead to permanently changed life course patterns, but – when external circumstances permitted this – to a return to normality" (ibid., p. 442).

Mittelschule) or – initially still in smaller numbers – the Gymnasium. In most cases, the intermediate school leaving certificate (Mittlere Reife) of the Realschule, which was obtained after six years, was followed by qualified vocational training, and the Abitur-certificate of the Gymnasium, which was obtained after nine years, was followed by university studies. The phase of (further) education was completed at the age of about 17–19 or, for academics, between the mid and late 20s. For men, this was followed by one to one-and-a-half years of military service (which was still compulsory at the time) or civilian service; high school graduates usually completed their service before beginning their studies.

The school system was differentiated into three types of school, the qualifications of which enabled or generated further differentiated educational trajectories and career and life opportunities. Differences in the educational path and status of individuals became the most important factor of social differentiation and functioned as a selection criterion for professional careers as well as in other areas of life. The (education) system was chronologically standardized throughout (with the exception of the quaternary sector), although standardization was less strict in the university sector. The internal differentiation and chronological standardization of the education and training system made educational pathways – including the associated options for connection – highly plannable and predictable.

After three to four years of vocational training, there was a rapid and smooth transition into the gainful employment system. For university graduates, too, labor market entry was unproblematic until the mid-1970s. Further employment histories were characterized by a high degree of employment security and continuity. Periods of unemployment were very rare; fixed-term employment contracts were an exception. Permanent full-time employment in an occupation appropriate to the training was the rule. Changes of occupation or company were rare, and when they did occur, they were usually initiated by the employees themselves. Increasingly qualified jobs were created in industry and the skilled trades, as well as in the context of tertiarisation. Measures for further and continuing vocational training were promoted by the state and career paths were established within companies. Professional advancement was widespread. Real wages and salaries rose continuously. In short, working life was on a steady upward trajectory.[43]

---

[43] In this context, reference should also be made to the so-called normal employment relationship and its much-discussed erosion since the 1980s (Mückenberger 1985; Osterland 1990; Kress 1998; Bosch 2013). Although the normal employment relationship was "never an empirical reality of the exclusive or even predominant form of performing work" (Mückenberger 1989, p. 211) in (West) Germany, it functioned for a long time as a point of reference for (labor) law regulations and interpretations and – especially against the background of the flexibilisation and precarisation of gainful employment since then – has partly remained a normative model for an employment relationship until today.

5.3 "Normal Life Course" and De-Standardization of the Life Course

In contrast to this completely work-centered male life course model, that of women was still strongly family-centered. Because in the course of the educational expansion women also acquired higher educational qualifications in growing numbers and increasingly completed qualified training, more and more women also took up qualified gainful employment (especially in the expanding civil service there were such jobs and career opportunities for women). However, most women interrupted their professional activity for a longer period of time with the birth of their first child. Being employed as a mother of young children was socially unacceptable (an attitude that only began to slowly change in the 1970s). After the childbearing phase – from an employment-centered point of view a career break – only some of the women resumed gainful employment, often on a part-time basis or no longer in the profession they had learned. The other women remained permanently in the female homemaker role (and thus in material dependence on their husbands).

A major goal in life at that time was to have a family of one's own: getting married and having children was the normal, almost universally accepted model of life. The age at (first) marriage fell steadily until the early 1970s, as did the age at birth of the first child, i.e. marriage and parenthood took place relatively early in the life course (for women between their early and mid-20s). Two children or even multiple-child families were the norm; after the "baby boom" in the mid-1960s, however, birth rates plummeted (("baby bust" due to antibaby pill). Until they started school at the age of six, children lived largely in the protected space of the family, primarily under the care of their mothers. The family functioned as the central instance of child rearing and care; in fact, this was primarily the mother's responsibility. Kindergartens played at best a supplementary secondary role with regard to the upbringing and care of children. Increasingly, families were in a position to fulfil their dream of owning their own home – the second major life goal of those years alongside having their own family – or at least to acquire their own apartment. Families were, at least formally, extremely stable, because divorce was socially frowned upon and because it would have resulted in serious material problems due to the male breadwinner/female homemaker model and its institutional-legal anchoring.

The standard age limit for the transition from working life to retirement was generally 65; women could already draw an old-age pension at 60. The pension reform of 1972 enabled those who had been insured for many years to draw their old-age pension from 63. As part of the pension reform of 1957, it was decided to adjust the pension level to the development of earned income – which resulted in an enormous increase in pensions. As a result of this dynamic linking of the pension level to the development of gross wages, which rose steadily in those years, the statutory pension insurance guaranteed a high standard of living even in old age, whereby the woman was financially secured primarily through her husband. While the average retirement age for men was initially slightly higher than the standard retirement age, it fell to 62.5 years (women: 61.9) by the end of the decade in the wake of this reform. If one takes not only the old-age pension but the insured pensions as a whole, i.e. if one also takes into account pensions due to reduced earning capacity, the average age of entry in 1980 was only 58.5 years (women: 59.8).[44]

In summary, it can be said that since the early 1950s the life courses of individuals have become "more continuous, more differentiated in their temporal structure and more homogeneous and standardized with regard to the spread and age dispersion of transition events" (ibid.). For the following two and a half to three decades, it is possible to speak of a "normal life course" that is employment-centered in its differentiation and chronologically standardized. In its institutional anchoring and its political-legal regulations, this concept of the tripartite "normal life course" was oriented solely towards the man, the male breadwinner. In this institutionalized life course regime, women's life courses were implicitly considered in the sense of their complementary role as female homemakers. In terms of individual life courses, the employment-centered male standard life course must therefore be supplemented by the family-focused female standard life course. In the heyday of the institutionalized life course, both the "normal" or standard male life course and the "derived" standard female life course were characterized by great stability, continuity and expectability. Subjectively-biographically, individuals experienced and interpreted their life courses as an upward development, i.e. as a continuous improvement in living standards, steady progress in their material prosperity and social security.

How was this chronologically standardized "normal life course" possible? What was the social precondition and basis of this gender-specific family and life course model? What made the life courses of individuals into quite homogeneous, typically male or female standard life courses, predictable in their continuity? The decisive socio-structural basis for this was a specific political-economic[45] situation

---

[44] Deutsche Rentenversicherung Bund (ed.): Rentenversicherung in Zeitreihen (Oct. 2016, p. 138).

[45] The male breadwinner/female homemaker family and life course model had a cultural foundation in the prevailing material mentality of the population, which was more than understandable on the basis of previous experience and oriented towards peace, order and security (as an emblematic source of zeitgeist, see for example election posters and slogans such as "Prosperity for all" or "No risk!", with which the Union parties went into the election campaign in 1957 and won an absolute majority in the third German Bundestag).

5.3 "Normal Life Course" and De-Standardization of the Life Course

and development: the enormous economic boom that began (not only) in Europe shortly after the Second World War and for which, in relation to (West) Germany, the term "economic miracle" has become established. This specific socio-historical phase was characterized by continuous economic growth together with welfare state support. The stable economic upswing was based on industrial mass production of standardized consumer goods and mass consumption. The development of wages and salaries was linked to the development of productivity. The rising level of education and skilled employment, which emerged in increasing numbers, guaranteed fairly secure and well-paid jobs. Full employment prevailed, upward mobility was widespread, and real wages rose steadily. The expanding welfare state cushioned risks in the life course and provided a high degree of social security beyond material subsistence. The relationship between capital, labor and politics was not determined by antagonistic interests but was oriented towards cooperation: Companies, employers' associations, trade unions and the state acted in a largely coordinated manner in matters of economic, labor market, employment, education and social policy.

In (West) Germany, the post-war economic boom outlined above ended – despite a first small recession in 1967 – in the wake of the "oil price shock" in the mid-1970s. This phase, which was shaped by the historically unique framework conditions of the "economic miracle", or the life course regime given in this specific socio-historical phase, is referred to as "Fordist" in life course research. The term "Fordist" or "Fordism" is thus not only used in the life course literature in an economic sense to designate a specific mode of production (mass production: standardized manufacture of goods), but – much more broadly – as a political-economic term that also encompasses the aspect of mass consumption, increasing welfare state and also a specific life course regime. "As a mode of societalization, Fordism refers to a distinctive pattern of social cohesion and integration, a social way of life" (Myles 1992, p. 172). That two-and-a-half to three-decade heyday of the institutionalized life course coincides with the Fordist phase; the chronologically standardized "normal life course" or standard male and female life course coincides with the Fordist life course regime.

In the long-term historical view of the institutionalization of the life course, four distinct life course regimes become visible according to the previous explanations. In his schematic summary of the periodizations mentioned in the literature, Mayer refers to these as traditional, industrial, Fordist and post-fordist (2001, p. 92 ff.). First of all, the traditional life course pattern, which was predominant until the end of the nineteenth century, was replaced by an industrial life course regime, which gave way towards the middle of the 1950s to the Fordist life course model (just described in more detail), which in turn gave way to a post-Fordist life course regime at the latest since the beginning of the 1980s. This periodization of the change of life course regimes or life courses will not be further discussed here. Such a periodization may have a certain heuristic utility, but it is fraught with a serious conceptual problem because the life courses of individuals extend beyond the period boundaries in their temporal span. To put this in concrete terms using the example of the Fordist phase, this is considered to be the formative period for the life courses of birth cohorts between the late 1930s and the mid-1950s. However, someone born in 1938, for example, has already experienced war years, a "messy" immediate postwar period, and the early reconstruction phase before this Fordist phase, and lived in and experienced the post-Fordist period for quite a few years after that. And the birth cohorts of the early 1950s lived the vast majority of their lives not in Fordist conditions but in post-Fordist conditions. The example illustrates that the life courses of individuals do not correspond in time to those – like all periodizations: theoretically constructed – periods of social history. Individuals normally live through and are shaped by not just one, but various socio-historical phases.

The problem inherent in this periodization would only not arise if a period of social history spanned the entire life course of an individual – which is rarely the case. Otherwise, one must either operate in terms of personality and developmental psychology with the assumption of a formative, i.e. lifelong formative effect of adolescence and young adulthood (an assumption that is, however, controversial, as already discussed in Chap. 4). Alternatively, from a sociological perspective, a kind of "life path dependency" can be assumed: in adolescence and young adulthood there are – at the same time – the end of education and training, the start of a career or gainful employment, moving out of the parental home, marriage/founding a common-law marriage, and parenthood. All these events are decisive moments in the life course, to which socially anchored and institutionally shaped connection options are linked. For example, initial occupational placement has serious structuring consequences for the entire subsequent course of employment (Blossfeld 1989; Mayer and Blossfeld 1990).[46] With regard to the birth cohorts from the end

---

[46] In terms of life course theory, the empirical phenomenon of "life course dependency" could be understood as an "endogenous causal connection" (Mayer 1990, p. 11), to use a life course concept from Mayer which, however, he did not elaborate further.

5.3 "Normal Life Course" and De-Standardization of the Life Course

of the 1930s to the mid-1950s, it should be noted that all the events of adolescence and young adulthood that set the course fell within the "economic miracle" phase of the Fordist period, which was favorable in terms of economic, educational and labor market structures as well as social policy.[47]

The heyday of the institutionalized life course in the form of the chronologically standardized "normal life course" began around the mid-1950s and ended in the early 1980s. This Fordist life course regime spanned just 25 to 30 years. By comparison, post-Fordist life courses are less standardized and expectable, and more discontinuous and uncertain. Of course, the Fordist period can be used as a frame of reference and evaluation for contemporary life courses. One should only be aware that one is then using an exceptional situation in social history as a normative point of reference (and perhaps ask oneself how sensible it is to want to continue dreaming this – to take up the apt title of Lutz's 1984 book again – "short dream of perpetual prosperity" against all reality). The Fordist life course regime, or rather its socio-structural, especially economic basis, was in any case an exception in the long history of industrial society's gainful employment (and of social modernity in general), and uncertain, discontinuous life courses were the norm. In this respect, the transition process from the Fordist to a post-Fordist life course regime, which has been observable since the beginning of the 1980s, can – depending on the chosen frame of reference – appear in a different light: if only the Fordist (exceptional) phase functions as a frame of reference, this transformation would have to be seen as an epochal structural change of individual life courses, which would have to be evaluated negatively, whereas in a larger frame of reference in social history it would rather have to be classified as a "return" or continuation of the normality of working society and its insecure, discontinuous life courses.

---

[47] This argument makes the (professional) careers of the 1940s cohorts plausible. By contrast, the birth cohorts of the second half of the 1920s, who were already in adulthood at the beginning of the Fordist phase, remained relatively disadvantaged in their careers as a result of their poorer educational and, in particular, occupational entry conditions, despite the "economic miracle" (Mayer 1988; Blossfeld 1989) – a finding that also supports the argument empirically (for those born after the mid-1950s, see the following subchapter).

One finding of the large intercultural comparative study "Project AGE" on the significance of the category "age" (Keith et al. 1994) was that our theoretical "ideas about the life course were not appropriate for non-industrialized communities ... or for those marginal to industry (...) The life course as we know it is but one variant of life courses" (Fry 2002, p. 283 f.). This is already obvious if one only thinks of the problematic phenomenon of child labor. A childhood and education phase, as the advanced (Western) industrial societies know it, still does not exist in many parts of the world. In 2012, 10.6% of all 5–17 year olds worldwide (168 million) or 9.9% of 5–14 year olds (over 120 million) or 8.5% of 5–11 year olds (73 million) lived as child laborers. Approximately half and a third and a quarter of these work in conditions "directly endangering their health, safety and moral development" (International Labor Organization 2013, p. 15).

- Where in the world is child labor particularly widespread? What is the data situation on the subject of "child labor"?
- Find out whether there is still (or also: again) child labor in Europe.

An institutionalized, secure retirement phase is also non-existent for many parts of the world; this is true not only for developing countries, but even – still – for emerging economies such as China (Leisering 2002). Even if one focuses only on the basic tripartite structure of the institutionalized life course: "the empirically observable life course patterns of the greater share of the earth's human population are – from childhood onward – quite different from the prevailing Eurocentric notions of either 'normal human development,' or of an institutionalized life course with sustained periods of schooling and retirement" (Dannefer 2002, p. 261).

- In light of this, what do you think about the following statement: "the description of life course patterns and other central preoccupations of the life course literature are largely irrelevant to the empirical reality of the existence of the majority of the present human population of the earth" (ibid., p. 259)?

There are no unstructured life courses. However, the institutionalization of the life course – as already shown by the example of the Tuareg, for whom the age of the individual does not function as the most important structuring factor, and the ignorance of one's own age, which was also widespread in Europe until the 19th century (see Sect. 3.1) – does not necessarily take place in the form of chronological standardization characteristic of modern industrial society. Even in the advanced (Western) industrial societies of today, there are subpopulations whose life course is structured quite differently.

The bestseller "Do or die" (Bing 1991) is an insider's report on the brutal world and life of the two opposing street gangs of the Crips and Bloods ("America's most notorious teenage gangs" – the subtitle) in the 1970/1980s. Dannefer (2002, p. 261) quotes the following sequence from a conversation between the 15-year-old Tiny Vamp and G-Roc, who is the same age:

Tiny Vamp: You still a little homie, or what?
G-Roc: Li'l Homie. I ain't probably gonna reach the O.G. stage for awhile yet. I got outta baby homie when I was like thirteen and a half. How 'bout you?
Tiny Vamp: I'm still a Tiny. In my set you get a rep by straight killin'. I been on drive-bys and I been stabbed.

And on the following page: It's like when I got jumped in – all my homeboys and my cousins told me "You in now, man ... Either you be down for it or get out now." Cause you KNOW you gonna have to go to jail.[48] You KNOW you might end up gettin' killed, gettin' stabbed, gettin' shot. You know all this. My homeboy, Li'l Lazy, just got killed, and he only sixteen.

- What stages in the life of a gang member can you identify on the basis of these statements? What does their biographical life plan look like and under what time horizon does it stand? What structures a *gang member's life course*?

---

[48] Research on crime and deviance has identified "incarceration as a new stage in the life course of young low-skill black men" (Pettit and Western 2004, p. 151): about one third of these men "had gone to prison by their mid-30s. Among black male high school dropouts, the risk of imprisonment had increased to 60%, establishing incarceration as a normal stopping point on the route to midlife. (…) Imprisonment now rivals or overshadows the frequency of military service and college graduation for recent cohorts of African American men. For black men in their mid-30s at the end of the 1990s, prison records were nearly twice as common as bachelor's degrees. In this same birth cohort of non-college black men, imprisonment was more than twice as common as military service" (ibid., p. 164).

5.3.2 "De-Institutionalizing" Individualization of the Life Course?

As already mentioned in the previous sub-chapter, since the end of the 1970s there has been talk of an increasing individualization of the life course. Empirical evidence for the increasing erosion of the institutionalized, chronologically standardized life course includes, for example, that marriage and parenthood are postponed in the younger birth cohorts; that family formation increasingly takes place in alternative forms of life (or no longer takes place at all); that more flexible transitions and more frequent changes between employment and education (with increasingly interspersed phases of social benefit receipt) are to be observed instead of a strict tripartite division of the life course; that an increasing number of employed persons are working part-time; that precarious employment relationships are on the increase; that normative ideas of age-appropriate behavior are losing significance. In view of these empirical findings, Kohli himself had already raised the question at the end of his fundamental essay on the institutionalization of the life course as to whether these were signs of a renewed structural change in the life course.

The interpretation and evaluation of such empirical findings initially took the form of two contrasting extreme positions: while one side perceived only signs of erosion of the institutionalized, chronologically standardized life course and postulated its end, the opposite side criticized this position as a view owing merely to "zeitgeist-hegemonic excitement" (Wohlrab-Sahr 1992, p. 1) and perceived continuity rather than tendencies of "de-institutionalization" in the life courses of individuals. In the meantime, both extreme positions have proven to be untenable and are no longer represented in this polarizing intensification. However, the question "institutionalization or individualization of the life course?" (ibid.) continues to divide sociological minds. Although the relevant literature can hardly be surveyed, no uniform picture has emerged to date in the sense that the empirical findings and statistical data can be combined into a clear and widely accepted trend statement in favor of or against individualization or institutionalization. Rather, empirical indications are found both for an individualization of life courses – dissolving chronological standardization – and for the continuity of institutionalized life courses (Brückner and Mayer 2005; Scherger 2007).[49] Secondly, empirical findings do not necessarily speak for

---

[49] Other important works on life courses even after the Fordist phase include Konietzka and Huinink 2003; Hillmert and Mayer 2004; Blossfeld et al. 2005; Fussel and Furstenberg 2005; Hillmert 2005; Macmillan 2005; Blossfeld and Hofmeister 2006; Blossfeld et al. 2006; Elchardus and Smits 2006; Elzinga and Liefbroer 2007; Buchholz 2008; Konietzka 2011; Simonson et al. 2011; Mortimer and Moen 2016.

themselves, but gain their significance in the light of theoretical perspectives – which means that an empirical result can, under certain circumstances, be an indication of both the erosion and the continuity of the institutionalized life course. In this respect, the following does not refer to individual empirical findings or studies on life courses after the Fordist phase, which are put forward for or against the thesis of institutionalization or individualization of the life course. In other words, it is not the aim of the following to prove that one of these theses is correct (or more plausible than the other). Rather, only a few results and insights are presented here that are sufficiently well-founded empirically and are largely consensual in life course research.

Individual life courses as the results of complex structure-agency interactions over time cannot remain unchanged if the structural framework conditions change significantly. In this respect, it is obvious that the life courses of individuals have changed in the wake of the structural changes in society – especially those caused by the economy, but also by (socio-)political and cultural changes – following the end of the "economic miracle". Since the late 1970s, the general conditions of the Fordist "economic miracle" phase, which guaranteed stability and were favorable in every respect, have given way to economic recessions and a general deterioration of the economic situation, problems with the structure of the labor market and employment policy, growing pressure from globalization, rapid technological and serious changes in the structure of occupations and sectors, demographic shifts with far-reaching consequences for the welfare state, catastrophic financial market crises, post-materialist values and the consequences of reunification. Compared to the Fordist phase, these post-Fordist conditions have tended to make individuals' life courses more discontinuous and consequently less predictable. The general statement that there has been a change in individual life courses in this direction since the end of the 1970s is completely undisputed – as I said, there is only dissent with regard to its extent and qualitative scope.

The historically given socio-structural conditions and institutional frameworks affect people at different stages of the life course. As Elder has shown (see Sect. 2.1), the life course effects resulting from social contexts or changes (also) depend to a large extent on the respective phase of life or age of an individual. As already mentioned in the previous sub-chapter, the birth cohorts of the late 1930s and the 1940s in particular were able to benefit from the generally (favorable) Fordist "economic miracle" phase. As a result of the agglomeration of life-course-relevant events in adolescence and young adulthood and the resulting "life-path dependency", the unfavorable post-Fordist framework conditions should be reflected in the life courses of those born since around the mid-1960s. In this context, the birth cohorts from the early 1990s onwards represent a "topicality frontier" for empirical life course research: the life courses of those born in 1995, for example, can now (i.e. 2017) only be surveyed and analyzed up to the age of 22 years. Thus, there is hardly anything that can be said on an empirical basis about the life courses of those born since 1990 after the education and training phase and the first years of employment, i.e. about by far the largest part of their lives.[50] In this respect, the following remarks essentially refer to the birth cohorts from around the mid-1960s to the early 1990s, who are now in their early 50s or the second half of their 20s. Beyond the general statement of a greater discontinuity of individual life courses, what can be said with empirical certainty about their life courses in post-Fordism?

It is a fact that the transition from the education system to the employment system has become longer, more complicated, more flexible and more diverse (Konietzka 2002; Buchholz 2008). Firstly, people rarely enter into stable employment after completing their education; fixed-term employment contracts, temporary work, part-time work, marginal and precarious employment, and even bogus self-employment have increased. Secondly, the discrepancy between the desired or trained occupation and the first job has grown. In order to be able to realize career biographical goals, further educational efforts are more frequently required, which is reflected in a growing number of second or multiple training courses, which are mostly close to the first vocational training and "continue" it (Jacob 2004). Thirdly, graduates of vocational training increasingly experience not only a short phase of search unemployment but also a longer period of unemployment. The increased uncertainties and problems in the transition from the education system to the employment system primarily affect school or training dropouts, the low-skilled, young people with a migration background and foreigners and young women. With regard to the post-Fordist school-to-work transition, a rough distinction can be made between three groups of people or life histories. The first group continues to make a smooth transition into the employment system and a stable working career.

---

[50] In the large-scale "German Life Course Study" (GLHS), the youngest birth cohorts are the cohorts born in 1964 and 1971, whose life courses were surveyed until the end of the 1990s (Hillmert and Mayer 2004); the younger of the two cohorts was surveyed again (and additionally qualitatively) in 2004/2005 (Mayer and Schulze 2009). This means that the life courses of the members of even these two early, or older, post-Fordist cohorts were only analyzed up to the age of 35 – the temporally larger part of the entire life span, important employment and family biographical events in the further course of life and the transition from the employment to the old-age security system could not be recorded at all.

5.3 "Normal Life Course" and De-Standardization of the Life Course

For example, around 70% of those who had completed vocational training in 2010 and 2012 (i.e. the core of the birth cohorts of the early 1990s) were already in full-time or part-time employment subject to social insurance contributions after one month as well as two years later, i.e. after a certain consolidation of employment status (Autorengruppe Bildungsberichterstattung 2016, p. 116).[51] University graduates were "predominantly employed in jobs appropriate to their degree. Differences are evident according to the type of degree, the university attended and the field of study (…) There is a very high degree of employment adequacy after a master's degree at a university" (ibid., p. 134 f.; Leuze 2010).[52] A second group also manages the transition into employment and entry into a working career, but only with a time delay and in a roundabout way. This group also maintains the fit between training and occupation or a high level of occupational commitment (Hillmert 2002). While transition problems for this group only arise after completion of training, i.e., at the second threshold, a third group often already has major problems finding a training place at all, i.e., already when facing the first threshold. Many of these youths go through measures in the so-called "transition system" (now established as a third pillar of the vocational education and training system) below the level of qualified vocational education and training – or are stuck in such (training) programs that are not aimed at acquiring a recognized training qualification but at addressing individual skills deficits in order to enable participants to take up vocational education and training in the first place (Lex and Geier 2010; Kohlrausch 2012). The percentage of those young people who end up in the transition system after leaving school as a proportion of all new entrants to the VET system grew steadily to 36.3% by 2005 and was still 28.3% in 2015, despite the easing that has occurred on the training market (Autorengruppe Bildungsberichterstattung 2016, p. 102). This group does not manage to enter the employment system and to have a reasonably stable career, or does so only with great difficulty.

---

[51] While there were almost no gender differences in this respect, there were considerable discrepancies between German and foreign graduates: after one month, only about 55% of foreign graduates were employed (the discrepancy between German and foreign graduates had, however, largely narrowed after two years; Autorengruppe Bildungsberichterstattung 2016, p. 116).

[52] The alarmist proclamation of a "generation of interns" can therefore only be spoken of, if at all, in terms of specific disciplines, but not as a mass phenomenon.

> Employers' representatives and associations have been complaining for years that more and more school leavers are not capable of undergoing training and that meanwhile around one in three apprenticeship places cannot now be filled. Since 2008, the number of training places has exceeded the number of training applicants; in 2016, the number of unfilled training places (43,478) was more than double the number of unplaced applicants (20,550; source: www.statista.com/statistik/daten/studie/36101/umfrage/freie-ausbildungsplaetze-vs-unversorgte-bewerber-seit-dem-jahr-1992/).
>
> - Find out about the (training) opportunities offered by the transition system and consider the possible effects of (repeated) participation in such measures on the life histories of the participants.
> - The measures of the transition system deal with individual (competence) deficits – which means that they see the causes for problems in the school-to-work transition in (competence) deficits of the young people. Discuss this individualizing view of the problem.
> - In view of the much-discussed shortage of skilled workers, what do you think about the ever-increasing academisation since the education reform (with a view to different – e.g. biographical, inequality-structural or economic – aspects of this academisation)?

After the transition to employment – and this is also a consensus – employment histories have become more dependent on (sector-specific) cyclical fluctuations under the post-Fordist framework conditions. Although employment histories have become more discontinuous and uncertain overall, they have done so to very different degrees for different social groups. The employment histories of men continued to be quite stable; until the end of the 1990s, occupational discontinuities tended to be of a temporary nature. Only after the turn of the millennium did men's employment careers also become more unstable, especially – as a result of fixed-term employment contracts – in their early stages (Diewald and Sill 2004). The situation is different for women: discontinuity and insecurity have become a permanent problem in women's employment histories. Employment instabilities are also and above all a problem of the low-skilled (Solga 2005; Buchholz et al. 2012) as well as of persons with a migration background. For these groups or their employment histories, an "erosion of the continuity paradigm" (Brose et al. 1993, p. 37) can indeed be observed after the Fordist phase. It is true that temporary employment relationships,

5.3 "Normal Life Course" and De-Standardization of the Life Course

changes of company and occupation as well as periods of unemployment or other interruptions of employment have tended to increase. However, the phenomenon of only precarious inclusion in the labor market or even permanent exclusion from the employment system, like that of inadequate employment, remains limited to certain social groups. The dramatizing notion often found in the mass media of complete job insecurity and unlimited flexibilisation of employment histories, which even leads to the precarisation of the majority of the population – symptomatically Bourdieu: "Precarity is everywhere" (1998)[53] – is empirically false and misleading. Although changes of company and also occupational mobility have increased, company and above all occupational loyalty is still high, and the risk of unemployment has also remained within limits (Erlinghagen 2004; Giesecke and Heisig 2010; Mayer et al. 2010). The unemployment rate had been trending upwards since 1980 (3.3%), but with large fluctuations (and especially reunification), peaking at 11.7% in 2005 (9.9% in West vs. 18.7% in East Germany) and then falling rapidly and significantly; in 2016 it was 6.1% (5.6% vs. 8.5%).[54] Among men in the 1971 birth cohort surveyed in the "German Life Course Study" (GLHS), the unemployment rate at the age of 25–34, i.e. in the period 1995–2005, fluctuated between 3% and 5% in West Germany and 5–10% in East Germany, among women between 5–10% and 10–15%, respectively (Mayer and Schulze 2009, p. 140 ff.).

Another empirically founded fact is that post-Fordist life course changes have mainly taken place in the private and family sphere. Compared to the – at least until the turn of the millennium – rather moderate changes in the education and employment system, the change of life courses in the family sphere is much more pronounced. Since the 1980s, a process of pluralization of lifestyles can be observed (Bien and Marbach 2003; Wagner 2008; Wagner and Valdés Cifuentes 2014). This pluralization does not result from structurally novel forms of living (since the 1960s, only same-sex cohabitation and living-apart-together have been able to establish themselves as new forms), but rather from a significantly changed distribution of the population across the existing structural forms (e.g. older people are also increasingly living in non-marital cohabitation; Schneider 2001).

---

[53] On precarity research see Castel and Dörre 2009 or Motakef 2015; also interesting in terms of welfare state and political theory is Neilson and Rossiter: "Precarity appears as an irregular phenomenon only when set against a Fordist or Keynesian norm. (…) If we look at capitalism in a wider historical and geographical scope, it is precarity that is the norm and not Fordist economic organization. Thus, in regulatory contexts where the social state has maintained less grip … precarity has not seemed an exceptional condition that can spark social antagonism" (2008, p. 54).v

[54] Source: www.bpb.de/nachschlagen/zahlen-und-fakten/soziale-situation-in-deutschland/61718/arbeitslose-und-arbeitslosenquote)

In particular, the life model of the 1950s and 1960s (marriage, two children, male sole breadwinner) has lost much of its importance, while non-marital cohabitation and single-person households have increased sharply (Klein and Lauterbach 1999; Lengerer 2011). The number of single parents and households without children has also increased (Konietzka and Kreyenfeld 2007; Krätschmer-Hahn 2012). Despite the declining numbers of marriages and rising numbers of divorces, marriage is still the most widespread form of living in adulthood and partner or cohabiting couples have not lost their importance (Klein et al. 2002). Among households with minor children, marriage remains by far the most common form of living: among these two-generation households, the share of married couples was 69% in 2014, while non-marital cohabiting couples accounted for 10% and single parents for 20% (Statistisches Bundesamt et al. 2016, p. 51).

It is also indisputable that women's life courses have changed much more than men's since the late 1970s. This "quiet revolution" (Goldin 2006) of female life courses is primarily related to the fact that girls and young women were the "winners" of the educational expansion of the 1960s, i.e. they were able to benefit considerably more from the increased educational opportunities and make better use of their educational chances than boys and young men. As the trend towards qualified training and higher education in general has continued unbroken to this day, the number of women with qualified vocational training and higher general school and university degrees has risen sharply. This has changed women's understanding of themselves and their roles as well as their (occupational) biographical plans (Geissler and Oechsle 1996): they also want to make appropriate use of the educational capital they have acquired. Gainful employment – and not in the sense of a mere "additional income job", but of a professional career – has become "normal" for women. This means not only that women's entry into the labor market has become almost universal, but also that their occupational biographies span a longer time horizon and that their employment histories have become longer. The male breadwinner model has given way to a dual earner model (Blossfeld and Drobnič 2001). The shift towards this dual earner model does not mean, however, that female and male life courses are converging, steadily becoming more similar. It is true, as has just been said, that there has been an alignment in terms of educational trajectories and also in terms of labor force participation. At the same time, however, there is not only a persistence of gender-specific differences (e.g. with regard to part-time employment), but also the "unfavorable" post-Fordist framework conditions – in relation to the Fordist phase – have a generally more negative impact on women's life histories, especially their employment histories, than on male employment careers (Levy and Widmer 2013; Blossfeld et al. 2015; McMunn et al. 2015; Hofferth and Goldscheider 2016).

5.3 "Normal Life Course" and De-Standardization of the Life Course

So much for the empirically verifiable change trends in life courses since the end of the 1970s. As far as the transition from the employment system to retirement is concerned, nothing can yet be said on an empirically sound basis for the birth cohorts since the mid-1960s – for the reason mentioned above. The effects of the post-Fordist framework on the biographical level of interpretation and the life planning of individuals are difficult to assess and far from undisputed. One position holds that the discontinuities and uncertainties that have grown steadily since the Fordist phase, especially in working life, have for more and more individuals, especially from certain social groups, destroyed the expectation of continuity in the everyday world as a prerequisite for planning one's own life,[55] or at least made it fragile. According to this position, post-Fordist insecurity has the biographical effect of "a virus that permeates everyday life, dissolves social relations and undermines the psychological structures of individuals" (Castel 2005, p. 8; Sennett 1998).[56] This is countered by the fact that discontinuity at the level of the "outer" life course does not necessarily mean that the institutionalized life course at the "inner" level of the biography loses its orientation function, because the two life course levels form a "contradictory unity" (Brose et al. 1993, p. 170), i.e. they do not have to be in a relationship of correspondence (as has already been emphasized in Sects. 2.2 and 3.2).[57] Empirical studies on the biographical processing of post-Fordist discontinuities and uncertainty often point to problematic consequences for the individual's identity and life planning that result from them (Wohlrab-Sahr 1993; Behringer 1998). However, these studies often work with an identity-theoretical perspective that regards uncertainty as problematic from the outset. If one abandons this fixed identity concept or an identity-focused study perspective altogether and instead examines in a constructivist doing biography perspective how individuals integrate insecurity into their own biographies and life plans, i.e. the problem of the biographical production of (expected) security, the negative evaluation immanent in that identity concept and the evaluation aspect in general

---

[55] For an orientation towards the future, the "and so on" idealization about the constancy of the lifeworld is fundamental (Schütz and Luckmann 1979, p. 42).

[56] The problem has been studied primarily using the example of unemployment or the experience of unemployment (Rogge 2013; classically the Mariental study by Jahoda et al. 1933).

[57] In biographical or life-planning terms, the "empirical erosion of the regularities of the course of life need not lead to the dissolution of normative orientations, which can continue to adhere to the counterfactual maintenance of the model of a life plan characterized by continuity" (Brose et al. 1993, p. 170).

also disappears.[58] Empirically, such a perspective reveals different biographical "strategies" with which individuals produce (expectational) security for themselves and the idea of life planability (Mutz 1997; Zinn and Eßer 2003; Wenzel 2008). The various strategic patterns of this doing biography can only ever be determined empirically and move between the poles of a resigned giving up and an innovative new beginning (and the question of "failure" or "success" can ultimately only be answered by the respective individual himself, i.e. from his biographical accounting perspective).[59]

> The previous sub-chapter ended by pointing out that the post-Fordist uncertainties and discontinuities are to be seen in a historically long-term perspective, going beyond or back beyond the Fordist (exceptional) phase, as a "return" or continuation of the normality of insecure, discontinuous life courses in working society. According to Kohli, however, there is a serious difference between the periods before and after the Fordist phase with regard to this "normal" life course insecurity: "Insofar as we again observe a de-standardization of the life course today, it can ... be based on structurally quite different reasons, namely compulsion or choice. Compulsion is the consequence of the fact that the continuity guarantees of the labor market and the welfare state security system are partially suspended. This gives rise to a situational form of life which, even in its deep structure, is a return to the 19th century – albeit above a social net (in the form of social welfare) which excludes any immediate material threat to existence. Choice, on the other hand, presupposes a corresponding material and cultural basis. Materially, beyond income security, the individualization tendency in the organization

---

[58] While the fixed identity concept (critically Keupp et al. 1999; Keupp and Hohl 2006) evaluates insecurity per se negatively and sees it as a problem to be eliminated, the constructivist doing biography perspective (non-judgmentally) regards insecurity as normal, as an omnipresent context and aspect of life.

[59] A biographical strategy which, e.g. after several phases of unemployment, does not lead to the continuation of the chosen occupational and employment career, but to a different life path associated with financial and prestige losses, may be classified by others as "failure", but by the individual himself as "success" (e.g. in the sense of a liberation from occupational or employment constraints and a gain in self-determination and life satisfaction).

of work is of particular concern, ... a development towards a holistic[60] use of labor power in which individualized work behavior in the sense of thinking along with others and independent use of competence is demanded and rewarded" (1986a, p. 202).

- First, clarify the meaning of Kohli's quote with concrete examples.
- Then discuss whether Kohli's statement can be sharpened to the effect that in post-Fordism "economic coercion ... has been replaced by individual choice" (ibid.).

The biographical expectation of continuity as a necessary prerequisite for one's own life planning (see above) "does not prevent professional mobility and individual initiative, it does not lead to a life without breaks and changes – on the contrary: the knowledge of potential instability is part of reflexive life planning. The link between life course patterns and individual life planning thus runs through the certainty of expectations with regard to material and symbolic support services provided by institutions: the life course pattern can only have a normative effect as an 'orientation scheme' and provide a basis for biographical decisions if individuals trust that possible breaks in continuity will be prevented or bridged" (Geissler 2004a, p. 116). With the transformation of the caring to the activating (welfare) state since the 1990s "central continuity mechanisms are weakened. (...) The crisis of the subjective experience of continuity or of trust in bridging discontinuity cannot be overlooked" (ibid., p. 119).

- Discuss whether the activating social and labor market policies, which also in crisis phases of life attribute the maintenance and restoration of the security of expectations and continuity in the life course "more strongly than before to the responsibility of the individual" (ibid., p. 121), lead to the fact that with the dwindling confidence in the security of expectations and continuity guaranteed by the welfare state, a basis for biographical life planning and thus ultimately the possibility of life planning at all for the individual dwindles.

---

[60] For an introduction to this discussion (conducted under the catchy buzzwords of the "labor entrepreneur", the "Ich-AG" or the "entrepreneurial self") on the dissolution of labor boundaries, see. Voß and Pongratz 1998; Diewald 2004; Bröckling 2007; Hardering 2011.

The outline of the empirically ascertainable tendencies of a post-fordist life course change shows considerable differences between different social groups, which "cast doubt on the validity of referring to de-standardization as a homogenous reality" (Widmer and Ritschard 2009, p. 37). Post-Fordist life course change is not a "monolithic" process that uniformly affects the life courses of individuals, but rather should be thought of in the plural: in terms of many and diverse life course changes that present themselves differently, for example, for university and secondary school graduates, women and men, skilled and unskilled workers, Germans and foreigners or persons with a migration background. For this reason, as Berger and Sopp rightly pointed out 25 years ago, life course research "will have to concentrate even more on working out characteristic mixing ratios of stability and instability for specific social groups, for historical phases and for (parts of) national societies" (1992, p. 181).

Before concluding the chapter by discussing how processes of erosion of the institutionalized life course can be empirically determined, it should be briefly noted that this phenomenon under discussion here is subsumed under a whole range of terms. The concept of "individualization" functions as a kind of general theoretical umbrella term; the term "flexibilization" is used primarily in labor market and occupational research[61] (Kress 1998; Szydlik 2008); the term "pluralization" is used preferentially in family and lifestyle research (Huinink and Wagner 1998; Brüderl 2004; Groß 2008, pp. 89 ff.); sometimes there is also talk of "diversification" or "differentiation" or "disintegration" (Buchmann 1989b, p. 101; Buchmann and Sacci 1995; Konietzka 1999, p. 133 ff.). In the discourse of life course theory – in the narrower sense – there is talk of the "de-structuring" (Hurrelmann 2003; Amrhein 2004), the "de-institutionalization" (Held 1986) or "de-standardization" (Guillemard 1991; Konietzka and Huinink 2003) of the life course. Here, no attempt will be made to clarify these terms, which are often used synonymously, theoretically and conceptually and to define them clearly.[62] Only the latter three terms require a brief commentary. If one takes the concept of "de-structuring" theoretically seriously and thinks from its empirical reference point – the unstructured life course – it becomes clear that this concept is not meaningful, but rather questionable, because life courses are always preformed by the socio-cultural formations in which individuals live. Unstructured life courses would presuppose that there are no longer any socio-cultural formations in which individuals move, but only atomized, isolated individuals – a more than questionable idea.

---

[61] See in this context also the discussion on so-called "flexicurity", a concept in which (the terms) "flexibility" and "security" merge (Kronauer and Linne 2005).

[62] For such an attempt see Brückner and Mayer 2005 or also Scherger 2007, p. 93 ff.

5.3 "Normal Life Course" and De-Standardization of the Life Course

The concept of "de-institutionalization" is the direct counter-concept to the institutionalized life course and in this respect radically questions the existence – and for sociological life course research constitutive idea – of the life course as an institution. The institutionalized life course is (as already stated in Sect. 2.2 and Chap. 3) a necessary concomitant of the social individualization process of modernity, which has increasingly freed people from their traditional ties to social collectives. This growing liberation is accompanied uno actu by the necessity of reintegrating the released individuals: the now fragile integration performance of categorial socialization, i.e., socialization based on the traditional and stable affiliations of individuals to social collectives, must be compensated – which in modern, individualized societies can no longer take place through the categorical mode of societalization, but only through a mode of societalization based on the individuals themselves. As potential starting points for this, only characteristics can function that are proper to each individual. Such a moment, common to all individuals, is aging: all individuals have an ("ongoing") lifetime. It is precisely on the basis of this that the institutionalized life course has been formed as a temporal mode of societalization in the social structural change of the last 250 years: the life course as an institution is an independent system of rules for the temporal dimension of life. It constitutes a life-time programme of events that structures and shapes life courses and to which individuals orient themselves. In this respect, talk of the "de-institutionalization" of the life course would only be appropriate if the question were also answered – or at least considered – as to which mode of societalization then takes or could take the place of the institutionalized life course.

In contrast, the term "de-standardization" does not imply this fundamental problem. This concept refers to the temporal structuring of life courses without questioning the societalization function of the institutionalized life course or the life course as an institution. In this respect, the concept of "de-standardization" can be used to appropriately conceptualize post-Fordist changes in the life course. The chapter concludes with the question of how the de-standardization of life courses can be empirically determined. To this end, some dimensions and indicators relevant for empirical studies of de-standardization processes are briefly presented (Konietzka and Huinink 2003; Brückner and Mayer 2005).

Processes of de-standardization can, for example, become apparent in the dimension of universality, namely when only an ever smaller proportion of a population undergoes certain events, states, transitions or specific sequences of events in life. In the universality dimension, quantitative indicators are relevant, i.e. empirical data are collected on whether the degree of spread of an event, state or transition or a specific sequence of events is reduced. The declining number of marriages and lifelong wedlocks can serve as an example here. In this context, it should be noted that processes of de-standardization may well be accompanied by re-standardizations (Billari and Liefbroer 2010; Huinink 2013): e.g. in the context of the de-standardization of marriage, non-marital cohabitation has simultaneously established itself as the first form of cohabitation in partnership as a normal standard phase in the life course.

Another important dimension for the empirical investigation of de-standardization processes is that of uniformity, which refers to the life-time location of events or transitions and in which time-related indicators are consequently used. If a pronounced age gradation can be determined in a given population for a certain event, this fact indicates standardization – if, on the other hand, the age of the individuals at this event is highly dispersed, this age heterogeneity indicates de-standardization. In the uniformity dimension, processes of de-standardization are empirically ascertained or statistically measured via measures of dispersion (such as standard deviation, interquartile range). This can be briefly illustrated using the example of the final age at which women left the parental home: for the 1919–21 birth cohort, the quartile difference (third minus first quartile) was 8.3 years; this gap has decreased continuously over the subsequent birth cohorts (and in particular since the 1939–41 cohort) to 3.8 years for women born in the mid-1950s (Konietzka and Huinink 2003, p. 297). The narrowing of the quartile gap attests to the growing standardization of move-out ages during the first two postwar decades. For female birth cohorts since the mid-1950s, the quartile difference then increased slightly again to 4.3 years for women born in 1975–78 (ibid.) – which may indicate a slight de-standardization trend in move-out age since the late 1970s.[63]

The dimension of the temporal coupling of (two or more) events is also relevant for the empirical survey of de-standardization tendencies. An increase in the degree of coupling indicates standardization, its weakening indicates de-standardization. Changes in the degree of coupling of two events can be measured by determining the development of the temporal distance between the median ages at these two events. If this distance grows, it means that the degree of linkage of the two events is weakening and i.e.: de-standardization. This can be illustrated by the example of the linkage of the events "moving out of the parental home" and "marriage": for men in the birth cohorts between 1919 and 1941, the distance between the median ages for the two events was extremely small, i.e. they were very closely linked;

---

[63] However, Konietzka and Huinink rightly emphasize that "the quartile gap remained at a comparatively low level of just over four years even in the younger cohorts" (2003, p. 296), i.e. the slight increase in the quartile gap is not yet convincing as evidence of de-standardization – for this the quartile gap would first have to increase significantly.

since then, the distance has grown steadily and considerably (in the 1959–61 cohort to more than seven years; ibid., p. 298), i.e. a de-standardization process has taken place. Quite similarly, one can operate with quartile gaps by measuring, for example, the quartile difference between "marriage" (third quartile) and "moving out of the parental home" (first quartile); this shows that these quartile differences were relatively constant for men born between 1919 and 1941, but then increased markedly with the birth cohorts after the end of World War II and almost doubled for men born in the mid-1950s compared to the oldest cohort (12.8 vs. 6.5 years; ibid., p. 300), i.e., the degree of linkage has weakened significantly and, consequently, de-standardization has taken place. Another way of determining changes in the degree of coupling between two events is to estimate event- or state-related transition rates for one event as a function of the time interval between it and the other transition event; for example, one can examine across the cohort sequence whether there are significant changes in the probability of moving out of the parental home for different time intervals as a function of, say, the "marriage" event (ibid., p. 302).

Another dimension relevant for the empirical survey of de-standardization tendencies is that of the sequence standardization of events or transitions.[64] This concerns the degree of distribution of certain sequences in a population: are the ascertainable sequences of events or transitions covered by only a few patterns (even by only one almost universally distributed pattern) – or is there rather a multitude of different sequence patterns? For the three events "employment", "marriage" and "parenthood", for example, six sequence patterns are theoretically conceivable. Empirically, however, the sequence "employment → marriage → parenthood" is found in at least 85% and 75% of men and women born between 1920 and 1979 (Scherger 2007, p. 173), i.e. with regard to these three events there is a highly standardized sequence pattern. The more events are taken into account, the greater the number of theoretically possible sequences (with five events, 120 combinations are already conceivable) and insofar the probability that even the most widespread sequence patterns represent significantly smaller population shares than in the example just mentioned. With regard to the five relevant events of the transition to adulthood, for example, the sequence "education → career entry/employment → final departure from the parental home → marriage → starting a family" was

---

[64] In this context, there is sometimes talk of the "reversibility" of life events and transitions. However, strictly speaking, a reversibility of life events and transitions, including their consequences, is not possible because of the unidirectional arrow of time (e.g. both the status "divorced" and the status "single" refer to unmarried individuals, but the biographical and social significance of the two statuses is not identical).

considered the normal pattern of progression until the 1970s. This sequence was most common among men born in 1939–41 – of whom, however, only one-third (33.8%) followed this sequence (in the 1919–21 birth cohort, the corresponding proportion was 17.5% and among men born in 1959–61 only 5.7%; Konietzka and Huinink 2003, p. 304; see also the important early study of "disorder in the life course" by Rindfuss et al. 1987).

In a more holistic perspective – in relation to the widespread event-analytical orientation – de-standardization is operationalized as growing heterogeneity (diversity, pluralization) of life courses. To detect decreasing similarity of life courses or larger life course sequences, one can, for example, transversally determine the entropy of the distribution of statuses (states) between individuals at each chronological age for several birth cohorts. Or one can measure the average difference of, i.e. the diversity in the life histories or in larger life history sequences of the individuals by comparing all life histories for different birth cohorts in pairs (on the basis of such distance measures, life history types are very often subsequently formed by means of a cluster analysis).[65]

So much for some dimensions and methodological possibilities relevant for the empirical survey of de-standardization processes. It was already said at the beginning of this sub-chapter that the question "institutionalization or individualization of the life course?" cannot be answered unequivocally on an empirically sound basis – at least not to date. Perhaps it is simply too early for a conclusive answer to this question: whether the changes in the life courses of individuals since the late 1970s represent a renewed structural change of the life course (in the sense of a de-institutionalizing individualization), i.e. a historical caesura, is perhaps not to be judged already during this period of upheaval (and by the contemporaries involved in it), but only from a greater historical distance. Perhaps, however, the question "institutionalization or individualization of the life course?" does not make sense at all, because the real changes in the life course as a whole do not follow the implied developmental logic of "either – or", but rather that of "both – and". At least, options beyond or between the two contrasting extreme positions are conceivable: Changes could, for example, affect only certain social milieus or be only temporary, relatively short-lived phenomena. Changes could, for example, erode the institutionalized life course in fact, but only to a small extent and not to a large extent, because they are rather "minor" deviations or variants within the framework

---

[65] An introduction to and empirical examples of the methodologically complex procedures of a holistic perspective are provided, for example, by Erzberger 2001; Elzinga and Liefbroer 2007; Widmer and Ritschard 2009; Aisenbrey and Fasang 2010; Anyadike-Danes and McVicar 2010; Robette 2010; Scherer and Brüderl 2010; Jäckle 2017; Zimmermann 2018.

5.3 "Normal Life Course" and De-Standardization of the Life Course

of the established life course patterns.[66] And changes could – as has already been briefly indicated – be reflected, for example, in a de-standardization and simultaneous re-standardization of new life course patterns. Instead of aiming at a grand interpretation à la either institutionalization or individualization of the life course – with possibly only little reality content – life course research should empirically elaborate in a convincing and precise way those "mixing relationships of stability and instability" (which have already been mentioned) and the factors and causalities that condition them. It is about "a more careful look at the life course as it is actually lived, not as we wish it to be for the sake of order in research" (ibid., p. 799).

---

[66] The outlined extension of the transition phase from training to employment or to the first permanent position may serve as an example: with regard to the overall career path of an individual, this is a rather small deviation from the Fordist life course pattern.

Life Course Research: A Conceptual Perspective 6

The previous chapters dealt with the life course as a – socially constructed – object of research that can be viewed and analyzed sociologically from different perspectives. Seen in this light, life course research is a "hyphenated sociology" among others, such as the sociology of education, economics, organization, religion, or family. However, it has already been pointed out in connection with the substantive life course definition developed in this book (see Sect. 2.2.1) that life course research is conceptually transverse to the established "hyphenated sociologies". Sociological life course research is thus also something else or more than a "hyphenated sociology": "There are basically two views social scientists hold when talking about life course research which can be labelled 'object-view' and 'paradigm-view'" (Wingens et al. 2011, p. 4; Mortimer and Shanahan 2003; George 2003). Thus, the life course is not only of interest to sociology as a research object, but also relevant in the sense of a research conception.[1] It is precisely this understanding of the life course in terms of a conceptual perspective for empirical research that this chapter is concerned with. "As a paradigm," – according to the editors of *the Handbook of the Life* Course – "the life course refers to an imaginative framework comprised of a set of interrelated presuppositions, concepts, and

---

[1] To speak of the life course not as a research object but as a research concept is irritating: Terms such as "education", "economy", "organization", "religion" or "family" usually refer to research objects or fields, i.e. they are used ontologically to designate specific subject areas; in normal language they are not used methodologically, i.e. they do not designate research concepts. In the English-language literature, however, talk of the "life course as a theoretical orientation" (Elder et al. 2003, p. 4), "as a paradigm" (Mortimer and Shanahan 2003, p. XI) or as an "imaginative framework" (Shanahan and Macmillan 2008, p. XIII) is commonplace.

© The Author(s), under exclusive license to Springer Fachmedien Wiesbaden GmbH, part of Springer Nature 2022
M. Wingens, *Sociological Life Course Research*,
https://doi.org/10.1007/978-3-658-37466-2_6

methods" (Mortimer and Shanahan 2003, p. XI). In the following, the set of basic assumptions of life course theory is presented first (Sect. 6.1). Subsequently, analytical concepts of life course research are discussed (Sect. 6.2; as already mentioned in the first chapter, methods of life course research are not dealt with in this book).

6.1 Principles of Life Course Research

Just as sociological theories of education or family represent conceptual perspectives for sociological education or family research, sociological theories of life course functioned as conceptual perspectives for sociological life course research. However – a life course theory that deserved this designation does not exist until today.[2] It is not uncommon in the relevant literature to speak of life course theory. Significantly, however, this term is not used when it comes to semantically specifying the concept of the life course as a research concept. Thus, when it comes to the meaning and understanding of this talk, i.e. to a definition and characterization of the life course as a research concept, the term life course theory strangely does not appear. Rather, it is said that the life course (as a research conception) "is fundamentally an imaginative framework" (Shanahan and Macmillan 2008, p. XIII), "a paradigm" (Mortimer and Shanahan 2003, p. XI) or a "theoretical orientation" (Elder et al. 2003, p. 4). There is obviously no sufficiently elaborated (sociological) life course theory that could do what theories generally do: namely, offer a conceptual perspective for empirical research, in this case: empirical life course sociology (see also the final chapter).

---

[2] "Life course study is typically described as a 'perspective' or 'approach' rather than a scientific theory in the conventional sense of linked hypotheses deduced from postulates tested by empirical evidence" (Bynner 2016, p. 27; see also the comment on Elder's attempted theorization in Sect. 2.1).

6.1 Principles of Life Course Research

Since there is no life course theory(s): How is this talk of the life course as a paradigm[3] to be understood? What is the theoretical orientation of life course research? What are its conceptual-theoretical basic assumptions? These are propagated in the form of "paradigmatic principles" (ibid., p. 10; see already Sect. 2.1). These basic conceptual principles of life course research were formulated by Elder as theoretical generalizations of empirical findings from his work on the "Children of the Great Depression" (1999, p. 302 ff.) and other empirical life course studies. According to Elder, there are five principles "that collectively define the analytical scope of life-course theory" (Elder and Shanahan 2006, p. 689):

- life-span development,
- human agency,
- timing,
- linked lives and
- historical time and place.

The life-span development principle states that "human development and aging are lifelong processes" (ibid., p. 692). It is directed against a division of the life course into a sequence of developmental and age stages (roughly: childhood, adolescence, adulthood, old age), which – as was customary until the 1960s – are viewed and analyzed separately. In contrast, it is emphasized that developmental psychological and behavioral changes (can) occur across the life span. Individual and personality development is a lifelong process, and socialization does not end with adolescence. Accordingly, the life course is "also an endogenous causal relationship. Later outcomes, as well as goals and expectations, are to be understood and explained from conditions, decisions, resources, and experiences of the preceding life history" (Mayer 1990, p. 11). One of the greatest challenges of life course research is to

---

[3] The highly problematic, much-discussed concept of the paradigm, which has meanwhile been abandoned in the epistemological and scientific-historical and -sociological discussion for good reasons, is not to be discussed further here. In life course research, this term is used simply in the sense that paradigms, "unlike theories, ... are not comprised of statements that are interrelated according to the rules of logic. Rather, paradigms are ideas, concepts, models, and analytic strategies that loosely fit together" (Shanahan and Macmillan 2008, p. 7).

determine and convincingly demonstrate effects of the preceding life history, e.g. certain deprivation experiences during childhood, on conditions, attitudes, behavior, and expectations at significantly later points in the life course (which is especially true with regard to cumulative effects).[4]

The human agency principle[5] states that "individuals construct their own life course through choices and actions they take within the opportunities and constraints of history and social circumstance" (Elder and Shanahan 2006, p. 692). Significantly, the subsequent explanations of this principle refer exclusively to the structural opportunities and constraints under which the individual realizes his agency, while this concept itself is not fleshed out further. Agency seems to be understood as a capacity inherent in every individual, given by his humanity, to be able to shape his life – within the framework of given circumstances – actively and in accordance with his own ideas. Agency is therefore not to be equated with an individual's motives or intentions for action or with his concrete actions, but rather with a capacity for self-directed action that is inherent in all individuals in principle. In this respect, the human agency principle is merely an anthropological background assumption – characteristically dubbed "existential agency" by Hitlin and Elder (2007, p. 176)[6] – without any explanatory potential. This understanding, which is predominant in life course research, also implies and generates a dualism or opposition of agency vs. structure, so that their factual entanglement and interrelation – neither is there any agency beyond any structure nor any structure that would not have to be permanently (re-)produced by agency – must then be concep-

---

[4] Empirical evidence and reflections on processes of cumulative advantage/disadvantage in the life course can be found, for example, in Sampson and Laub 1997; Dannefer 2003; Elman and O'Rand 2004; DiPrete and Eirich 2006; Willson et al. 2007; O'Rand 2009; Schafer et al. 2011.

[5] Agency is not only a much-discussed but also a highly controversial concept in social theory (see e.g. Giddens 1984; Collins 1992; Emirbayer and Mische 1998; Archer 2000; Barnes 2000; Meyer and Jepperson 2000; Fuchs 2001; Sewell 2001). This general or social theoretical discussion will not be discussed further here; we are only concerned here with agency in life course research.

[6] Agency in this understanding is a kind of counterpart to the philosophical concept of free will.

tually recaptured (Settersten and Gannon 2005).[7] In this common understanding of agency in life course theory, it functions as a kind of mere residual category for what cannot be explained by structural factors.[8]

In empirical life course research, the human agency principle is usually operationalized by means of established psychological control constructs such as self-efficacy, locus of control, mastery, or coping (Crockett 2002; Skinner 1996 provides an overview systematizing along the agent-means-end relationships). Another psychological concept used in life course research to measure agency is planful competence (Clausen 1991, 1993), i.e. the ability to make biographically relevant decisions in a reflective manner, especially those with long-term consequences. It is obvious that the two measurement constructs do not operationalize this understanding of agency in a seamless or comprehensive manner. The psychological control constructs do not measure agency as defined, but rather an individual's self-assessment of his own agentic capacity (which is, of course, relevant to action).[9] And planful competence is only one (albeit important) moment of agency. In order to capture the (long neglected) essential temporality of agency (Emirbayer and Mische 1998; Hitlin and Elder 2007)[10] – which is particularly important for life

---

[7] The work of Settersten and Gannon is typical of this: first, the models of a structure without agency and agency without structure are presented, respectively, in order to then criticize these two "straw man" models as questionable and replace them with "blended models of agency within structure" (2005, p. 36) that are appropriate to reality.

[8] So too Marshall: "In one way, agency functions in this theoretical perspective in the same way that 'unexplained variance' functions in statistical models: if behavior is not patterned structurally, then it must reflect resistance to structure" (2005, p. 63).

[9] Self-efficacy, for example, refers to "beliefs in one's capabilities to organize and execute the courses of action required to produce given attainments" (Bandura 1997, p. 3).

[10] The theoretically most elaborate conception of the fundamental temporality of agency is found in Emirbayer and Mische, who define the latter "as the temporally constructed engagement by actors of different structural environments – the temporal-relational contexts of action – which, through the interplay of habit, imagination, and judgment, both reproduces and transforms those structures in interactive response to the problems posed by changing historical situations" (1998, p. 970). Accordingly, there are three – only analytically distinguishable – "constitutive elements of human agency: iteration, projectivity, and practical evaluation. In broad terms, these correspond to … forms of action that are more oriented (respectively) toward the past, the future, and the present. (…) The iterational element … refers to the selective reactivation by actors of past patterns of thought and action, as routinely incorporated into practical activity, thereby giving stability and order to social universes and helping to sustain identities, interactions, and institutions over time. The projective element … encompasses the imaginative generation by actors of possible future trajectories of action, in which received structures of thought and action may be creatively

course research, for which the time dimension is constitutive (see Sect. 2.2.2) – either those psychological control constructs and their items must be temporalized, i.e. formulated in such a way that a present as well as a past and future reference is possible (Pearlin et al. 2007). Alternatively, other specific constructs need to be formulated to operationalize the temporality of agency, such as optimism (Hitlin and Elder 2006) or life course expectations (Hitlin and Johnson 2015) for the future reference.

> "They always say you can do anything if you want to. Well ... I don't know. As I said, the retraining didn't work out because I was too old. You run into a wall, you can't do anything. (*longer period of silence*) And now I just have to see what comes, no, if something comes up so. That's how it is. Well, I have to make ends meet somehow".
>
> - Is this statement (taken from an interview with a person who has been unemployed for a long time) to be interpreted as meaning that the person in question has only a low level of agency or even: no agency at all? Give reasons for your answer or position.
> - Discuss your positions, becoming aware of your understanding of agency against which you measure the quoted statement.
> - Reflect on your discussion in light of an essay on "Social Conditions of Agency" (Scherr 2012, esp. p. 110 ff.; see also Hoggett 2001).

---

reconfigured in relation to actors' hopes, fears, and desires for the future. The practical-evaluative element ... entails the capacity of actors to make practical and normative judgments among alternative possible trajectories of action, in response to the emerging demands, dilemmas, and ambiguities of presently evolving situations" (ibid., p. 970 f.; Hitlin's and Elder's attempt at a typology is not theoretically convincing against the background of Emirbayer's and Mische's considerations). It should also be noted that Emirbayer and Mische do not represent an individualistic conception of agency – as is common in life course research – but a relational one; see also the critique of the individualistic understanding of agency by Raithelhuber (2011), who attempts to make the concept usable for life course research by passing through the general and social theoretical discussion of agency.

6.1 Principles of Life Course Research

> Modern society demands agency from the individual: to see oneself as (at least: co-)shaping one's own life course (see Sect. 3.2).[11] The lack of such agency was postulated as an obstacle to transformation in the transformation process of the "real socialist societies" after the collapse of the USSR. For example, with regard to the GDR and its citizens, among others, it was said: "People who grew up in a perfectly integrated society and were subject to fixed external controls were at the same time expected to act and feel only as members of a collective. As a result, they did not learn to act autonomously, to take responsibility of their own free will, and to rely on internal directives instead of being guided by the threats of external sanctions – all factors that make it difficult to adapt to the new situation of freedom" (Mayntz 1992, p. 23).
>
> - Do you find this argument convincing? Give reasons for your opinion. Discuss Wingens' empirical study on the "trained GDR citizen" (1999, esp. pp. 265–276) with regard to the agency question.
> - According to Goffman it is true that, even for total institutions (such as the mental institutions he studied), "whenever worlds are laid on, underlives develop" (1961, p. 305) – what do you think about this statement?

The timing principle states that the "developmental antecedents and consequences of life transitions, events, and behavior patterns vary according to timing in a life course" (Elder and Shanahan 2006, p. 694). Elder had shown in his well-known study of the "Children of the Great Depression" that the impact of even such a massive event as the Great Depression on the life courses of individuals also depended on the age at which an individual was hit by it (see Sect. 2.1): although there was only an age difference of a few years between the two cohorts studied, the Great Depression had a significantly more negative effect on the life courses and personality development of members of the Berkeley cohort (born in 1928/1929) than on the Oakland cohort, which was only eight years older. Biographical status transitions, such as parenthood or unemployment, can also initiate divergent trajectories and development patterns depending on the age or life stage in which they occur. Parenthood in the teenage years is off-time, i.e. it does not correspond to the normatively and institutionally or socially structured "normal life course" model (see Sect. 5.2) and thus usually

---

[11] In this context, the "Lebensführung" (conduct of life) concept is also interesting (Voß 1991; Kudera and Voß 2000).

entails negative consequences which – mutually reinforcing – often accumulate in the further course of life. In relation to on-time parents, teenage parents, especially teenage mothers, are disadvantaged in terms of life course structure. The biographical significance of the onset of unemployment is different for a 30 year old than for a mid-50 year old.

The linked lives principle states that "lives are lived interdependently and socio-historical influences are expressed through this network of shared relationships" (ibid., p. 695). It refers to the fundamentally social character of individuals' lives: to the fact that individuals do not live their lives alone, as an "isolated Robinson" so to speak, but are always in many and varied relationships with other people (as individuals as well as members of social groups and organizations). This inescapable social interdependence means that the actions of one person (almost) always have an impact on other individuals as well. For example, becoming a mother or father at the age of 16 makes one's own parents grandparents – which can be problematic for them because the behavioral expectations associated with grandparent status do not fit with the (age) self-image and life trajectories of women and men who are in their 40s. That the life(s) of individuals are "linked" is an everyday experience: I know that, for example, with regard to a joint holiday, I should coordinate with my partner or my clique of friends, because a "solitary" decision on my part about where to go on holiday would almost certainly end in a (relationship) conflict. The fact that people are in principle involved in social networks of relationships also means – "conversely" – that the individual is influenced by them in terms of the structure of his life. For example, someone who grows up in a dysfunctional family, in problematic urban areas or neighborhoods, or in contact with youth gangs with an affinity for crime is more likely to go off the rails than someone who grows up in an intact family, a well-off neighborhood and non-deviant peer groups. The biographical significance of an event for the individual is also mediated by his social relationship structure: being made redundant and unemployed, for example, is likely to be less problematic for a person who has close family ties and a circle of good friends, i.e. lives embedded in a network of strong ties, than for a person who has neither close family ties nor deep friendships.[12]

The historical time and place principle states that the "individual life course is embedded in and shaped by historical times and places over a lifetime" (ibid., p. 697). Human life beyond space and time does not exist – in this respect, all individuals live in a specific here and now and life courses are necessarily

---

[12] Yet, in terms of life course structure, weak-tie relationships can be a more advantageous resource than strong-tie networks for re-entering the labor market (Granovetter 1973).

embedded in and shaped by specific historical and social contexts. The structural contexts of the economic, political and cultural conditions of different phases of social history or situations open up specific possibilities for individuals to shape their lives or impose specific restrictions on them. The life courses of people born around 1950, for example, differ significantly according to whether they lived in West Germany or in the GDR. And working careers in West Germany, for example, differ markedly according to whether people entered the labor market at the beginning of the 1960s, i.e. during the "economic miracle" phase, or at the beginning of the 1980s, i.e. in a recession phase followed by solidified structural basic unemployment.

> - Clarify Elder's five paradigmatic principles of life course research using specific examples from any area of life and society.
> - In a second step, do not relate your examples to different areas, but to one and the same (research) field, e.g. the integration of migrants: What shows the importance of time and place? Which facts refer to the linked lives principle? How does the timing principle manifest itself? How is human agency manifested? How can the relevance of the life-span development principle be recognized?

Elder's five principles have been repeated like a prayer wheel for a quarter of a century when it comes to the theoretical orientation of life course research (only their number and designation varies somewhat in the literature). It must be stated that life course research has largely – and extremely productively – concentrated on empirical work, while life course theoretical work has been sidelined and (almost) completely neglected (the consequence of this theoretical "self-sufficiency" of life course research for the field of life course research will be addressed in the final chapter). The paradigmatic principles formulated by Elder are – as already mentioned – not a life course theory. But what about their paradigmatic quality: do they have a corresponding potential, i.e. are they able to offer theoretical orientation to empirical life course research? The abundance of empirical studies claiming a life course perspective seems to confirm this at any rate. And indeed: the conceptual invocation of Elder's paradigmatic principles[13] goes beyond a mere methodological reference to a micro analytical longitudinal design – which is widespread, but can-

---

[13] Most of these empirical studies do not use all five principles, but only certain ones, the combination of which depends on the research question.

not define life course research (see Sect. 2.2) – and gives these empirical studies a certain theoretical grounding.

The fact that these principles are themselves dependent on "theory imports" in order to fulfil the function of a theoretical orientation at all – e.g. the human agency principle only functions in empirical studies by recourse to a theory of action; the linked lives principle requires a network- or social capital-theoretical translation and implementation – does not speak against their paradigmatic quality.

It is problematic, however, that the paradigmatic principles postulated by Elder formulate little more than sociological truisms. Not only life courses, but all social phenomena and processes are embedded in specific spatio-temporal contexts and are influenced by them (historical time and place). Not only life courses, but all social phenomena and processes exhibit interdependencies – this is, so to speak, the "essence" of the social and constitutes a "socio-logic" (or sociology) (linked lives). Not only in life courses, but for all social phenomena and processes, the time at which something is done or experienced plays a role for the further course of things (timing). Not only life courses, but all social phenomena and processes are not totally structurally determined, but are always also shaped by the actions of actors (human agency). And that – as the life-span development principle says – human (individual) development and ageing are life-long processes is certainly true. But if or because these paradigmatic principles postulated by Elder are ultimately sociological truisms, they cannot establish an independent field called "life course research", or in other words: they cannot be a theoretical orientation specific to it. As sociological truisms, these principles are not only paradigmatic for life course research, but for empirical social research in general.

One only has to ask oneself whether sociological research on inequality, family, deviance, education or mobility, for example, can adequately explain different risks of poverty in old age, the decision to have a child, criminal behavior patterns among young people, the academic performance of children with a migration background or the lower proportion of women in management positions without taking those principles into account. Because Elder's paradigmatic principles are not specific – "exclusive" – to life course research, but apply to empirical social research in general, to all "hyphenated sociologies", it was possible for their theoretical orientation to give rise to the abundance of empirical studies. It was precisely the conceptual "non-specificity" or openness of these principles that enabled any empirical work that invoked them (and then worked with micro analytical longitudinal data) to sail under the label of "life course research". Much of this empirical work could just as well have been (and continues to be) labelled as inequality or poverty, family or fertility, deviance, education or migration/integration or mobility research in sociology, to take up the examples just mentioned again (and will probably increasingly do so again; see the final chapter on this). In this respect, there is still a great deal of work to be done on life course theory before we can really speak of a theoretical orientation of life course research (or even of an elaborate life course theory).

6.2 Analytical Concepts of Life Course Research

Elder not only defined the "theoretical" framework of life course research with his paradigmatic principles, but also formulated its basic analytical concepts in a seminal contribution that is important for empirical work: "The concepts of trajectory and transition are central themes in contemporary studies of life course dynamics ... They represent both the long and short view on analytic scope" (1985, p. 31). For Elder, the two concepts differ only in temporal terms: the trajectory pursues a long-term analytical perspective, i.e. takes a look at life course dynamics over a longer period of time – the transition focuses on quite short periods of time, i.e. captures short-term life course dynamics. Elder sees no difference in the research-logical relevance of the two concepts: for him, trajectory and transition are equivalent analytical concepts in this respect. As with their merely repetitive treatment of those paradigmatic principles, life course research has largely adopted Elder's definition of these two basic concepts unquestioned. As the following discussion shows, however, Elder's conceptual determinations prove theoretically ambiguous and imply conceptual inconsistencies. The discussion also shows that Elder's two fundamental concepts of analysis need to be expanded to include a third basic analytical concept, that of the turning point.[14]

Elder defines the transition concept in direct connection with another term: life event[15] and defines transitions as well as events as "changes in state that are more or less abrupt" (1985, p. 31 f.). First of all, it must be clarified what is meant by a "change in state". The literal translation, which is common in German-language life course research, means a change in state. However, this is a formal-technical

---

[14] The following discussion is based on Sackmann and Wingens 2001; Wingens and Reiter 2011; Wingens et al. 2011, p. 13 ff. and further develops considerations formulated there.

[15] In this context (this should only be noted), it must be stated that the life event concept – despite its importance for life course research (one thinks, for example, of the important method of life event analysis) – has not been discussed at all in life course theory up to now (but see Hoerning 1987).

term[16] under which sociologically irrelevant changes in life can also be subsumed. For example, someone who goes to a party sober and goes home drunk has experienced a sociologically irrelevant change of state. Similarly, buying a squeaky duck for the bathtub, for example, would not be of interest to sociological life course research. Changes of state occur continuously and in all possible respects in the life of an individual[17] – but only a part of them is sociologically relevant. Of interest and relevant for sociological life course research are those changes of state that take place in the form of socially defined – and mostly institutionally framed – transitions or events. This does not apply to the rise in alcohol levels just mentioned, but it does apply to transitions or events such as unemployment, parenthood, starting school, changing jobs, divorce, invalidity, widowhood, etc. In order to distinguish such transitions or life events from the broad stream of sociologically irrelevant changes in the life of an individual, "change in state" is here (as generally in this book) not simply translated and understood as "change of state", but as "change of status".[18]

> Every act of purchase – be it the purchase of a small squeaky duck or an expensive sailboat – is a socially defined and institutionally framed event. In this respect, the purchase of a squeaky duck just mentioned would also be of interest for sociological life course research, if one follows the delimitation of (ir)relevant transitions and events in the sociology of life courses as described above. What do you think about this? Does it make a difference for life course sociological relevance whether it is the purchase of a squeaking duck or a sailing yacht? Why or why not?

---

[16] Think, for example, of the states of aggregation of water and its change of state (solid – liquid – gaseous).

[17] This is evident for inner-psychic states of the individual, but applies to changes in life in general: for example, every purchase, whether of an expensive sailboat or just a squeaky duck, represents a change of state in the buyer's life with respect to his financial and property circumstances.

[18] To prevent any irritation: the term "change of status" (or "status") is thus not used here in the inequality-theoretical (hierarchical) sense customary in sociology, but – as stated above – in the sense of a socially defined, usually institutionally framed change of state in the life course.

6.2 Analytical Concepts of Life Course Research

The above restriction to socially defined (and institutionally framed) changes of status is about life course sociological relevance: surviving a serious traffic accident unharmed, for example, is certainly a serious biographical experience – but as such it is not of interest for sociological life course research. This biographical experience can, of course, have consequences relevant to the sociology of life courses: the person concerned could, for example, interpret the experience in the sense of a "second life given to him" and, in order to be able to live this "new" life, give up what has become only a "matter of habit wedlock" and his "60-hour week" job – (only) this divorce or dismissal represents a sociologically relevant "change in state".

According to Elder, transition differs from event in temporal terms. He specifies his "more or less abrupt" formulation to the effect that a change of status in the form of transition "may take place over a substantial period of time" (ibid., p. 32), whereas as a life event it "would be dated according to when the new state is reached" (ibid.). Thus, the transition concept is conceived in terms of process, while the event concept is punctual. Before discussing the transition and event concepts further, it is worth briefly pointing out a theoretical ambiguity regarding Elder's two basic analytical concepts, which results from his temporal determination of transition just cited. In view of the cited determination, it must be asked in what way the "substantial period of time" of a transition differs from the "extended span of time" (ibid., p. 31) of a trajectory. Elder does not seem to be aware of the fact that the question of where or how the temporal boundary between a "substantial period of time" and an "extended span of time", i.e. between his two basic analytical concepts, is to be drawn, poses a theoretical problem for their understanding as propagated by him – at any rate, this question is not discussed by him (or by his adepts), let alone answered. Such a discussion is indispensable, however, because the two characterizations of a period as "substantial period" and "extended span" are taken in the ordinary understanding of language to be largely semantically equivalent. If, however, the two periods characterized as "substantial period" and "extended span" are of roughly the same length, the provision cited above undermines Elder's earlier definitional distinction between the trajectory and transition concept by means of the criterion of a "long and short view on analytic scope" or in the sense of an analytic focus on long-term or short-term life course dynamics.

Back to the (procedural) concept of transition and (punctual) event. An example of a life event would be widowhood as a result of a fatal accident of the spouse (punctual change of status). As an example of a transition, Elder mentions the divorce of a marriage, because a divorce is preceded by a certain, usually longer period of living apart (procedural change of status). At the same time, however, divorce as a legal act represents a punctual change of status, and is thus also to be understood as a life event. As the examples show, the relationship between transition and life event is more complicated than Elder's merely temporal distinction suggests. "Becoming widowed" stands as an event in its own right, while "divorce" can be understood both as a life event in its own right and as a partial moment of a transition – specifically, as the moment that concludes the transition process. In the one case, the event concept is research-logically equivalent to the transition concept, in the other case it is subordinate to it. Moreover, the example of divorce makes it clear that events that are defined in terms of points can certainly also have a prehistory – and therefore should perhaps better be analyzed in a processual perspective. In the quantitative life course studies that predominate in life course research, this does not usually happen. Although it is certainly methodologically possible, for example, to model a preceding period of arbitrary duration for the event of "divorce", divorce – contrary to Elder's stipulation – is usually not treated methodologically as a transition in terms of process, but rather as a selective event.[19] This is unproblematic if the antecedents of the divorce were sociologically irrelevant.

This question, whether the prehistory of an event is sociologically of interest or only subjectively-biographically relevant, is to be addressed here using the example of "marriage". Here is a short love story (from the pre-Tinder era): Svenja and Martin got married in a civil ceremony on 03.09.2002. They had met five and a half years earlier, when Svenja, after graduating from university, took a job in the same department of a company where Martin had been working for several years. They only got to know each other more closely two years later. On whatever occasion or in whatever context there was a "spark" (company party, business trip, by chance while jogging or at an open-air concert): they "suddenly" found each other likeable and interested in each other. The first date was soon followed by others, sympathy turned into infatuation. In the following time a deep affection and fulfilling relationship developed. In mid-2001, the two moved in together. Since their relationship and love did not suffer from the mundane demands of running a household together, they developed a trusting idea of a future together, i.e. growing old together, and gradually also a desire to have children. And so it happened that Svenja and Martin stood in front of the registrar on 03.09.2002 (and – who knows – happily survived the "darned seventh year" and still live "in the seventh heaven").[20]

---

[19] If – in the sense of a transition – different time periods are modelled for the divorce event, the problem would remain that these are "empty" in terms of content, i.e.: one does not know what happened in these time periods and ultimately led to the divorce.

[20] Most divorces of the 2001 marriage cohort (no statistical data could be found for Svenja's

6.2 Analytical Concepts of Life Course Research

Svenja and Martin's marriage is a socially defined and also institutionally framed change of state (single → married). As a legal act, it takes place at the exact moment when the registrar certifies the marriage. Svenja and Martin's marriage was in this respect a life event that took place on 03.09.2002. Are the five and a half years preceding this event of interest for life course research or only relevant for Svenja and Martin? And – if this period is not only subjectively-biographically relevant – what is its sociological relevance? The first two years after Svenja's entry into Martin's department are probably uninteresting for sociological life course research, because the two of them only "lived side by side". In contrast, the move into the shared apartment or the establishment of the shared household is obviously of sociological interest because this is a socially defined "change in status" associated with social consequences; methodologically, this change in status can again be treated as an event without any problems. But what about the period, or rather "events", between spring 1999 and mid-2001? A first date, followed by further, eventually regular dates; first kisses, first sex, followed by further, eventually regular physical intimacies; a few short trips to trendy cities and a longer holiday in a romantic hotel; activities with Svenja's and Martin's circle of friends; the initially emphatically neutral behavior at work; Christmas Eve at Svenja's, Christmas Day at Martin's parents', etc. – the list of the mostly completely unspectacular (Svenja and Martin may see it differently) events during this period could easily be continued. Much of it is not sociologically relevant, some of it is.

Sociologically irrelevant is everything that takes place in a "Svenja & Martin private world" shielded from the others. But as soon as the two leave their shielded "private world" (either voluntarily or because they feel compelled to do so[21]), it becomes visible to the outside world: the others, that they are lovers. And this has social consequences – and is therefore also sociologically of interest and relevance. The fact that such an "outing" does indeed have social consequences becomes particularly clear in the much-discussed topic of "love at work" (a complex problem for the persons concerned as well as for companies or employers). But already in the circle of friends, in which a love relationship probably first becomes "public" – the respective circle of friends is likely to ask themselves relatively soon why he or she

---

and Martin's 2002 marriage cohort) took place after six years of marriage (www.bib.bund.de/ DE/Fakten/Fakt/L133-Scheidungsziffer-Ehedauer-Westdeutschland-ab-1991.html/). If one takes into account the legally prescribed year of separation and the longer crisis phase that usually precedes the application for divorce, it is not the seventh but rather the third or fourth year of marriage that is the "darned" one.

[21] Be it because the two no longer want to "hide" their love affair from others or forced to do so because, for example, two work colleagues happened to spend their Mallorca vacation in the same hotel as Svenja and Martin.

almost only appears together with him or her –, becoming visible that Svenja and Martin are lovers (and making it visible: look – we are a couple) has social and insofar sociologically relevant consequences. Svenja and Martin behave differently, present themselves to others as a couple – and the behavior of others towards Svenja and Martin also changes. Their friends, acquaintances, colleagues perceive them in a new role, and they ascribe new roles to them: Svenja and Martin experience a "role change"[22] with socially significant consequences, which is to be understood as a sociologically relevant "change in status". But when in that period between spring 1999 and mid-2001 did this "change in status" occur? And is it even possible to specify an exact point in time when Svenja and Martin became lovers? If a precise point in time could be determined, the event that triggered it and caused it would automatically be named,[23] and the change in status of "becoming a couple" could methodically be treated as such again without any problems. Perhaps, however, the two – if a sociologist were to ask them about it – would not themselves know when exactly they "became a couple"; it could also be that the two refer to two different points in time or events (which for the sociologist is only a technical measurement problem, but for Svenja and Martin could possibly become a relationship problem). If one leaves Svenja's and Martin's subjective-biographical point of view and takes an external perspective, there will certainly not be only one point in time of their "becoming a couple", but several points in time depending on the respective social context (e.g. circle of friends, parents, relatives, workplace), which mark the transition of both into the "couple state" for the others. Perhaps, then – to conclude the considerations on the relationship between transition and life event – no specific point in time or singular event is relevant for the sociologically relevant change of status of Svenja and Martin's "becoming a couple" nor with regard to a possible causality construction concerning their marriage on 03.09.2002, but rather the entire period between spring 1999 and mid-2001: the internally and externally motivated process of their "becoming a couple" in its entirety, which took place over the course of these two years, or the cumulative and consolidating events during this time that resulted in their "couple status".

---

[22] A descriptively interesting study of role changes that is rooted in the structural-functionalist role-theoretical perspective is Ebaugh's study of the process of "Becoming an Ex" (1988), in which she interviewed former police officers, prisoners, alcoholics, nuns, and transsexuals, among others, about their role exit and the formation of a new role identity.

[23] In Svenja's and Martin's subjective-biographical perspective, this might be, for example, their second or fifth date, when they had sex for the first or fourth time, or their first holiday as a couple. In the external perspective, i.e. from the point of view of the others, it could be, for example, the first visit to the partner's parents or the day when a colleague sees them taking a walk holding hands.

6.2 Analytical Concepts of Life Course Research

Notwithstanding the problems outlined above, the transition concept, or rather its empirical basis of status change, is regarded as clearly defined in life course research.[24] The transition concept is also easy to operationalize – at least if such status changes are not understood in terms of processes as transitions stretched out over time, but rather (without circumstance) in terms of points as life events. This can be well illustrated by the empirically often studied transition to adulthood: this transition process is analyzed in life course research as "a series of transition events" (Buchmann and Kriesi 2011, p. 482).[25] The transition process to adulthood, which as a process is not easy to operationalize, is thus conceptually dissected or methodologically subdivided into selective and thus easy-to-operationalize events that function as markers of adulthood. The – seemingly problem-free – easy operationalizability of the transition concept and, above all, its direct methodological translatability into the powerful instrument of event analysis have led to the fact that empirical life course research, or more precisely: the quantitative life course research that dominates it, is mostly transition research (or actually: event research). This concentration on individual transitions (and events) at the expense of the analysis of longer trajectories was initially unavoidable, because longitudinal data sets and statistical analysis methods covering larger periods of time or trajectories were lacking.[26] "The data and data-analysis techniques currently at our disposal" – said Hagestad in her overview article in the early 1990s – "are more likely to improve our understanding of transitions than they are to produce significant new knowledge about life trajectories" (1991, p. 31; George 1993). In the meantime, however, there is a whole series of corresponding longitudinal data sets and methodological innovations for the analysis of

---

[24] This conceptual statement does not contradict the empirical observation that in the course of growing tendencies towards de-standardization, transitions are becoming more diffuse, unclear and reversible (see Sect. 5.3.2); on "de-standardized" transitions, see also the "Handbuch Übergänge" (Transitions Handbook) published by Schröer et al. in 2013, which is oriented towards social education, and Stauber et al. 2007.

[25] And is traditionally considered "complete when an individual has experienced all events" (Buchmann and Kriesi 2011, p. 482; on this transition and its "transition events" see the corresponding paragraph in Sect. 5.2.1).

[26] In this context, reference should also be made to the sequence type concept of Sackmann and Wingens (2001, p. 32 ff., 2003), which is situated between the transition and trajectory concepts and which, although it does not allow longer life course phases to be analyzed, allows more than just singular events and transitions to be analyzed. The concept comprises at least two status changes (e.g. the sequence "employed → unemployed → in retraining") and can be formally typified with regard to the relationship between the respective statuses. Empirically, Brzinsky-Fay (2007), for example, has worked with the formal sequence types proposed by Sackmann and Wingens.

life course dynamics over longer periods of time. In other words, the fact that life course research is still predominantly transitional research can no longer be legitimized (with that data and methodological argument). Nevertheless, studies of life course dynamics over long periods of time, i.e. holistic analyses of trajectories or even entire life courses, can still be found predominantly in (qualitative) biographical research, while life course research largely examines singular transitions and life events. Although there have been important methodological advances in recent years with regard to the recording of longer life course phases, this "second wave" of sequence pattern analysis methods (Aisenbrey and Fasang 2010) are descriptive-explorative, but not causal-analytical methods.[27]

Some transitions and life events can be expected – and can therefore be included by individuals in their life plans – while some status changes occur unexpectedly. An unexpected change of status occurs, for example, when a professional becomes incapacitated or even unable to work as a result of an accident, or when he enters a monastic order as a result of an epiphanic experience (conversion experience). An expectable change of status is expectable because it is an age- or time-dependent transition: for example, one starts school at the age of six or (from birth year 1964) retires regularly at the age of 67; a time-dependent change of status is given, for example, with the separation year to be observed before a divorce. The age- and time-dependency and thus the expectability of certain status changes ultimately result from their institutional framing and their embedding in socio-structurally preformed trajectories (see Chap. 5 and Sect. 2.2.1).

Some transitions and life events prove to be extremely consequential for the further course of life, because they suggest certain follow-up options or subsequent courses, while making other subsequent course sequences improbable or even ruling them out. The effects of such transitions represent moments in the life (course) of the individual which are difficult to revise. In this context, Blossfeld speaks of "sensitive phases" in the life course – such as the transition to a lower secondary school – and has shown for the field of education that, as a result of the institutional differentiation of the German education and school system, "in the course of an educational career there are 'sensitive' and 'less sensitive' phases in which differ-

---

[27] On the possibility of combining sequence pattern and event analysis or holistic life course analysis, see recently Piccarreta and Studer 2019; Han and Moen (1999), using the dependence of retirement age on different employment history types, showed early on that sequence pattern-analyzed history types can be incorporated as an explanatory variable in causal analytic methods.

6.2 Analytical Concepts of Life Course Research

ent birth cohorts are affected differently by historically current influences" (1988, p. 60; with regard to the phase of entry into working life, see Scherer 2004). The fact that some transitions and events have such a decisive effect on life courses results from the fact that the options and subsequent courses associated with them are anchored and pre-programmed in the structure of society. Or, to put it another way, it ultimately results from the embeddedness of individual status changes or transitions and life events (micro level) in patterns of progression that are preformed by the structure of society (macro level). These social pathways (Shanahan and Macmillan 2008, p. 66), which are predefined by social structures and institutions in particular, can in principle be abandoned, but in fact only with considerable individual effort.

Before discussing the trajectory concept, a brief comment is in order on a term related to the transition concept: the term "status passage". Originally developed in ethnology, this concept became popular in sociology mainly through the book of the same name by Glaser and Strauss (1971) (whose attempt to categorize properties of status passages for the purpose of developing a formal status passage theory, however, proved unconvincing in terms of life course theory). In life course research, the status passage concept became the guiding concept of a DFG Collaborative Research Centre entitled "Status Passages and Risks in the Life Course" (Sfb 186; 1988–2001). In Heinz's understanding, this term refers not only to an individual change of status, but also to the socio-structural embedding and institutional framing of such a transition. Status passages – according to Heinz – "link institutions and actors … On the micro level status passages are constructed by biographical actors … On the macro level status passages refer to institutional resources and guidelines for life course transitions" (1996, p. 58 f.). Thus, while the transition concept is located solely at the micro level of individual action, the status passages concept of Sfb 186 refers both to this and to the macro level of social structures.

- What do you think makes more sense: to keep the two levels or individual transitions and societal transition structures analytically separate or to draw them together in one term (status passage)? What advantages and disadvantages do you see in each case?

Elder's concept of trajectory is already unclear and only vaguely defined at first glance. He defines what is meant by a trajectory rather en passant in the context of a statement on the term "career", which has been established in sociology from the beginning,[28] and whose uses "all ... fall within the more inclusive definition of a life trajectory, a pathway defined by the aging process or by movement across the age structure" (1985, p. 31). First, to avoid any possible misunderstanding, it should be made clear that the "pathway" paraphrase used by Elder to define a trajectory is not identical with the term "social pathway" mentioned in the previous paragraph. The latter denotes socially structured paths, i.e. it is a macro-sociological concept; Elder's description of a trajectory as a "pathway", on the other hand, is micro-sociological from the perspective of the actors living their lives. This micro-sociological understanding of the concept becomes clear when Elder methodically explains that "life trajectories can be charted by linking states across successive years, the states of employment, for example" (ibid.). The trajectory concept also does not denote a life course in its entirety. Rather, Elder understands the life course as a whole as consisting of a whole series of trajectories: a life course "entails multiple, interlocking trajectories" (ibid., p. 45), e.g. an educational trajectory, an employment trajectory, a family trajectory, etc. A trajectory thus refers to a person's life over a period of time. Thus, a trajectory denotes life course dynamics in a particular area of life that extend over a longer period of time; for example, the occupational trajectory represents the occupational course or occupational changes in the life course of an individual. Trajectories represent domain-specific "sub-courses" in the overall life course of an individual.[29] However, by far the majority of trajectories are not only area-specific, but also "partial life courses" in a double sense: limited in terms of content and also in terms of time. For example, an individual's career or marriage trajectory does not refer to his entire life span. This aspect of the temporal delimitation of a trajectory will be taken up later; here we are concerned for the moment only with the area-specificity or content-related delimitation of a trajectory.

---

[28] The career concept was already used by the Chicago School – within the framework of its life history approach – in its investigations of (in the broadest sense) deviant behavior, as the title of Shaw's study on "The natural history of a delinquent career" (1931) already shows; it was not until the end of the 1950s that the primary reference of the career concept to the field of work and occupation became established (Barley 1989).

[29] The fact that the various trajectories that make up a life course are more or less intertwined has become clear in the previous chapters and does not need to be explained here.

6.2 Analytical Concepts of Life Course Research

A first theoretical inconsistency of Elder's remarks already results from his casual metaphorical definition of the trajectory as a path defined by the process of aging: this aging process as such, by itself alone, does not differentiate any specific (and also no temporally limited) "partial life courses". The process of aging of an individual does not produce different trajectories – the aging of individual's results only in their overall life courses from birth to death. That is, Elder's notion that the life course of an individual consists of a whole series of more or less interdependent trajectories is incompatible with his definition of the trajectory as a path constituted by the process of aging, and his understanding of the trajectory concept is thus inherently contradictory – a theoretical inconsistency that has not been noticed (or simply ignored) by life course research.

Formally, according to Elder, each trajectory is "marked by a sequence of life events and transitions" (ibid., p. 31), i.e. those more or less abrupt status changes in the life of the individual. For example, a marriage trajectory might consist of the status change sequence "single → married → divorced → living apart together → remarried → widowed." If now – as Elder determines – a trajectory consists of a sequence of events and transitions, i.e. if these are constitutive for trajectories, the transition concept takes constitutional-logical priority over the – then secondary, derived – trajectory concept. Life course research then needs theoretical ideas about how events AND transitions form or are joined together to form a trajectory. However, Elder fails to provide corresponding life course theoretical considerations on the constitution of trajectories. Even more: Elder's further remarks on trajectories lead to a theoretical contradiction with regard to the research-logical relation of his two basic analytical concepts. Indeed, he also claims that "transitions are always embedded in trajectories that give them distinctive form and meaning" (ibid.). This is immediately obvious: for example, it makes a considerable difference whether a married 30-year-old woman or a 15-year-old girl becomes a mother, or whether someone marries for the first time or for the fourth time, or becomes unemployed at 55 or 25. But if – as Elder claims – events and transitions only acquire their distinct form and meaning through the trajectory in which they are embedded, this statement implies constitutionally logical priority of the trajectory concept over the transition concept. In this respect, Elder's explanations of his two basic concepts of life course analysis contain a conceptual inconsistency with regard to the research-logical relationship between trajectory and transition.[30]

---

[30] What Elder does not seem to be aware of (at least there are no indications of this in his work) – and because life course research has simply, i.e. uncritically, adopted his concepts, this problem of life course theory has also remained virtually unaddressed to date.

> Elder's last quoted statement points – as just mentioned (and as does Mayer's talk of the life course as an endogenous causal connection, which is also not elaborated further theoretically) – to an empirical and research-logical priority of the trajectory over life events and transitions.
>
> - How do you think about this in terms of the empirical level of real individual life courses?
> - Discuss whether the trajectory concept with its (tendentially) holistic analysis perspective has research-logical priority, i.e. greater analytical relevance than the transition concept, and why or why not.

From Elder's last quoted statement results another problem of life course theory. In order to be able to give transitions a distinct form and meaning, trajectories themselves must have a distinct form and meaning – and it must therefore be clarified what this consists of and how it arises. However, Elder does not elaborate further on this question, which is central to life course theory (as was already the case with the constitutional-logical priority of the transition concept). Empirical life course research – theoretically limited to the uncritical adoption of Elder's life course principles and basic analytical concepts – uses the trajectory concept quite pragmatically. Which events and transitions in the life of an individual (in their succession) are defined and treated as a "trajectory" depends on the particular research question. Depending on this, the researcher determines a subset from the total of life events and transitions in the life of an individual: namely, the events and transitions that the individual experiences in the area of life relevant to the research question of the empirical study. If, for example, the life events and transitions of individuals in the life domain "education" are of interest, we speak of an education trajectory; if we are concerned with changes in health status in the life of an individual, we speak of a health trajectory. In principle, any sociologically meaningfully delimitable life domain, or more precisely: the sequence of events and transitions of an individual therein, can be defined as a trajectory: for example, one can define and analyze educational, health, marriage, employment, income, occupation, business, family, or residential trajectories, etc. Which – and how many – trajectories make up an individual's overall life course cannot be determined in general or a priori, but varies individually. With regard to someone who, for example, lives in the same apartment all his life, one cannot meaningfully speak of a housing trajectory; strictly speaking, one can only speak of a marriage trajectory with regard to persons who have married at least once. However, a marriage trajectory

6.2 Analytical Concepts of Life Course Research

is often understood to include not only an individual's marital relationships, but also his non-marital partnerships. Therefore, any empirical work on this area of life must make clear and justify whether and, of course, why it distinguishes between a "marriage trajectory" and a "partnership trajectory" or whether these terms are understood as equivalent in meaning and are only used for reasons of stylistic variety (the same applies, for example, with regard to the occupational or gainful employment trajectory or to the income and wealth trajectory).

It has already been said that trajectories are not only content-related, i.e. related to specific areas of life, but in the vast majority of cases also represent "partial life courses" limited in time (as e.g. the occupational or marriage trajectory illustrate). It is obvious that the vast majority of trajectories do not cover the entire life span but are limited in time. However, the question of the temporal delimitation of a traject becomes interesting when it is directed towards the (sequence of) life events and transitions of individuals within a specific life domain. In other words, if one asks whether the longer-term life course dynamics in a substantively delimited life domain are captured and represented by one, i.e. only and precisely one, trajectory. Is there only one trajectory for each content-defined "partial life course" of an individual – or are several trajectories possible within these specific life spheres? The question will be discussed on the basis of two fictitious examples, a family trajectory and an employment trajectory.

Born in 1960, Sven marries his childhood sweetheart Martina in 1987 after completing his training as a dental technician and taking a job in the local dental laboratory; the following year their first daughter is born, followed a year later by their second; for whatever reason, Sven and Martina's marriage begins to crumble in 1995; In 2003, the two finally separate; a year later, Sven moves in with Marie, ten years his junior, with whom he had a brief affair before his divorce; when Marie becomes pregnant in 2005, the two marry, and a year later they have a second child; Sven and Marie's marriage lasts to this day. So much for that example. The question is whether, in view of this sequence of events and transitions, we can speak of only one family trajectory with regard to Sven – or whether this sequence of life events and transitions represents two family trajectories in Sven's life.

The same problem also arises, for example, in the case of employment trajectories. This is obvious in the case of a radical change of activity: for example, when a social pedagogue who has worked for many years at a hotspot school gives up this position or her profession – for whatever reason – and then earns her living as a physiotherapist, yoga teacher or stablehand, for example. But even in the case of less radical changes of activity in working life, the question arises as to whether these are (or should be) subsumed under one or more than one employment trajectory. The following example: Ms. Meyer (born 1950) – after completing her teaching degree in "German/History for Secondary Level II" – takes up a post as a teacher at one of the then still new comprehensive schools in 1975; in 1988 she becomes deputy headmaster there; six years later she receives an enquiry from the Ministry of Education and Cultural Affairs as to whether she would be interested in taking over the management of the "Quality Development" department in the education authority – an offer which Ms. Meyer accepts in 1995; As head of the department, however, she is not only responsible for the quality development of the schools, but also sets up the department "Inclusion", which she takes over in 2000; four years later, Ms. Meyer – for whatever reason – leaves the Ministry of Education and, at the age of 54, sets up her own business as an organizational consultant (focusing on "Change Management in Educational Institutions"); she pursues this activity until an illness makes her unable to work in 2016. The question is whether these activities of Ms. Meyer are to be appropriately understood in the sense of only one employment trajectory – or whether it would be more "appropriate" to see more than just one employment trajectory in their sequence.

> What do you think: is there only one trajectory for each content-defined "partial life course" of an individual, or can there be several trajectories within such a specific life course? Discuss the reasons for or against the two positions.

If one affirms the latter and assumes – generally speaking – that the sequence of life events and transitions within a "partial life course" of an individual that is delimited in terms of content does not always represent only one trajectory or can be grasped as a single trajectory, but that the sequence of events and transitions in a specific area of life can also form two or more trajectories, the question of the beginning and end of a trajectory arises in terms of life course theory. More precisely – because the beginning of the first trajectory is unproblematic (in the two examples this would be Sven's marriage in 1987 and Mrs. Meyer's start of employment in 1975) –: the problem of determining the end of a trajectory (and thus the beginning of a new trajectory). With regard to this question – as already pointed out at the beginning of the subchapter – the concept of the turning point gains analytical and life course theoretical relevance. Elder briefly mentions the turning point concept in the context of some remarks on the (endogenous causal) interconnection of life events and transitions in life that are far apart in time: "Another way of phrasing such interconnections over the life course is to say that events and transitions modify life trajectories. Some events are important turning points in life –

6.2 Analytical Concepts of Life Course Research

they redirect paths" (ibid., p. 35). But how can the "lifetime effects of ordinary events and turning points" (ibid.) be captured, that is, how can "normal" life events and transitions be distinguished from turning points? Elder only says that, in addition to the biographical resources, experiences and plans of the individual (agency) and the structural embedding or definition of the situation (structure), "the nature of the event or transition" (ibid.) must also be taken into account. Elder does not provide an answer to the then central question of what immanent properties life events and transitions must have in order to represent not only "ordinary", i.e. "normal" events and transitions in life, but to be able to function and apply as direction-changing turning points.

However, trying to classify and identify events or transitions as turning points on the basis of an immanent quality is also likely to be a futile endeavor. Hareven and Masaoka rightly emphasized early on that "all transitions are potential turning points" (1988, p. 274), i.e. every event and every transition can be a turning point, but need not be. That there are no events or transitions that are turning points per se is evident from even a brief look at empirical studies: whether dramatic or inconspicuous, positive or negative, self-initiated or externally induced, expected or unexpected, abrupt or gradual, etc. – one time corresponding life events and transitions are turning points, another time they are not.[31] This empirical fact has the consequence in life course theory that "there is little agreement" (Settersten 1999, p. 139) about what constitutes a turning point and how it is to be defined. A theoretically significant difference exists between the various understandings of the turning point concept in terms of whether it is situated at the level of an individual's biographical experiences or at the level of the 'external' trajectory of his life. Or in other words: whether the turning point concept refers to the "subjective" life history of the individual or to his "objective" life course.

The life-historical understanding of turning points is anchored in an identity-theoretical perspective: turning points mark transformations of the self, of an individual's identity.[32] This conceptual foundation can already be found in the late 1950s in Strauss, who defines turning points as "critical incidents that … force a person to recognize that 'I am not the same person as I was, as I used to be'" (1959, p. 93). In this understanding, the existence of a turning point is indispensably linked to the experience and interpretation of biographical (dis)continuities by the

---

[31] See, in addition to Hareven and Masaoka 1988, e.g., Elder 1986; Clausen 1995; Rutter 1996; Sampson and Laub 1993, 1996; Wheaton and Gotlib 1997; Uggen 2000; Roos 2002; Wethington et al. 2003.

[32] Which explains that this turning point understanding is fundamental and predominant in relevant studies of life span development and developmental psychology.

individual himself: beyond the self-reflexive-biographical consciousness of an individual, independently, there are no turning points. In terms of methodology, this means that turning points are to be grasped within the framework and on the basis of the life story of an individual. The prototype for this is the life story approach,[33] according to which "identity formation ... is largely about formulating a story for one's life ... that selectively reconstructs the past and imagines the future as an integrated temporal whole, to provide life with meaning" (McAdams 2005, p. 243). In such a life history narrative, turning points function as a quasi "causal" hinge or connector between divergent events, transitions, and trajectories in life. They serve to establish a certain narrative and that means: life-historical coherence[34] (and in this respect are biographically continuity- and identity-providing). The following four remarks are not to be understood in the sense of a rejecting criticism of the life-historical turning point concept: turning points conceived in biographical or identity-theoretical terms do indeed represent an interesting object area in life course research that has relevance and independent justification.

The first remark refers to the fact that the life story of an individual has in principle no definitive version, but is subject to an ongoing (re)construction process. Each individual permanently makes new biographical experiences and plans, which he incorporates into his life story – and in the process continuously changes it. Individuals constantly tell new (usually only slightly, but sometimes significantly revised) versions of their life stories over the life span. The point here is that the biographical meaning of a turning point can change depending on the version of the life story that is told: the individual may present a transition with a short time lag as a serious turning point, but 20 years later tell of it only in the sense of a marginal interruption or deviation within a trajectory.[35] A second comment concerns the fact that interviewees often refer to transitions that are expected (e.g. moving out of the parental home, marriage) or even pre-programmed in terms of social structure, above all institutionally (e.g. completing education, starting work, retirement) as turning points. This is understandable insofar as such status changes are accompanied by a change in the self-image of the individual, who falls back on the

---

[33] See Bertaux 1981; Harrison 2009; Goodson 2016. The term life story approach suggests a degree of conceptual uniformity that is not present among its representatives; rather, the term refers to a research perspective under whose umbrella diverse theoretical accentuations and methodological characteristics can be found.

[34] Consider, however, Geertz's well-known warning that "there is nothing so coherent as a paranoid's delusion or a swindler's story" (1973, p. 18).

[35] What – this should be emphasized here – is not to be understood in the sense of a retrospective memory error: such biases cannot exist in the context of the life story approach (unlike in retrospective surveys of life course data; Reimer 2003).

6.2 Analytical Concepts of Life Course Research

narrative and interpretation schemes culturally given in society for the narration of his life story.[36] However, the turning point concept loses its distinctiveness from "normal" life events and transitions. Another note is related to what has just been said. Often in life history narratives, "non-normal" events and transitions (e.g., a friend's accident, a spiritual experience, a sojourn in a foreign culture) are mentioned as biographical turning points only when the individual interviewed is given a lot of space for detailed narratives or the researcher inquires intensively. Here, empirical studies are in danger of motivating the individual to excessively name life-historically pseudo-relevant turning points, thus methodically producing turning point artifacts. The fourth and last remark refers to the fact that in the life-historical understanding of turning points, events and transitions can also be considered turning points that, contrary to the common semantics of the word, do not mark biographical discontinuity. On the contrary, "sometimes continuity accentuated is seen as a turning point" (Clausen 1995, p. 369). Even if this is conclusive in this turning point conception[37] – perhaps it would be better to speak of "advancing points" (connoting both continuity and change) with regard to such life events and transitions instead of turning points.

The understanding of the turning point in terms of the "external" course of life retains the common semantics of the word: "What defines a turning point as such is the fact that" – as Abbott, who has arguably formulated the most advanced thinking on this concept,[38] summarizes his discussion of the logical and formal characteristics of turning points definitionally – "the turn that takes place within it contrasts with a relative straightness outside (both before and after). Thus, ... what matters is the separation of relatively smooth patterns by a turn that is by compari-

---

[36] To illustrate this: the widespread saying (especially strained at graduation ceremonies) about the "seriousness of life", which – depending on the occasion of the speech – begins with school enrolment or the start of studies or the entry into a profession, suggests to the individual to adapt his self-image to the new role and phase of life that the corresponding transition marks – and this biographical change is the reason why the change of status associated with the entry into school, studies or a profession is also experienced and presented by the individual as a turning point in life history.

[37] Fundamental is – as already mentioned in the quotation from Strauss – the identity-theoretical-biographical experience of no longer being the same person as before – for the individual no biographical discontinuity in the sense of a change in direction of his life (course) is necessary "to feel that a turning point has occurred. But one must have a feeling that new meanings have been acquired, whether or not life experiences are much changed" (Clausen 1995, p. 371).

[38] Abbott addresses turning points not only from the perspective of life course theory, but in their general sociological and social theoretical relevance; the life course literature serves him only as a hook for his reflections.

son abrupt" (1997, p. 89). Abbott's definition makes it clear that there is a constitutive or logical connection between a turning point and the preceding as well as the following pattern, i.e.: trajectory.[39] For this very reason, Elder's two basic analytical concepts – transition and trajectory – must be supplemented not only from an empirical-pragmatic perspective (as illustrated by the fictitious example of Sven's family trajectory and Mrs. Meyer's employment trajectory), but rather in a theoretically compelling way by the turning point concept.

In contrast to the life-historical understanding, in which the existence of turning points is anchored in the self-reflexive-biographical consciousness of the individuals and dependent on it, turning points in Abbott's "objective" understanding exist independently of the life-historical interpretations of the individuals. His conception of turning points in terms of "objective" life histories is structural in nature – turning points have a "social structural character" (ibid., p. 93). This understanding does not deny the relevance of biographical experiences and interpretations of turning points, nor the fact and necessity that turning points only become real at all in micro-sociological terms through the actions of individuals. It does, however, methodologically emphasize that turning points cannot be identified on the basis of the life-historical narratives of the individuals themselves. But how, in Abbott's "objective" or structural understanding of turning points, can turning points be identified and thus the end of an old trajectory and the beginning of a new one be determined?

As the first part of this term says, it is about a "turn", i.e.: the trajectories separated by a turning point "differ in direction ... or in nature (one is 'trajectory-like', the other is random)" (ibid., p. 94). However, the fact that such a change of direction[40] has taken place in the course of life can only be determined after a certain period of time has elapsed. Whether an event or transition merely represents a marginal deviation within a trajectory or whether it changes the direction of this trajectory, i.e. represents a turning point, cannot be determined at the moment when the event or transition takes place – it is logically impossible to say at this moment "since it is the arrival and establishment of a new trajectory ... that defines

---

[39] So also Wheaton and Gotlib: "Indeed, the essential characteristic of a turning point is that it changes the direction of a trajectory. The concepts of trajectories and turning points require each other in order to be understood" (1997, p. 1).

[40] The difference "in nature" between preceding and following trajectory is subsumed here – because the aspect of interest here is then easier and more space-saving to represent linguistically – under the concept of change of direction. This is quite justified, because Abbot means by it either the "turn" from a stable pattern of progression to random sequences of events and transitions – in which case he speaks of a "randomizing turning point" (1997, p. 94), or the reverse turn – in which case he speaks of a "focal turning point" (ibid.).

6.2 Analytical Concepts of Life Course Research

the turning point itself" (ibid., p. 95). A turning point can in principle and always only be determined retrospectively: only after a change of direction in the course of life has become apparent. The fact that a turning point separates the trajectory preceding it from the trajectory following it, i.e. that it lies between two trajectories, implies a further characteristic: turning points have two temporal reference points (to the preceding and to the following trajectory). By referring to both the past and the future, turning points link past, present and future. They separate trajectories and concatenate them simultaneously. Abbott combines the two aforementioned turning point characteristics in the illustrative statement that, "if … turning points could be identified merely with reference to the past and the immediate present, algorithms locating turning points could beat the stock market. It is precisely the 'hindsight' character of turning points – their definition in terms of future as well as past and present – that forbids this" (ibid., p. 89).

A final, particularly important property of a turning point is that (contrary to what the second part of the term misleadingly suggests) it is not to be thought of as punctual, but processual: "turning points in fact have extension in time" (ibid., p. 96).[41] Empirically, the fact that a turning point is ultimately not a point in time without extension, but has a certain duration in time, is easy to see: imagine, for example, a person who (inspired by the idea of improving the world) took up a sociology degree, did a compulsory internship of several months in a social project in a developing country, noticed that engineers change the world more than sociologists, gave up the sociology degree and henceforth studied and successfully completed "mechanical engineering". A turning point in this progression example would (only) be easy to determine, if one follows that misleading selective connotation: that would then simply be the date of the change of subject. But – was this really the turning point for this person's course of study? Can one attribute his change of subject causally to a point in time at all, i.e. to a specific moment during the internship?

---

[41] For: "Indeed, if we follow a causal theory of the social world, of whatever sort, it seems necessary to believe in this duration. Without it, we would have to assume that the social process sometimes took on new directions instantaneously. But then, there would be no source, in some sense, for change. It would simply arise de novo" (ibid., p. 96). Abbott sees very well that this "problem of the beginning" also arises for processually conceived turning points: "this issue of instants actually arises even if we allow for turning points with finite duration. That beginning is either instantaneous or extended, and if extended, must have a beginning, and so forth. (…) The problem, again, is how it is that change begins. In particular, if turning points are the embodiment or extended process of change, how is it that they get started? This start must take place at a moment, and yet it would seem that given normal ideas about causality, an instant cannot see the production of enduring change" (ibid., p. 96 f.). His considerations on the "solution" of this general social theoretical problem are not further relevant here.

Or is it not rather a whole series of (experiential) moments or even the totality of all experiences made during the internship that led to this?[42] There is a simple reason why the question of the "turn" that separates two trajectories is not easy to answer: turning points are not, in fact, life events or transitions that are shrunk down to a single moment, but are rather to be understood as processes that have a certain temporal duration? Even if turning points are comparatively – namely in relation to the two trajectories separated by them – abrupt: they have a temporal duration, a beginning and an end.[43] Precisely therein lies the problem of determining a turning point: "turning points – if extended – may have little trajectories in them. This fractal interpenetration will make identification difficult" (ibid., p. 103). Whether a certain event or a specific transition is to be located as the beginning of a turning (point) process or in its initial phase, or whether it is still in the final phase of the preceding trajectory – and likewise: whether a certain event or a specific transition is still in the final phase of a turning (point) process or to be located as its end or already lies in the initial phase of the following trajectory – can logically only be determined ex post: only after the entire turning (point) process has been completed and a new course direction has become established and recognizable.

- What turning points have there been in your life so far and what kind of turning points were they?
- Reflect on the biographical and social significance that these turning points had (or still have).

As has already been pointed out, there is a constitutive connection between turning points and trajectories. Or, to put it differently: the turning point concept and the trajectory concept are not logically independent of each other, but are theoretically mutually dependent. What does the outlined understanding of turning point mean

---

[42] A comparable problem was already apparent in the fictional love story of Svenja and Martin: the question of the point in time, the one moment in which they became a couple, was not easy to answer or could not be answered independently of the respective question context, i.e. there was not just one "objective" answer to it.

[43] Of course, the temporal duration of a turning point must not be "overstretched", i.e. so broadly defined that the difference to social processes of change that take place over longer periods of time becomes blurred – this is precisely the point of the turning point concept in the first place: "that is the point of having a concept of turning point, as opposed to simply one of change or causality or succession, all of which would cover a turning point of this extremely gradual kind" (ibid., p. 104).

6.2 Analytical Concepts of Life Course Research

for the trajectory concept (defined by Elder only vaguely and above all: problematically)? Abbot defines turning points as relatively abrupt "turns" between relatively smooth patterns of relative straightness. These patterns or trajectories consist of a whole series of life events and transitions. If the various life events and transitions were simply to represent additively arbitrary, i.e. only disparate and discontinuous sequences of events and transitions, there could be no question of a course pattern or trajectory. In order to form a trajectory, life events and transitions must rather (re-)produce a double continuity: namely, a developmental ("smooth") as well as a – self-reinforcing – directional continuity ("straightness") must be established and maintained. This double continuity is fundamental to trajectories, the defining characteristic of them. In a processual perspective, one can also speak (instead of continuity) of the fundamental inertia of a traject. What constitutes a trajectory is its inherent moment of inertia: theoretically decisive is the "inertial, historicist character of the trajectories. These are life episodes with a capacity for self-regeneration and self-perpetuation. (…) What makes the trajectories is their inertial quality, their quality of enduring large amounts of minor variation without any appreciable change in overall direction" (ibid., p. 92 f.).

Where does this defining "inertial quality" of the trajectory come from? What causes its inertia (or double continuity)? How is it that life events and transitions do not simply form discontinuous, disparate sequences of events and transitions, but rather produce a continuity of development and above all: continuity of direction? Already at the beginning of the discussion of the trajectory concept it was said that life course research needs a theoretical conception of how life events and transitions form or are formed into trajectories. Abbott's answer to this central life course theoretical question is – like his turning point concept – structural: as "self-regenerating and self-perpetuating" life course episodes, trajectories are "widely programmed into our social institutions" (ibid., p. 92). This is evident, for example, with regard to the education system: the Gymnasium course of education after primary school is such an institutionally pre-programmed life course episode, as is vocational training in the dual system or university studies after lower or upper secondary school. The internal labor markets or career paths that exist, for example, in the public sector or in large companies, also illustrate the socio-structural pre-programming of temporary parts of life courses (for a detailed discussion of these socio-structural, in particular institutional, preformations of life course episodes, see Sect. 5.2). In the discussion of the transition concept, the embedding of the various life events and transitions in social contexts was already emphasized (see also the remarks on the theoretical conception of life course research and on a substantial definition of the term "life course" in Sect. 2.2). This social-structural embedding of events and transitions suggests to individuals certain connection options for their life courses, while making others unlikely, i.e. this embedding – above all in the form of institutionally anchored "social pathways" – represents a pre-programming of life course phases from which individuals can deviate only with difficulty, at considerable individual effort and cost. The inertia that characterizes trajectories results from precisely this social embeddedness of the life events and transitions that constitute them, and from the accompanying social-structural preformation of life course phases.

This social-structural embedding of life events and transitions, especially in the form of institutionally predefined "social pathways", does indeed shape the life course of an individual – but not in the sense of a deterministic concatenation of events and transitions into trajectories. Rather, trajectories are formed – according to the basic theoretical assumption of life course research (see Sect. 2.2.2) – in an always contingent process of a complex structure-agency interplay over time: in that individuals (actively) bring about and (passively) experience certain life events and transitions under given social-structural framework conditions, above all within the framework of preformed "social pathways", whereby their "linking" – whether initially biographically planned or imposed by structural constraints – generates a self-reinforcing path dependency (or continuity of direction) over time.[44] The individual links up – again oscillating between the poles of biographical self-direction and active shaping of his own life on the one hand and merely reacting to and being rather passively "processed" by external factors on the other – these temporally parallel, successive and partially overlapping trajectories, in turn, to the specific totality of his life course. This largely takes place in trajectories, i.e. the life of an individual usually runs along relatively stable, steady paths. Occasionally, however, the individual finds himself forced by biographically motivated or externally induced turning points to leave his familiar trajectory and "leap to a new steady trajectory" (ibid.).[45]

---

[44] It is important to keep in mind that this path dependency or continuity of direction is contingent at any point in time, because the term "trajectory" is used in everyday language to describe the trajectory of a projectile – if one were to transfer this understanding, which comes from ballistics, to life course research, trajectories would be determined by an initial moment that shapes the trajectory. This deterministic conception is not compatible with the basic theoretical assumption of life course research (see also the critical discussion of the assumption of a "formative phase" in the cohort and generation approach that shapes individuals throughout their lives in Chap. 4).

[45] An example of this is the divorce of a long-term marriage and the start of a new relationship, or the successful completion of studies or vocational training and entry into a corresponding gainful employment.

6.2 Analytical Concepts of Life Course Research

So much for the – not just two, but – three basic analytical concepts of life course research, with whose presented discussion the chapter on life course research as a conceptual perspective is concluded.

> In connection with his structural understanding of the trajectory and turning point concept, Abbott has pointed out an interesting methodological and theoretical consequence. According to Abbott, the double continuity or inertia characteristic of trajectories gives them a "causal character, in particular their comprehensibility under the image of cause implicit in regression thinking" (1997, p. 93). This means that the causal analytical tools of sociology are applicable to trajectories (and indeed causal relations between life events and transitions within a trajectory and between trajectories have been empirically analyzed and established many times by life course research, with the temporal internal structure of trajectories in their aspects of timing, sequencing, spacing, density and duration being particularly relevant).[46] In contrast, turning points represent "'random' periods" (ibid.) in the life of an individual, are "chaotic" (ibid.). Methodologically, it follows for Abbott that the causal-analytical arsenal of methods of sociology is not applicable to turning points.
>
> This methodological consequence, that trajectories can be causally analyzed, whereas turning points cannot, is particularly interesting because the relationship between the trajectory and the turning point concept also implies a theoretically and conceptually relevant consequence: it is true – as already mentioned – that an individual's life largely proceeds along regular paths, i.e. trajectories. But: "paradoxically, individual actors experience the causally comprehensible trajectories as less important and less consequential than the less comprehensible turning points" (ibid., p. 102). The fact that, from the biographical perspective of the individual, the causally incomprehensible (or poorly comprehensible) turning points are more important and more consequential than the trajectories results from the fact that turning points "give rise to changes in overall direction or regime, and do so in a determinate fashion. Thus, while we may want

---

[46] "Timing ... refers to the age at which experiences occur. Sequencing refers to the order in which experiences occur, spacing to the amount of time between two or more ordered experiences, and density to the compression of transitions within a bounded period of time. Duration refers to the length of time spent in any particular role or 'state'" (Settersten 1999, p. 138).

to think of them as 'abrupt' and 'chaotic,' and indeed we may discover them because they appear as irregularities in what has hitherto been a stable trajectory or regime, in fact they are the crucial sites of determination in the overall structure of a life course ... because they change its parameters" (ibid., p. 93).
- Discuss Abbot's methodological as well as his theoretical-conceptual argument.

Life Course Research, Quo Vadis? 7

The history of life course research since the 1970s is without question a success story. Life course studies have produced a wealth of empirical results and findings. On the one hand, with regard to the life course itself and its social and biographical continuity-founding function as an institution, its modern structure, its formation, important structuring factors, current change tendencies, group-specific life course patterns, and historical and intercultural variations. In a second – and numerically much larger – strand of life course research, problems, phenomena and developments in all kinds of social domains (such as education, labor market, family, inequality, social policy, health, migration, etc.) were investigated by means of the analysis of (aggregated) individual life courses. Beyond analyses of area-specific social issues and developments, the research field has produced empirically grounded insights into processes of social change in general.

Conceptually, the prominent role of life course research for a dynamic analysis of social phenomena must be emphasized. The general theoretical "time matters" (Abbott 2001), i.e. the insight that an investigation of social phenomena or the fundamental structure-agency interplay must conceptually always pursue and apply a time-sensitive analytical perspective, has been taken seriously and successfully implemented by this field of research: life course research "has brought a fresh perspective to many classical domains of sociology ... by demonstrating the temporality of what had long been conceptualized as positions and states" (Kohli 2007, p. 253).

In this context, life course research has stimulated important methodological innovations such as event analysis or sequence pattern analytic procedures (life course research methods were not dealt with in the context of this book – in this respect, reference is made to the relevant methodological literature). An indispensable prerequisite and basis for the time-sensitive analyses of the dynamic life course approach are micro analytical longitudinal data. The development and expansion of corresponding data sets as well as international collaborations has been enormously driven by life course research (Bynner 2016). Today, microanalytically based longitudinal analyses are part of the standard repertoire of empirical social research.

Since 2009, life course research has had its own international professional society, the Society for Longitudinal and Life Course Studies (SLLS), which promotes the internal and external relevance of life course research through annual international conferences and the journal "Longitudinal and Life Course Studies". A second journal for this field of research, "Advances in Life Course Research", has been published since 2000. In summary, life course research is an established and growing field of empirical social research and sociology. Given the increasing number of life course publications – which have shown a quadratic growth rate since 1990 (Shanahan et al. 2016b, p. 1)[1] – one can assume that this success story will continue in the future.

However, this success story of life course research also includes a not unproblematic aspect. Four decades after Cain's systematic overview of early life course research and three decades after Elder's groundbreaking study of the "Children of the Great Depression", the *Handbook of the Life Course was* published in 2003. In their foreword, the editors point out that life course research is now diffusing into all areas of empirical social research and into other disciplines.[2] They attribute this diffusion to the "generalized nature of this paradigm" (Mortimer and Shanahan 2003, p. XI), i.e. to the fact that the research field does not have any elaborated life course theory(s), but only something like an imaginative framework, a theoretical orientation (see Sect. 6.1). The increasing diffusion of life course research proves its usefulness and relevance, but also confronts life course researchers with the problem "to maintain a core identity and to evaluate the development of their field" (ibid.). With regard to this question of the intellectual core distinguishing (and

---

[1] In 2013, nearly 400 life course sociology papers appeared in journals alone (if we add life course psychology and biomedical epidemiology journal articles, this figure rises to over 900; Shanahan et al. 2016b, p. 2); in addition, there are life course sociology articles in edited volumes (the number of which is likely to be substantial) and monographs.

[2] The word "dissipate" used by them in quotation marks (Mortimer and Shanahan 2003, p. XI f.) also has the meaning "to get out of hand" or "to get bogged down", i.e. a negative connotation (the neutral word "diffuse" is used here).

constituting in the first place) life course research as a distinct research field, the editors were optimistic and of the opinion that "a common core of generalized concepts and premises is now taking hold and giving definite form to the life course paradigm" (ibid.). As its intellectual core were presented – it must be said: once again and only – the life course principles propagated by Elder.[3] However, Elder's paradigmatic principles are – as explained in Sect. 6.1 – insufficient as a theoretical orientation of life course research due to their "unspecificity" in terms of life course theory – and thus cannot function as a distinct intellectual core of this field of research.

Almost a decade and a half later, the *Handbook of the Life Course, Volume II* (2016) was published. Its introductory article also addresses the connection between the increasing diffusion of life course research, especially "in fields beyond sociology" (Shanahan et al. 2016b, p. 1), including the associated problem of a "coherent, paradigmatic core", (ibid.) with the "status of the life course as a paradigm" (ibid., p. 3), which is insufficient in terms of life course theory. In other words, the editors again state that this paradigm, i.e. Elder's life course principles, do not offer a clearly defined research perspective and a distinct intellectual core of life course research, but on the contrary promote a "fraying" of this research field. Life course research, however, still seems to be exhausted in defining its intellectual core in Elder's paradigmatic principles. In any case, the second handbook does not contain any contribution that documents progress in this respect, i.e. an intellectual core for this field of research that is elaborated in terms of life course theory.[4] This fact – as well as the result of a thematic review of the articles published in the two journals of the research field: not one of them contains the term "life course theory" (or the corresponding adjective) in its title – is an indication that life course research is still largely limited to "conducting empirical studies, theoretically accompanied by a prayer-wheel like reeling off of Elder's life course principles" (Wingens and Reiter 2011, p. 188).

---

[3] The first section of the handbook, entitled "The Life Course Perspective", served to present the intellectual (paradigmatic) core: it contained only one article (Elder et al. 2003) and – like other contributions touching on the question of the intellectual core of life course research – did not go beyond the repetition of Elder's paradigmatic principles in terms of life course theory.

[4] Moreover, while the first handbook contains review articles on the state of research in a specific problem or area as well as methodological and conceptual contributions, the second handbook contains no theoretical or conceptual contribution at all (and if the problem is touched upon en passant in an article, it remains a recitation or brief reference to Elder's life course principles).

The editors of the second handbook describe the relationship between the increasing diffusion of life course research and its core, which is insufficient in terms of life course theory, as a polar alternative: "the coherent core versus interdisciplinary diffusion" (Shanahan et al. 2016 b, p. 3). That is: according to them, life course research is at a crossroads. Although their diagnosis of a polar alternative is a strong claim, the editors do not discuss their "either-or" scenario of the further development of this research field in any detail. More than that – and this is more than unsatisfactory – they do not even seem to bother with a brief justification of their opposition scenario, but without hesitation delegate all reflection on it with the nice invitation: "we invite readers to consider this tension between cohesiveness and cross-pollination" (ibid.). The problem raised in the previous two paragraphs will be addressed at least briefly in the following – and concluding the present book (it goes without saying that the reader should form his or her own opinion).

The editors of the second handbook describe this problem – as already mentioned – antagonistically: as a tension between the contrary poles of a "challenge of intellectual cohesiveness" (ibid.) on the one hand and the "opportunities for intellectual cross-pollination" (ibid.) on the other. Does this antagonistic understanding adequately and meaningfully grasp and describe the problem to be discussed here? Is life course research really faced with the two opposing options of a coherent intellectual core on the one hand, or (versus!) a mutually enriching diffusion into all possible areas of empirical social research and other disciplines? This antagonistic view is rooted in the accurate observation that the life course theoretical "unspecificity" of the life course paradigm in the form of Elders' paradigmatic principles not only promotes but inevitably produces such diffusion. From this fact, however, no contradiction can be derived between an elaborated intellectual core of life course research and its diffusion (including cross-pollination). It cannot be logically concluded from this fact that a theoretically-conceptually elaborated core of life course research makes its fruitful diffusion impossible. Logically, such a conclusion is not compelling, i.e. it is wrong; empirically, it is at least problematic and would first have to be proven – which, however, is not possible because this intellectual core does not yet exist. In this respect, this antagonistic alternative (intellectual core versus fruitful diffusion) does not adequately comprehend and describe the problem of life course research, but rather in a problematic way. In contrast to this questionable antagonistic view, the following comments focus on the lack of an intellectual core as the central problem for life course research. There is consensus on the fact that it does not have an elaborated life course theory(s). But what does this deficit in life course theory, the lack of an intellectual core, mean for the field of research?

Life course research could only do without such a theoretical-conceptual core if it focused solely on the life course itself as its "actual" object of research. In this focus, life course research would (only) see itself as a hyphenated sociology. The field of life course research would then, like any hyphenated sociology, be ontologically defined by (its) object or object area – and the methodological question of an intellectual core defining the research field (and constituting it in the first place) would be invalid. In this case, life course research, like all hyphenated sociologies, could make use of the entire fund of sociological theories and concepts and apply these, as well as self-developed theses and field-specific theoretical approaches, in empirical investigations without running the risk of becoming unrecognizable as a distinct research field. However – such a focusing (or massive self-limitation) is possible, but in view of the factual development of the research field over the last almost five decades, it is an extremely unlikely option. The primary issue here, however, is not how likely this option – or another scenario – is (and even less about normatively propagating a desirable direction of development, such as overcoming the divide between life course and biographical research criticized in Sect. 2.2.1); rather, the issue here is whether this option – or another scenario – is at all possible, conceivable.

Life course research in the sense of a hyphenated sociology is also quite conceivable in the future. It is true that the life course itself is now well researched as a research object and that there is a wealth of empirical results and findings on the integrative function of the modern life course, its structure and structuring factors, its formation and socio-historical as well as intercultural variations, group-specific life course patterns and current changes. Nevertheless, the life course itself will remain a relevant object of sociological research in the future. First, there are still questions and problems that require more detailed empirical analysis (such as the issue of the long-term consequences of events and imprints that occurred early in life and their revisability in later life course phases, or the issue of diverse institutional life course effects and their interactions). Moreover – and secondly – societies are subject to permanent and accelerated social change. Since life courses and biographies are a part of this, the question of a renewed structural change of the life course, which was already raised in Kohli's fundamental article on the institutionalization of the life course, remains topical and an interesting research topic.

Life course research, however, has always wanted to be more than (just) a hyphenated sociology: from the beginning, it also understood itself in the sense of a research conception, i.e. as a paradigm or theoretical orientation for empirical social research in general. The development of this research field since the 1970s has proceeded accordingly, i.e. as a (also interdisciplinary) diffusion. In this respect, there is much to be said for a continuation scenario of further and increasing – also interdisciplinary – diffusion. What does that life course theoretical deficit of the lack of an intellectual core mean for this option? Two positions can be taken on this question.

One position was succinctly advocated as early as 2003 in George's contribution to the concluding section of the first handbook, entitled "The Future of the Life Course". George sees the future innovative knowledge potential of life course research less in its understanding as a hyphenated sociology. Rather, its future lies in the "integration of life course principles with the total range of theoretical and substantive themes of social and behavioral research" (2003, p. 673). For this scenario, however, the lack of an elaborated conceptual core of life course theory is not a problem at all. On the contrary, George not only concedes this indisputable fact, but even welcomes it: according to her, there are "basic principles that characterize life course perspectives,[5] but there is not an integrated theory of the life course; nor ... should there be one" (ibid., p. 671). However, this normative postulate is argumentatively supported by George's diffusion scenario only if that questionable antagonistic alternative "intellectual core vs. diffusion" is implicitly assumed. Apart from this weakness in argumentation logic, what is more interesting here is the consequence that George draws from her diffusion scenario for the field of life course research. She clearly states that there is a price to pay for its fruitful diffusion: "As this happens, life course research will become increasingly less distinctive. And that will be a marker of its success rather than its failure" (ibid., p. 678). Accordingly, life course research becomes unrecognizable as such to the extent that it successfully diffuses, dissolves as a distinctive field of research. A lethal success, so to speak. One can argue for this position, but then one can no longer say that one is doing life course research.[6]

---

[5] According to George, these are Elder's paradigmatic principles.

[6] Consequently, Bynner, who proposes such an overcoming of disciplinary perspectives in life course research: a fusion of "life course sociology, life span psychology and human biol-

The second position understands the life course theoretical deficit of the lack of an intellectual core as a fundamental problem for diffusing life course research.[7] From this position, Bernardi, Huinink, and Settersten have recently made a commendable attempt to initiate the long overdue life course theoretical discussion beyond Elder's inadequate paradigmatic principles and "to provide a theoretical foundation to guide the development of interdisciplinary life course research and help to integrate and unify the field" (2019, p. 2). The authors see this foundational life course theoretical perspective in a "dynamic … theory of agency" (ibid.).[8] This theory, they argue, is based on the axiomatic assumption that individuals strive to improve – at least maintain – their physical and psychological well-being. As central aspects, the authors briefly mention the individuals' search for certainty of action and the relevance of their previous life histories as well as future expectations. In terms of life course theory, this remains the case for the time being – "a concise and comprehensive dynamic theory of agency over the life course has yet to be formulated" (ibid.). In this respect, it (only) remains to be seen whether the outlined approach – if it is eventually available in a form elaborated in terms of life course theory – can and will function as an integrative, holistic intellectual core of interdisciplinary life course research.

Instead of elaborating the postulated fundamental agency theory in terms of life course theory, Bernardi, Huinink and Settersten essentially present in their paper a synthetic representation of the life course as a complex set of interdependencies in the form of their titular "life course cube" (ibid., p. 3 ff.). The three axes of the life course cube stand for the dimensions of time, life domains and life course levels,

---

ogy" (2016, p. 50) – in addition, Bynner also mentions demography, epidemiology, criminology, history and geography (ibid, p. 28); economics and anthropology should also not be forgotten as relevant disciplines – has in mind to call this integrative-holistic research perspective "applied developmental science" (ibid., p. 50).

[7] "Precisely because life course scholarship is a multidisciplinary and interdisciplinary enterprise, there is a great need to integrate our disparate and complex research area" (Bernardi et al. 2019, p. 2).

[8] It is therefore surprising that the theoretically most elaborate conception of agency and its fundamental temporality, namely Emirbayer and Mische's essay "What is agency?" (1998; see also the corresponding remarks in Sect. 6.1), is not even mentioned by the authors.

i.e. they represent the three "first-order interdependencies" (ibid., p. 3) between past, present and future, between different life domains (such as work, family, health, leisure, etc.) and between intra-individual, individual and supra-individual factors. This results in the three "second-order interdependencies" (ibid., p. 6) between the time dimension and the diverse life domains, between the time dimension and the multilevel structure, and between the multilevel structure and the diverse life domains. And finally, the stage of "third-order interdependencies" (ibid., p. 7), i.e. the mutual relations of all three dimensions, is reached, which is ultimately crucial, because "this means understanding how such interdependencies work in combination" (ibid.) – one can then understand or explain how life courses form and why they form the way they do.

Whether this is the case or not remains to be seen here. The construction-logical problem of this life course cube in the form of the analytical difference between the time dimension and the other two dimensions is also not relevant here.[9] Nor is the fact that the "life course cube" itself obviously does not formulate a life course theory, but rather functions as a scheme or instrument for "locating"[10] studies from the field of life course research of interest here (although it should be emphasized that this classification scheme is indirectly productive in terms of life course theory, because it raises questions such as, for example, why the results of empirical studies that are to be located in the same sector of the life course cube diverge). The sole point at issue here is an argumentative turn that Bernardi, Huinink, and Settersten make with their life course cube that is insightful in terms of life course theory. This point at issue here can be clothed in the question of the life course theoretical relationship between the dynamic agency theory initially promoted by

---

[9] But Mayer is clear about this: "Time ... is just a marker, it is empty. Levels and domains are substantive; time is not, or at least not in the same way. A first order time-related life course dependency is always one in at least one domain. One cannot formulate a life course research question or hypothesis without specifying at least one substantive domain plus time. Time might therefore be more fruitfully constructed as the basis of all first order interdependencies. (…) That fault could easily be corrected: as first order interdependencies, then, we should denote changes in any given domain on the individual level, the intra-individual level and the collective level ... Consequently, second order interdependencies can then be formulated as inter-domain effects across life time, and inter-level interaction across life time" (2019, p. 1 f.).

[10] As Bernardi, Huinink and Settersten themselves see it and say: the life course cube "serves as an ordering structure into which all specific mechanisms relevant to study life course dynamics can be integrated" (2019, p. 8).

the authors and their "life course cube". Whereas the authors initially argued for a dynamic agency theory (albeit one that has yet to be elaborated) as a fundamental life course theoretical perspective, they postulate in the concluding part of their essay that it is "seemingly impossible to develop a single and complete life course theory" (ibid., p. 8) – thus rowing back a bit in terms of life course theory. At the same time, however, their "life course cube" is intended to make a life course theoretical contribution beyond those "guiding principles that some scholars might argue approximate theory" (ibid.). To this end, they must theoretically enhance the life course cube, because it is admittedly not itself a life course theory. They do this by abruptly declaring the interdependencies captured and expressed in it to be mechanisms: "The life course cube provides a parsimonious set of basic mechanisms" (ibid.). The – very scanty – argumentation with which the authors attempt to justify the sudden transformation of interdependencies into mechanisms containing explanations is not convincing. What is interesting, however, is the conclusion they draw from their consideration: "When we study and explain the outcomes of particular life course dynamics, which are necessarily entangled in the interdependencies of the cube, we need to employ additional, specific theories from different disciplines" (ibid.). The authors conclude that inter- and transdisciplinary life course research is thus dependent on elaborate disciplinary theories.

Perhaps one should abandon the notion of a cross-disciplinary, or more precisely: merging integrative-holistic life course theory. Perhaps the nowadays generally popular idea of a unified research perspective as a result of inter- or transdisciplinary convergence is not only difficult but impossible to realize. Illustrative of this is the decades-old demand to integrate sociological life course and psychological life span development research – an attempt that has not yet succeeded despite the relatively close proximity of the two perspectives. On the contrary: "life span psychology and life course sociology, with few exceptions, did not come together at all but now seem to stand further apart than in the 1970s" (Diewald and Mayer 2009, p. 5). It is absolutely indisputable that there are common interests, overlaps, and opportunities for fruitful cooperation between these two research perspectives; it is equally indisputable – and also self-evident – that such cooperation potentials should be better exploited than they have been so far. However, to want to integrate life course sociology and life span development psychology into one (holistic) research perspective means something different and much more than such a meaningful cooperation. The fact that an integration or, more precisely, a fusion of sociological life course and psychological life span development perspectives has not succeeded so far (and will probably not succeed in the future either), despite all commonalities, is not a contingent fact, but has a systematic or epistemological reason – overlooked or ignored by the heralds of inter- and transdisciplinarity.

The philosophy of knowledge and science shows – as already stated in Chap. 1 – that there is no such thing as a-theoretical observation and knowledge, and that a research object or problem is not simply given "in itself", but only becomes such (in each case) in a (specific) theoretical perspective. In this respect, then, sociological life course and psychological life span development research are "quite distinct in both the main explananda and the prevailing explanatory factors" (Diewald and Mayer 2009, p. 5; Mayer 2003; Dannefer and Daub 2009; Settersten 2005, 2009). In other words – and varying a formulation from the first chapter – sociological life course research conceives and explains its respective research object or problem "socio-logically" and precisely not "psycho-logically" (whereas for life span development psychology no "socio-logic" but a "psycho-logic" is constitutive). These fundamental disciplinary perspectives cannot be merged any more than an electric motor and an internal combustion engine can be merged (which – to emphasize this once again – does not mean that there cannot be meaningful interdisciplinary cooperations: of course, an electric motor and an internal combustion engine can be "integrated" into a hybrid drive – but even in such a hybrid drive, the electric motor is an electric motor and the internal combustion engine remains an internal combustion engine).

Bernardi's, Huinink's, and Settersten's commendable initiation of a discussion of life course theory stands decidedly in an interdisciplinary perspective. The present book is concerned solely with sociological life course research – as outlined in Chap. 1. Ten years ago, Mayer came to a similar, albeit less apodictic, conclusion as those authors in the concluding part of their essay: "Indeed, because there is not just one mechanism underlying the social structuring of human lives, but rather manifold mechanisms operating on the individual, meso, and macro levels, one might contend that a simple, unified sociological theory of the life course is not possible" (2009, p. 423). This leaves room for hope – especially since nowhere is it written that it has to be a "simple theory" or only one (single) "unified theory". For sociological life course research, it would already be a great theoretical step forward if it could develop elaborate, robust life course sociological theories on specific aspects of the life course and have them at its disposal – comparable to disciplines such as psychology or economics. But it would also be appropriate to – finally! – start working on general life course theory(s) which go beyond such "partial theories". Perhaps Mayer's concept of the life course as an endogenous causal relation could be elaborated. Or the idea of a dynamic agency theory first pursued by Bernardi, Huinink, and Settersten could be expanded into a sociological life course theory. Such a dynamic agency theory perspective is certainly a promising, perhaps even the most promising, approach to a general sociological life course theory. This need not – as Bernardi, Huinink and Settersten suggest – operate within the framework of theories of rational choice or a model of the individual as a "resourceful, restricted, evaluating, expecting, maximizing man"[11] and his social production functions (such an approach would, however, have the advantage of being able to build on an elaborate theoretical foundation). Following Emirbayer and Mische (1998), it could also be elaborated in the sense of a relational concept of agency, which understands the relationship between structure and agency as a reciprocal constitutional relationship – i.e. structure not only as a relevant contextual variable – which is conceived dynamically and takes account of the different time dimensions (Abbott's "time matters") and which models life courses as endogenous causal relationships (path dependencies) without excluding breaks or turning points.

In whatever direction theoretical approaches and perspectives of sociological life course research may go – the main thing is that a serious life course theoretical discussion and work begins that goes beyond those inadequate paradigmatic principles or even the vague talk of an imaginative framework.

---

[11] Thus Lindenberg's sociological extension of the homo economicus model of classical microeconomics (1985, p. 100).

References

Abbott, Andrew. 1997. On the concept of turning point. *Comparative Social Research* 16 (Methodological issues in comparative social science): 85–105.
———. 2001. *Time matters. On theory and method*. Chicago: University of Chicago Press.
Abbott, Andrew, and Angela Tsay. 2000. Sequence analysis and optimal matching methods in sociology. Review and prospect. *Sociological Methods & Research* 29 (1): 3–33.
Abels, Heinz, et al. 2008. *Lebensphasen. Eine Einführung*. Wiesbaden: VS.
Advances in Life Course Research (2000ff).
Aisenbrey, Silke. 2000. *Optimal Matching Analyse. Anwendung in den Sozialwissenschaften*. Opladen: Leske + Budrich.
Aisenbrey, Silke, and Anette Fasang. 2010. New life for old ideas: The "second wave" of sequence analysis. Bringing the "course" back into the life course. *Sociological Methods & Research* 38 (3): 420–462.
Alheit, Peter. 1995. Biographizität als Lernpotential: Konzeptionelle Überlegungen zum biographischen Ansatz in der Erwachsenenbildung. In *Erziehungswissenschaftliche Biographieforschung*, Hrsg. H.-H. Krüger und W. Marotzki, 276–307. Opladen: Leske + Budrich.
Alheit, Peter, und Morten Brandt. 2006. *Autobiographie und ästhetische Erfahrung Entdeckung und Wandel des Selbst in der Moderne*. Frankfurt: Campus.
Alheit, Peter, und Bettina Dausien. 2000. Die biographische Konstruktion der Wirklichkeit. Überlegungen zur Biographizität des Sozialen. In *Biographische Sozialisation*, Hrsg. E. Hoerning, 257–283. Stuttgart: Lucius & Lucius.
Allmendinger, Jutta. 1989. Educational systems and labor market outcomes. *European Sociological Review* 5 (3): 231–250.
———. 1994. *Lebensverlauf und Sozialpolitik. Die Ungleichheit von Mann und Frau und ihr öffentlicher Ertrag*. Frankfurt: Campus.
Alwin, Duane. 1994. Aging, personality and social change. The stability of individual differences over the adult life-span. In *Life-span development and behavior*, ed. D. Featherman, R. Lerner, and M. Perlmutter, vol. 12, 135–185. Hillsdale: Erlbaum.

———. 1995. Taking time seriously: Social change, social structure and human lives. In *Examining lives in context: Perspectives on the ecology of human development*, ed. P. Moen, G. Elder, and K. Lüscher, 211–262. Washington: American Psychological Association.

Alwin, Duane, and Ryan McCammon. 2003. Generations, cohorts, and social change. In *Handbook of the life course*, ed. J. Mortimer and M. Shanahan, 23–49. New York: Kluwer/Plenum.

Amrhein, Ludwig. 2004. Der entstrukturierte Lebenslauf? Zur Vision einer "altersintegrierten" Gesellschaft. *Zeitschrift für Sozialreform* 50 (1–2): 147–169.

Anderson, Nels. 1923. *The Hobo: The sociology of the homeless man*. Chicago: University of Chicago Press.

Anderson, Michael. 1985. The emergence of the modern life cycle in Britain. *Social History* 10 (1): 69–87.

Anyadike-Danes, Michael, and Duncan McVicar. 2010. My brilliant career. Characterizing the early labor market trajectories of British women from Generation X. *Sociological Methods & Research* 38 (3): 482–512.

Archer, Margaret. 2000. *Being human. The problem of agency*. Cambridge: Cambridge University Press.

Ardelt, Monika. 2000. Still stable after all these years? Personality stability theory revisited. *Social Psychology Quarterly* 63 (4): 392–405.

Ariès, Philipp. 1975. *Geschichte der Kindheit*. München: Hanser (frz. Orig.: 1960).

Arnett, Jeffrey. 2000. Emerging adulthood. A theory of development from the late teens through the twenties. *American Psychologist* 55 (5): 469–480.

Autorengruppe Bildungsberichterstattung. 2016. *Bildung in Deutschland 2016. Ein indikatorengestützter Bericht mit einer Analyse zu Bildung und Migration*. Bielefeld: Bertelsmann.

Back, Kurt. 1980. Introduction. In *Life course: Integrative theories and exemplary populations*, ed. K. Back, 1–5. Boulder: Westview Press.

Balsiger, Philipp. 2005. *Transdisziplinarität. Systematisch-vergleichende Untersuchung disziplinenübergreifender Wissenschaftspraxis*. München: Fink.

Baltes, Paul, Ulman Lindenberger, and Ursula Staudinger. 1998. Life-span theory in developmental psychology. In *Theoretical models of human development (Handbook of child psychology; vol. 1)*, ed. R. Lerner, 5th ed., 1029–1143. New York: Wiley.

Bandura, Albert. 1997. *Self-efficacy. The exercise of control*. New York: Freeman.

Barley, Stephen. 1989. Careers, identities, and institutions: The legacy of the Chicago school of sociology. In *Handbook of career theory*, ed. M. Arthur, D. Hall, and B. Lawrence, 41–65. Cambridge: Cambridge University Press.

Barnes, Barry. 2000. *Understanding agency. Social theory and responsible action*. London: Sage.

Baumert, Jürgen, et al. 2001. *PISA 2000. Basiskompetenzen von Schülerinnen und Schülern im internationalen Vergleich*. Opladen: Leske + Budrich.

Beck, Ulrich. 1983. Jenseits von Stand und Klasse? Soziale Ungleichheit, gesellschaftliche Individualisierungsprozesse und die Entstehung neuer sozialer Formationen und Identitäten. In *Soziale Ungleichheiten*, Hrsg. R. Kreckel, 35–74. Göttingen: Schwartz (Soziale Welt-Sonderband 2).

———. 1986. *Risikogesellschaft. Auf dem Weg in eine andere Moderne*. Frankfurt: Suhrkamp.

Beck, Ulrich, und Elisabeth Beck-Gernsheim. 1994. Individualisierung in modernen Gesellschaften – Perspektiven und Kontroversen einer subjektorientierten Soziologie. In *Riskante Freiheiten. Individualisierung in modernen Gesellschaften*, Hrsg. U. Beck und E. Beck-Gernsheim, 10–39. Frankfurt: Suhrkamp.

Becker, Michael. 2009. *Kognitive Leistungsentwicklung in differenziellen Lernumwelten. Effekte des gegliederten Sekundarschulsystems in Deutschland*. Berlin: MPI für Bildungsforschung.

Becker, Rolf. 2016. Bildungseffekte vorschulischer Erziehung und Elementarbildung. Bessere Bildungschancen für Arbeiter- und Migrantenkinder?. In *Bildung als Privileg. Erklärungen und Befunde zu den Ursachen der Bildungsungleichheit*, Hrsg. R. Becker und W. Lauterbach, 145–181. Wiesbaden: Springer VS.

Becker, Rolf, und Wolfgang Lauterbach. 2004. Vom Nutzen vorschulischer Kinderbetreuung für Bildungschancen. In *Bildung als Privileg? Erklärungen und Befunde zu den Ursachen der Bildungsungleichheit*, Hrsg. R. Becker und W. Lauterbach, 127–160. Wiesbaden: VS.

Beckermann, Ansgar (2012): Willensfreiheit – ein Überblick aus kompatibilistischer Sicht. In *Aufsätze (Bd. 2)*, Hrsg. A. Beckermann, 267–287. Bielefeld: Universitätsbibliothek Bielefeld. https://pub.uni-bielefeld.de/download/2306223/2306226.

Beekes, Albert. 1990. The development of cohort analysis. In *Life histories and generations*, ed. H. Becker, 547–562. Utrecht: ISOR (Rijksuniversiteit).

Behrens, Johann, und Wolfgang Voges. 1996. Kritische Übergänge. Statuspassagen und sozialpolitische Institutionalisierung. In *Kritische Übergänge. Statuspassagen und sozialpolitische Institutionalisierung*, Hrsg. J. Behrens und W. Voges, 16–42. Frankfurt: Campus.

Behringer, Luise. 1998. *Lebensführung als Identitätsarbeit. Der Mensch im Chaos des modernen Alltags*. Frankfurt: Campus.

Bellenberg, Gabriele. 2012. *Schulformwechsel in Deutschland. Durchlässigkeit und Selektion in den 16 Schulsystemen der Bundesländer innerhalb der Sekundarstufe I*. Gütersloh: Bertelsmann.

Bengtson, Vern, and Robert Harootyan, eds. 1994. *Intergenerational linkages. Hidden connections in American society*. New York: Springer.

Berger, Bennet. 1960. How long is a generation? *British Journal of Sociology* 9 (1): 10–23.

Berger, Peter A. 1996. *Individualisierung. Statusunsicherheit und Erfahrungsvielfalt*. Opladen: Westdeutscher Verlag.

Berger, Peter A., und Ronald Hitzler, Hrsg. 2010. *Individualisierungen. Ein Vierteljahrhundert "jenseits von Stand und Klasse"?* Wiesbaden: VS.

Berger, Peter A., und Peter Sopp. 1992. Bewegtere Zeiten? Zur Differenzierung von Erwerbsverlaufsmustern in Westdeutschland. *Zeitschrift für Soziologie* 21 (3): 166–185.

Berger, Peter L., Brigitte Berger, und Hansfried Kellner. 1975. *Das Unbehagen in der Modernität*. Frankfurt: Campus (am. Orig.: 1973).

Bernardi, Bernardo. 1985. *Age class systems. Social institutions and polities based on age*. Cambridge: Cambridge University Press.

Bernardi, Laura, Johannes Huinink, and Richard Settersten. 2019. The life course cube. A tool for studying lives. *Advances in Life Course Research* 41: 100258. https://doi.org/10.1016/j.alcr.2018.11.004.

Bertaux, Daniel, ed. 1981. *Biography and society. The life history approach in the social sciences*. Beverly Hills: Sage.

Bertaux, Daniel, and Martin Kohli. 1984. The life story approach: A continental view. *Annual Review of Sociology* 10: 215–237.
Best, Fred. 1980. *Flexible life scheduling. Breaking the education-work-retirement lockstep.* New York: Praeger.
———. 1990. Does flexible life scheduling have a future? In *Rethinking worklife options for older persons*, ed. J. Habib and C. Nusberg, 217–242. Washington: International Federation on Ageing.
Best, Heinrich. 2003. Geschichte und Lebensverlauf. Theoretische Modelle und empirische Befunde zur Formierung politischer Generationen im Deutschland des 19. Jahrhunderts. In *Generationswechsel und historischer Wandel*, Hrsg. A. Schulz und G. Grebner, 57–69. München: Oldenbourg.
Bien, Walter, und Jan Marbach, Hrsg. 2003. *Partnerschaften und Familiengründung. Ergebnisse der dritten Welle des Familien-Survey*. Opladen: Leske + Budrich.
Billari, Francesco, and Aart Liefbroer. 2010. Towards a new pattern of transition to adulthood? *Advances in Life Course Research* 15 (2–3): 59–75.
Bing, Leon. 1991. *Do or die (for the first time, members of L.A.'s most notorious teenage gangs – The Crips and the Bloods – Speak for themselves)*. New York: Harper Collins.
Blau, Peter, and Otis Duncan. 1967. *The American occupational structure.* New York: Wiley.
Blome, Agnes, Wolfgang Keck, und Jens Alber. 2008. *Generationenbeziehungen im Wohlfahrtsstaat. Lebensbedingungen und Einstellungen von Altersgruppen im internationalen Vergleich*. Wiesbaden: VS.
Blossfeld, Hans-Peter. 1985. *Bildungsexpansion und Berufschancen. Empirische Analysen zur Lage der Berufsanfänger in der Bundesrepublik.* Frankfurt: Campus.
———. 1988. Sensible Phasen im Bildungsverlauf. Eine Längsschnittanalyse über die Prägung von Bildungskarrieren durch den gesellschaftlichen Wandel. *Zeitschrift für Pädagogik* 34 (1): 45–63.
———. 1989. *Karriereprozesse und Kohortendifferenzierung. Eine Längsschnittstudie über die Veränderung der Bildungs- und Berufschancen im Lebenslauf.* Frankfurt: Campus.
Blossfeld, Hans-Peter, and Sonja Drobnič, eds. 2001. *Careers of couples in contemporary society. From male breadwinner to dual earner families.* Oxford: Oxford University Press.
Blossfeld, Hans-Peter, and Heather Hofmeister, eds. 2006. *Globalization, uncertainty and women's careers.* Cheltenham: Elgar.
Blossfeld, Hans-Peter, und Johannes Huinink. 2001. Lebensverlaufsforschung als sozialwissenschaftliche Forschungsperspektive. Themen, Konzepte Methoden und Probleme. *BIOS* 14 (2): 5–31.
Blossfeld, Hans-Peter, and Götz Rohwer. 1995. *Techniques of event history modeling. New approaches to causal analysis.* Mahwah: Erlbaum.
Blossfeld, Hans-Peter, et al., eds. 2005. *Globalization, uncertainty, and youth in society.* London: Routledge.
Blossfeld, Hans-Peter, Melinda Mills, and Fabrizio Bernardi, eds. 2006. *Globalization, uncertainty and men's careers. An international comparison.* Cheltenham: Elgar.
Blossfeld, Hans-Peter, Thorsten Schneider, und Jörg Doll. 2009. Die Längsschnittstudie Nationales Bildungspanel: Notwendigkeit. *Grundzüge und Analysepotential. Pädagogische Rundschau* 63 (2): 249–259.

Blossfeld, Hans-Peter, Hans-Günther Roßbach, and Jutta von Maurice, eds. 2011. *Education as a lifelong process. The German National Educational Panel Study (NEPS)*. Wiesbaden: VS.
Blossfeld, Hans-Peter, et al., eds. 2015. *Gender, education and employment. An international comparison of school-to-work transitions*. Cheltenham: Elgar.
———., eds. 2016. *Methodological issues of longitudinal surveys. The example of the National Educational Panel Study*. Wiesbaden: Springer VS.
BMBF. 2015. *Weiterbildungsverhalten in Deutschland 2014. Ergebnisse des Adult Education Survey – AES Trendbericht*. Bonn: BMBF.
Born, Claudia. 2001. Modernisierungsgap und Wandel. Angleichung geschlechtsspezifischer Lebensführungen? In *Individualisierung und Verflechtung. Geschlecht und Generation im deutschen Lebenslaufregime*, Hrsg. C. Born und H. Krüger, 29–53. Weinheim: Juventa.
Born, Claudia, und Helga Krüger. 2001. Das Lebenslaufregime der Verflechtung: Orte, Ebenen und Thematisierungen. In *Individualisierung und Verflechtung. Geschlecht und Generation im deutschen Lebenslaufregime*, Hrsg. C. Born und H. Krüger, 11–26. Weinheim: Juventa.
Bosch, Gerhard. 2013. Normalarbeitsverhältnis. In *Lexikon der Arbeits- und Industriesoziologie*, Hrsg. H. Hirsch-Kreinsen und H. Minssen, 376–382. Berlin: edition Sigma.
Bourdieu, Pierre. 1998. Prekarität ist überall. In *Gegenfeuer. Wortmeldungen im Dienste des Widerstands gegen die neoliberale Invasion*, Hrsg. P. Bourdieu, 96–102. Konstanz: UVK.
Brandtstädter, Jochen, und Ulman Lindenberger, Hrsg. 2007. *Entwicklungspsychologie der Lebensspanne. Ein Lehrbuch*. Stuttgart: Kohlhammer.
Bright, Jim, and Joanne Earl. 2011. *Brilliant CV: What employers want to see and how to say it*. 4th ed. Harlow: Prentice Hall.
Brim, Orville. 1966. Socialization through the life cycle. In *Socialization after childhood: Two essays*, ed. O. Brim and S. Wheeler, 1–49. New York: Wiley.
Bröckling, Ulrich. 2007. *Das unternehmerische Selbst. Soziologie einer Subjektivierungsform*. Frankfurt: Suhrkamp.
Brose, Hanns-Georg, und Bruno Hildenbrand. 1988. Biographisierung von Erleben und Handeln. In *Vom Ende des Individuums zur Individualität ohne Ende*, Hrsg. H.-G. Brose und B. Hildenbrand, 11–30. Opladen: Leske + Budrich.
Brose, Hanns-Georg, Monika Wohlrab-Sahr, und Michael Corsten. 1993. *Soziale Zeit und Biographie. Über die Gestaltung von Alltagszeit und Lebenszeit*. Opladen: Westdeutscher Verlag.
Brückner, Erika, and Karl Ulrich Mayer. 1998. Collecting life history data. Experiences from the German Life History Study. In *Methods of life course research: Qualitative and quantitative approaches*, ed. J. Giele and G. Elder, 152–181. London: Sage.
Brückner, Hannah, and Karl Ulrich Mayer. 2005. De-standardization of the life course: What it might mean? And if it means anything, whether it actually took place? In *The structure of the life course: Standardized? Individualized? Differentiated?* ed. R. Macmillan, 27–53. Amsterdam: Elsevier.
Brüderl, Josef. 2004. Die Pluralisierung partnerschaftlicher Lebensformen in Westdeutschland und Europa. *Aus Politik und Zeitgeschichte* 54 (19): 3–10.
Brzinsky-Fay, Christian. 2007. Lost in transition? Labour market entry sequences of school leavers in Europe. *European Sociological Review* 23 (4): 409–422.

Buchholz, Sandra. 2008. *Die Flexibilisierung des Erwerbsverlaufs. Eine Analyse von Einstiegs- und Ausstiegsprozessen in Ost- und Westdeutschland.* Wiesbaden: VS.
Buchholz, Sandra, et al. 2012. Sind leistungsschwache Jugendliche tatsächlich nicht ausbildungsfähig? Eine Längsschnittanalyse zur beruflichen Qualifizierung von Jugendlichen mit geringen kognitiven Kompetenzen im Nachbarland Schweiz. *Kölner Zeitschrift für Soziologie und Sozialpsychologie* 64 (4): 701–727.
Buchmann, Marlis. 1989a. *The script of life in modern society entry into adulthood in a changing world.* Chicago: University of Chicago Press.
———. 1989b. Die Dynamik von Standardisierung und Individualisierung im Lebenslauf. Der Übertritt ins Erwachsenenalter im sozialen Wandel fortgeschrittener Industriegesellschaften. In *Handlungsspielräume Untersuchungen zur Individualisierung und Institutionalisierung von Lebensläufen in der Moderne*, Hrsg. A. Weymann, 90–104. Stuttgart: Enke.
Buchmann, Marlis, and Irene Kriesi. 2011. Transition to adulthood in Europe. *Annual Review of Sociology* 37: 481–503.
Buchmann, Marlis, und Stefan Sacci. 1995. Zur Differenzierung von Berufsverläufen. Ein mehrdimensionaler Kohortenvergleich. In *Sozialstruktur und Lebenslauf*, Hrsg. P. Berger und P. Sopp. 49–64. Opladen: Leske + Budrich.
Büchtemann, Christoph, Jürgen Schupp, und Dana Soloff. 1993. Übergänge von der Schule in den Beruf – Deutschland und USA im Vergleich. *Mitteilungen aus der Arbeitsmarkt- und Berufsforschung* 26 (4): 507–520.
Bude, Heinz. 1987. *Deutsche Karrieren. Lebenskonstruktionen sozialer Aufsteiger aus der Flakhelfer-Generation.* Frankfurt: Suhrkamp.
———. 1995. *Das Altern einer Generation. Die Jahrgänge 1938 bis 1948.* Frankfurt: Suhrkamp.
———. 2000. Die biographische Relevanz der Generation. In *Generationen in Familie und Gesellschaft*, Hrsg. M. Kohli und M. Szydlik, 19–35. Opladen: Leske + Budrich.
———. 2005. "Generation" im Kontext Von den Kriegs- zu den Wohlfahrtsstaatsgenerationen. In *Generationen. Zur Relevanz eines wissenschaftlichen Grundbegriffs*, Hrsg. U. Jureit und M. Wildt, 28–44. Hamburg: Hamburger Edition.
Bühler, Charlotte. 1933. *Der menschliche Lebenslauf als psychologisches Problem.* Leipzig: Hirzel.
Bynner, John. 2005. Rethinking the youth phase of the life course. The case for emerging adulthood? *Journal of Youth Studies* 8 (4): 367–384.
———. 2016. Institutionalization of life course studies. In *Handbook of the life course*, Hrsg. M. Shanahan, J. Mortimer, und M. Johnson, 27–58. Cham: Springer.
Bynner, John, et al. 2009. Editorial: Longitudinal and life course studies. *Longitudinal and Life Course Studies* 1 (1): 3–10.
Cain, Leonard. 1964. Life course and social structure. In *Handbook of modern sociology*, ed. R. Faris, 272–309. Chicago: Rand McNally.
Caspi, Avshalom, Brent Roberts, and Rebecca Shiner. 2005. Personality development: Stability and change. *Annual Review of Psychology* 56: 453–484.
Castel, Robert. 2005. *Die Stärkung des Sozialen. Leben im neuen Wohlfahrtsstaat.* Hamburg: Hamburger Edition.
Castel, Robert, und Klaus Dörre, Hrsg. 2009. *Prekarität, Abstieg, Ausgrenzung. Die soziale Frage am Beginn des 21. Jahrhunderts.* Frankfurt: Campus.

Chanfrault-Duchet, Marie-F. 1995. Biographical research in former West Germany. *Current Sociology* 43 (2): 209–219.
Chudacoff, Howard. 1984. *How old are you? Age consciousness in American culture*. Princeton: Princeton University Press.
Clausen, John. 1986. *The life course. A sociological perspective*. Englewood Cliffs: Prentice-Hall.
———. 1991. Adolescent competence and the shaping of the life course. *American Journal of Sociology* 96 (4): 805–842.
———. 1993. *American lives. Looking back at the children of the Great Depression*. New York: Free Press.
———. 1995. Gender, contexts, and turning points in adults' lives. In *Examining lives in context: Perspectives on the ecology of human development*, ed. P. Moen, G. Elder, and K. Lüscher, 365–399. Washington: American Psychological Association.
Collins, Randall. 1992. The romanticism of agency/structure versus the analysis of micro/macro. *Current Sociology* 40 (1): 79–97.
Comte, Auguste. 1974. *Die Soziologie. Die positive Philosophie im Auszug*, 2. Aufl. Stuttgart: Kröner (frz. Orig.: 1839).
Cornwell, Benjamin. 2015. *Social sequence analysis. Methods and applications*. Cambridge: Cambridge University Press.
Corsten, Michael. 2001. Biographie, Lebenslauf und das "Problem der Generation". *BIOS* 14 (2): 32–59.
Cressey, Paul. 1932. *The taxi-dance hall: A sociological study in commercialized recreation and city life*. Chicago: University of Chicago Press.
Crockett, Lisa. 2002. Agency in the life course. Concepts and processes. In *Agency, motivation, and the life course*, ed. L. Crockett, 1–29. Lincoln: University of Nebraska Press.
Cunningham, Hugh. 2006. *Die Geschichte des Kindes in der Neuzeit*. Düsseldorf: Artemis & Winkler.
Dannefer, Dale. 2002. Whose life course is it, anyway? Diversity and "linked lives" in global perspective. In *Invitation to the life course. Toward new understandings of later life*, ed. R. Settersten, 259–268. Amityville: Baywood.
———. 2003. Cumulative advantage/disadvantage and the life course. Cross-fertilizing age and social science theory. *Journal of Gerontology (Social Sciences)* 58B (6): 327–337.
———. 2011. Age, the life course, and the sociological imagination: Prospects for theory. In *Handbook of aging and the social sciences*, ed. R. Binstock and L. George, 3–16. Amsterdam: Elsevier.
Dannefer, Dale, and Antje Daub. 2009. Extending the interrogation: Life span, life course, and the constitution of human aging. *Advances in Life Course Research* 14 (1–2): 15–27.
Dannefer, Dale, and Jessica Kelley-Moore. 2009. Theorizing the life course: New twists in the paths. In *Handbook of theories of aging*, ed. V. Bengtson et al., 2nd ed., 389–411. New York: Springer.
Dannefer, Dale, and Peter Uhlenberg. 1999. Paths of the life course: A typology. In *Handbook of theories of aging*, ed. V. Bengtson and K. Schaie, 306–326. New York: Springer.
Diewald, Martin. 2004. Die neue Arbeitsgesellschaft als ICH-AG. In *Das individualisierte Ich in der modernen Gesellschaft*, Hrsg. G. Nollmann und H. Strasser, 110–129. Frankfurt: Campus.

———. 2006. Spirals of success and failure? The interplay of control beliefs and working lives in the transition from planned to market economy. In *After the fall of the wall. Life courses in the transformation of East Germany*, ed. M. Diewald, A. Goedicke, and K.U. Mayer, 214–236. Stanford: Stanford University Press.
Diewald, Martin, and Karl Ulrich Mayer. 2009. The sociology of the life course and life span psychology: Integrated paradigm or complementing pathways? *Advances in Life Course Research* 14 (1–2): 5–14.
Diewald, Martin, und Stephanie Sill. 2004. Mehr Risiken, mehr Chancen? Trends in der Arbeitsmarktmobilität seit Mitte der 1980er Jahre. In *Beschäftigungsstabilität im Wandel?* Hrsg. O. Struck und C. Köhler, 39–62. München: Hampp.
Diewald, Martin, Heike Solga, and Anne Goedicke. 2006. Old assets, new liabilities? How did personal characteristics contribute to labor market success or failure after 1989? In *After the fall of the wall. Life courses in the transformation of East Germany*, ed. M. Diewald, A. Goedicke, and K.U. Mayer, 65–88. Stanford: Stanford University Press.
Dilthey, Wilhelm. 1961. Über das Studium der Geschichte der Wissenschaften vom Menschen, der Gesellschaft und dem Staat. In *Gesammelte Schriften*, Bd. V, 3. Aufl., Hrsg. W. Dilthey, 31–73. Stuttgart: Teubner (Orig.: 1875).
DiPrete, Thomas. 2002. Life course risks, mobility regimes, and mobility consequences. A comparison of Sweden, Germany, and the United States. *American Journal of Sociology* 108 (2): 267–309.
DiPrete, Thomas, and Gregory Eirich. 2006. Cumulative advantage as a mechanism for inequality. A review of theoretical and empirical developments. *Annual Review of Sociology* 32: 271–297.
Dobischat, Rolf. 2010. Schulische Berufsbildung im Gesamtsystem der beruflichen Bildung. Herausforderungen an der Übergangspassage von der Schule in den Beruf. In *Das Berufsbildungssystem in Deutschland Aktuelle Entwicklungen und Standpunkte*, Hrsg. G. Bosch, S. Krone, und D. Langer, 101–131. Wiesbaden: VS.
Easterlin, Richard. 1980. *Birth and fortune: The impact of numbers on personal welfare*. New York: Basic Books.
Ebaugh, Helen. 1988. *Becoming an ex. The process of role exit*. Chicago: University of Chicago Press.
Eisenstadt, Shmuel. 1956. *From generation to generation: Age groups and social structure*. Glencoe: Free Press.
Elchardus, Mark, and Wendy Smits. 2006. The persistence of the standardized life cycle. *Time & Society* 15 (2/3): 303–326.
Elder, Glen. 1974. *Children of the Great depression. Social change in life experience*. Chicago: University of Chicago Press.
———. 1975. Age differentiation and the life course. *Annual Review of Sociology* 1: 165–190.
———. 1979. Historical change in life patterns and personality. In *Life-span development and behavior*, ed. P. Baltes and O. Brim, vol. 2, 117–159. New York: Academic Press.
———. 1985. Perspectives on the life course. In *Life course dynamics: Transitions and trajectories, 1968–1980*, ed. G. Elder, 23–49. Ithaca: Cornell University Press.
———. 1986. Military times and turning points in men's lives. *Developmental Psychology* 22 (2): 233–245.

———. 1999. *Children of the Great depression. Social change in life experience*, (25th anniversary) ed. Bolder: Westview Press.
Elder, Glen, und Avsholm Caspi. 1990. Die Entstehung der Lebensverlaufsforschung. In *Lebensverläufe und sozialer Wandel*, Hrsg. K. U. Mayer, 22–57. Opladen: Westdeutscher Verlag (KZfSS-Sonderheft 31).
Elder, Glen, and Michael Shanahan. 2006. The life course and human development. In *Theoretical models of human development (Handbook of child psychology; vol. 1)*, ed. R. Lerner, 6th ed., 665–715. Hoboken: Wiley.
Elder, Glen, Monica Johnson, and Robert Crosnoe. 2003. The emergence and development of life course theory. In *Handbook of the life course*, ed. J. Mortimer and M. Shanahan, 3–19. New York: Kluwer/Plenum.
Elias, Norbert. 1992a. Entwurf zu einer Theorie der Zivilisation. In *Über den Prozess der Zivilisation. Soziogenetische Soziogenetische und psychogenetische Untersuchungen*, Bd. 2, 17. Aufl., Hrsg. N. Elias, 312–454. Frankfurt: Suhrkamp (Orig.: 1939).
———. 1992b. *Über den Prozess der Zivilisation. Soziogenetische und psychogenetische Untersuchungen*, Bd. 2, 17. Aufl. Frankfurt: Suhrkamp (Orig.: 1939).
Elman, Cheryl, and Angela O'Rand. 2004. The race is to the swift. Socioeconomic origins, adult education, and wage attainment. *American Journal of Sociology* 110 (1): 123–160.
Elwert, Georg, und Martin Kohli. 1990. Einleitung. In *Im Lauf der Zeit*, Hrsg. G. Elwert, M. Kohli, und H. Müller, 3–9. Saarbrücken: Breitenbach.
Elwert, Georg, Martin Kohli, und Harald Müller, Hrsg. 1990. *Im Lauf der Zeit. Ethnologische Studien zur gesellschaftlichen Konstruktion von Lebensaltern*. Saarbrücken: Breitenbach.
Elzinga, Cees, and Aart Liefbroer. 2007. De-standardization of family-life trajectories of young adults. A cross-national comparison using sequence analysis. *European Journal of Population* 23 (3/4): 225–250.
Emirbayer, Mustafa, and Ann Mische. 1998. What is agency? *American Journal of Sociology* 103 (4): 962–1023.
Erikson, Erik. 1959. *Identity and the life cycle: Selected papers*. New York: International University Press.
Erlinghagen, Marcel. 2004. *Die Restrukturierung des Arbeitsmarktes. Arbeitsmarktmobilität und Beschäftigungsstabilität im Zeitverlauf*. Wiesbaden: VS.
Erzberger, Christian. 2001. Sequenzmusteranalyse als fallorientierte Analysestrategie. In *Strukturen des Lebenslaufs. Übergang – Sequenz – Verlauf*, Hrsg. R. Sackmann und M. Wingens, 135–162. Weinheim: Juventa.
Esping-Anderson, Gøsta. 1990. *The three worlds of welfare capitalism*. Cambridge: Polity Press.
Ette, Andreas, Kerstin Ruckdeschel, und Rainer Unger, Hrsg. 2010. *Potenziale intergenerationaler Beziehungen. Chancen und Herausforderungen für die Gestaltung des demografischen Wandels*. Würzburg: Ergon.
Falk, Susanne. 2005. *Geschlechtsspezifische Ungleichheit im Erwerbsverlauf. Analysen für den deutschen Arbeitsmarkt*. Wiesbaden: VS.
Feller, Gisela. 2002. Leistungen und Defizite der Berufsfachschule als Bildungsgang mit Berufsabschluss. In *Bildung und Berufsausbildung und berufsstruktureller Wandel in der Wissensgesellschaft*, Hrsg. M. Wingens und R. Sackmann, 139–157. Weinheim: Juventa.
Fietze, Beate. 2009. *Historische Generationen. Über einen sozialen Mechanismus kulturellen Wandels und kollektiver Kreativität*. Bielefeld: transcript.

Fischer, Wolfram, und Martin Kohli. 1987. Biographieforschung. In *Methoden der Biographie- und Lebenslaufforschung*, Hrsg. W. Voges, 25–49. Opladen: Leske + Budrich.
Fischer-Rosenthal, Wolfram. 1990. Von der "biographischen Methode" zur Biographieforschung: Versuch einer Standortbestimmung. In *Biographieforschung Eine Zwischenbilanz in der deutschen Soziologie*, Hrsg. P. Alheit, W. Fischer-Rosenthal, und E. Hoerning, 11–32. Bremen: Universität Bremen.
Flaherty, Michael, and Gary Fine. 2001. Present, past, and future. Conjugating George Herbert Mead's perspective on time. *Time & Society* 10 (2/3): 147–161.
Fogt, Helmut. 1982. *Politische Generationen. Empirische Bedeutung und theoretisches Modell*. Opladen: Westdeutscher Verlag.
Foner, Anne, and David Kertzer. 1978. Transitions over the life course: Lessons from age-set societies. *American Journal of Sociology* 83 (5): 1081–1104.
Friebel, Harry, et al. 2000. *Bildungsbeteiligung: Chancen und Risiken. Eine Längsschnittstudie über Bildungs- und Weiterbildungskarrieren in der "Moderne"*. Opladen: Leske + Budrich.
Fry, Christine. 2002. The life course as a cultural construct. In *Invitation to the life course. Toward new understandings of later life*, ed. R. Settersten, 269–294. Amityville: Baywood.
Fuchs, Werner. 1983. Jugendliche Statuspassage oder individualisierte Jugendbiographie? *Soziale Welt* 34 (3): 341–371.
Fuchs, Stephan. 2001. Beyond agency. *Sociological Theory* 19 (1): 24–40.
Fuchs-Heinritz, Werner. 1998. Soziologische Biographieforschung: Überblick und Verhältnis zur allgemeinen Soziologie. In *Biographische Methoden in den Humanwissenschaften*, Hrsg. G. Jüttemann und H. Thomae, 3–23. Weinheim: Beltz.
———. 2009. *Biographische Forschung: Eine Einführung in Praxis und Methoden*, 4. Aufl. Wiesbaden: VS.
Fussel, Elizabeth, and Frank Furstenberg. 2005. The transition to adulthood during the twentieth century. Race, nativity, and gender. In *On the frontier of adulthood. Theory, research, and public policy*, ed. R. Settersten, F. Furstenberg, and R. Rumbaut, 29–75. Chicago: University of Chicago Press.
Gamoran, Adam, and Robert Mare. 1989. Secondary school tracking and educational inequality. Compensation, reinforcement, or neutrality? *American Journal of Sociology* 94 (5): 1146–1183.
Geertz, Clifford. 1973. Thick description. Toward an interpretive theory of culture. In *The interpretation of cultures selected essays*, ed. C. Geertz, 3–30. New York: Basic Books.
Geissler, Birgit. 2004a. Das Individuum im Wohlfahrtsstaat. *Lebenslaufpolitikund Lebensplanung. Zeitschrift für Sozialreform* 50 (1–2): 105–125.
Geißler, Rainer. 2004b. Die Illusion der Chancengleichheit im Bildungssystem – von PISA gestört. *Zeitschrift für Soziologie der Erziehung und Sozialisation* 24 (4): 362–380.
Geissler, Birgit, und Mechthild Oechsle. 1996. *Lebensplanung junger Frauen. Zur widersprüchlichen Modernisierung weiblicher Lebensverläufe*. Weinheim: Deutscher Studien-Verlag.
George, Linda. 1993. Sociological perspectives on life transitions. *Annual Review of Sociology* 19: 353–373.
———. 2003. Life course research. Achievements and potential. In *Handbook of the life course*, ed. J. Mortimer and M. Shanahan, 671–680. New York: Kluwer/Plenum.

References

Gestrich, Andreas. 1999. *Geschichte der Familie im 19. und 20. Jahrhundert.* München: Oldenbourg.
Giddens, Anthony. 1989. *The constitution of society. Outline of the theory of structuration.* Cambridge: Polity Press.
Giele, Janet, and Glen Elder. 1998. Life course research: Development of a field. In *Methods of life course research: Qualitative and quantitative approaches*, ed. J. Giele and G. Elder, 5–27. London: Sage.
Giesecke, Johannes, und Jan Heisig. 2010. Destabilisierung und Destandardisierung, aber für wen? Die Entwicklung der westdeutschen Arbeitsplatzmobilität seit 1984. *Kölner Zeitschrift für Soziologie und Sozialpsychologie* 62 (3): 403–435.
Gillis, John. 1980. *Geschichte der Jugend.* Weinheim: Beltz.
Glaser, Barney, and Anselm Strauss. 1971. *Status passage: A formal theory.* Chicago: Aldine-Atherton.
Glenn, Norval. 1977. *Cohort analysis.* Beverly Hills: Sage.
———. 2003. Distinguishing age, period, and cohort effects. In *Handbook of the life course*, ed. J. Mortimer and M. Shanahan, 465–476. New York: Kluwer/Plenum.
Goffman, Erving. 1961. *Asylums. Essays on the social situation of mental patients and other inmates.* Chicago: Aldine.
Goldin, Claudia. 2006. The quiet revolution that transformed women's employment, education, and family. *American Economic Review* 96 (2): 1–21.
Goodson, Ivor, ed. 2016. *The Routledge international handbook on narrative and life history.* Milton: Taylor and Francis.
Gottschall, Karin. 2000. *Soziale Ungleichheit und Geschlecht. Kontinuitäten und Brüche, Sackgassen und Erkenntnispotentiale im deutschen soziologischen Diskurs.* Opladen: Leske + Budrich.
Granovetter, Mark. 1973. The strength of weak ties. *American Journal of Sociology* 78 (6): 1360–1380.
Groß, Martin. 2008. *Klassen, Schichten, Mobilität. Eine Einführung.* Wiesbaden: VS.
Guillemard, Anne-Marie. 1991. Die Destandardisierung des Lebenslaufs in den europäischen Wohlfahrtsstaaten. *Zeitschrift für Sozialreform* 37 (10): 620–639.
Hagestad, Gunhild. 1991. Trends and dilemmas in life course research: An international perspective. In *Theoretical advances in life course research*, ed. W. Heinz, 23–57. Weinheim: Deutscher Studien-Verlag.
Hall, Anja. 2012. Lohnen sich schulische und duale Ausbildung gleichermaßen? Bildungserträge von Frauen und Männern im Vergleich. In *Soziologische Bildungsforschung*, Hrsg. R. Becker und H. Solga, 281–301. Wiesbaden: Springer VS (KZfSS-Sonderheft 52).
Hall, Peter, and David Soskice. 2001. An introduction to varieties of capitalism. In *Varieties of capitalism. The institutional foundations of comparative advantage*, ed. P. Hall and D. Soskice, 1–68. Oxford: Oxford University Press.
Han, Shin-Kap, and Phyllis Moen. 1999. Clocking out. Temporal patterning of retirement. *American Journal of Sociology* 105 (1): 191–236.
Hardach, Gerd. 2006. *Der Generationenvertrag – Lebenslauf und Lebenseinkommen in Deutschland in zwei Jahrhunderten.* Berlin: Duncker & Humblot.
Hardering, Friedericke. 2011. *Unsicherheiten in Arbeit und Biographie. Zur Ökonomisierung der Lebensführung.* Wiesbaden: VS.

Hareven, Tamara. 1982. *Family time and industrial time. The relationship between the family and work in a New England industrial community.* Cambridge: Cambridge University Press.
Hareven, Tamara, and Kanji Masaoka. 1988. Turning points and transitions. Perceptions of the life course. *Journal of Family History* 13 (3): 271–289.
Harrison, Barbara, ed. 2009. *Life story research (Bd. 1–4).* Los Angeles: Sage.
Hausen, Karin. 1976. Die Polarisierung der "Geschlechtscharaktere" – eine Spiegelung der Dissoziation von Erwerbs- und Familienleben. In *Sozialgeschichte der Familie in der Neuzeit Europas: Neue Forschungen,* Hrsg. W. Conze, 363–393. Stuttgart: Klett-Cotta.
Havighurst, Robert. 1948. *Developmental tasks and education.* Chicago: University of Chicago Press.
Heckhausen, Jutta. 1990. Erwerb und Funktion normativer Vorstellungen über den Lebenslauf. Ein entwicklungspsychologischer Beitrag zur sozio-psychischen Konstruktion von Biographien. In *Lebensverläufe und sozialer Wandel,* Hrsg. K.U. Mayer, 251–373. Opladen: Westdeutscher Verlag.
———. 1999. *Developmental regulation in adulthood. Age-normative and sociostructural constraints as adaptive challenges.* Cambridge: Cambridge University Press.
Heinz, Walter. 1996. Status passages as micro-macro linkages in life course research. In *Society and biography. Interrelations between social structure, institutions and the life course,* ed. A. Weymann and W. Heinz, 51–65. Weinheim: Deutscher Studien-Verlag.
———. 2000. Selbstsozialisation im Lebenslauf. Umrisse einer Theorie biographischen Handelns. In *Biographische Sozialisation,* Hrsg. E. Hoerning, 165–186. Stuttgart: Lucius & Lucius.
———. 2003a. From work trajectories to negotiated careers. The contingent work life course. In *Handbook of the life course,* ed. J. Mortimer and M. Shanahan, 185–204. New York: Kluwer/Plenum.
———. 2003b. Introduction. In *Social dynamics of the life course. Transitions, institutions, and interrelations,* ed. W. Heinz and V. Marshall. New York: Aldine de Gruyter.
Heinz, Walter, and Helga Krüger. 2001. Life course: Innovations and challenges for social research. *Current Sociology* 49 (2): 29–45.
Heinz, Walter, et al. 2009. General introduction. In *The life course reader. Individuals and societies across time,* ed. W. Heinz et al., 15–30. Frankfurt: Campus.
Held, Thomas. 1986. Institutionalization and deinstitutionalization of the life course. *Human Development* 29 (3): 157–162.
Hendricks, Jon. 2001. It's about time. In *Aging and the meaning of time,* ed. S. McFadden and R. Atchley, 21–50. New York: Springer.
Herbert, Ulrich. 2003. Drei politische Generationen im des 20. Jahrhunderts. In *Generationalität und Lebensgeschichte im 20. Jahrhundert,* Hrsg. J. Reulecke, 95–114. München: Oldenbourg.
Hesse, Jürgen, und Hans Schrader. 2007. *Praxismappe: So schreiben Sie einen überzeugenden Lebenslauf.* Frankfurt: Eichborn.
Hillmert, Steffen. 2001. *Ausbildungssysteme und Arbeitsmarkt. Lebensverläufe in Großbritannien und Deutschland im Kohortenvergleich.* Wiesbaden: Westdeutscher Verlag.
———. 2002. Stabilität und Wandel des "deutschen Modells". Lebensverläufe im Übergang zwischen Schule und Beruf. In *Bildung und Beruf Ausbildung und berufsstruktureller*

Wandel in der Wissensgesellschaft, Hrsg. M. Wingens und R. Sackmann, 65–82. Weinheim: Juventa.

———. 2005. From old to new structures. A long-term comparison of the transition to adulthood in West and East Germany. In *The structure of the life course: Standardized? Individualized? Differentiated?* ed. R. Macmillan, 151–173. Amsterdam: Elsevier.

Hillmert, Steffen, und Marita Jacob. 2003. Bildungsprozesse zwischen Diskontinuität und Karriere: Das Phänomen der Mehrfachausbildungen. *Zeitschrift für Soziologie* 32 (4): 325–345.

Hillmert, Steffen, und Karl Ulrich Mayer, Hrsg. 2004. *Geboren 1964 und 1971. Neuere Untersuchungen zu Ausbildungs- und Berufschancen in Westdeutschland*. Wiesbaden: VS.

Hitlin, Steven, and Glen Elder. 2006. Agency – An empirical model of an abstract concept. *Advances in Life Course Research* 11: 33–67.

———. 2007. Time, self, and the curiously abstract concept of agency. *Sociological Theory* 25 (2): 170–190.

Hitlin, Steven, and Monica Johnson. 2015. Reconceptualizing agency within the life course. The power of looking ahead. *American Journal of Sociology* 120 (5): 1429–1472.

Hoerning, Erika. 1987. Lebensereignisse Übergänge im Lebenslauf. In *Methoden der Biographie- und Lebenslaufforschung*, Hrsg. W. Voges, 231–259. Opladen: Leske + Budrich.

Hofäcker, Dirk. 2015. In line or at odds with active ageing policies? Exploring patterns of retirement preferences in Europe. *Ageing & Society* 35 (7): 1529–1556.

Hofferth, Sandra, and Frances Goldscheider. 2016. Family heterogeneity over the life course. In *Handbook of the life course*, ed. M. Shanahan, J. Mortimer, and M. Johnson, vol. II, 161–178. Cham: Springer.

Hogan, Dennis. 1978. The variable order of events in the life course. *Annual Sociological Review* 43 (4): 573–586.

———. 1980. The transition to adulthood as a career contingency. *Annual Sociological Review* 45 (2): 261–276.

Hogan, Dennis, and Nan Astone. 1986. The transition to adulthood. *Annual Review of Sociology* 12: 109–130.

Hoggett, Paul. 2001. Agency, rationality and social policy. *Journal of Social Policy* 30 (1): 37–56.

Honig, Michael. 1999. *Entwurf einer Theorie der Kindheit*. Frankfurt: Suhrkamp.

Huinink, Johannes. 1995. *Warum noch Familie? Zur Attraktivität von Partnerschaft und Elternschaft in unserer Gesellschaft*. Frankfurt: Campus.

———. 2013. De-standardisation or changing life course patterns? Transition to adulthood from a demographic perspective. In *The demography of Europe*, ed. G. Neyer et al., 99–118. Dordrecht: Springer.

Huinink, Johannes, und Michael Wagner. 1998. Individualisierung und die Pluralisierung der Lebensformen. In *Die Individualisierungs-These*, Hrsg. J. Friedrichs, 85–106. Opladen: Leske + Budrich.

Huinink, Johannes, Karl Ulrich Mayer, et al. 1995. *Kollektiv und Eigensinn. Lebensverläufe in der DDR und danach*. Berlin: Akademie.

Hurrelmann, Klaus. 2003. Der entstrukturierte Lebenslauf. Die Auswirkungen der Expansion der Jugendphase. *Zeitschrift für Soziologie der Erziehung und Sozialisation* 23 (2): 115–126.

Imhof, Arthur. 1984a. Von der unsicheren zur sicheren Lebenszeit. Ein folgenschwerer Wandel im Verlaufe der Neuzeit. *Vierteljahresschrift für Sozial- und Wirtschaftsgeschichte* 71 (2): 175–198.

———. 1984b. *Die verlorenen Welten. Alltagsbewältigung durch unsere Vorfahren – und weshalb wir uns heute so schwer damit tun*. München: Beck.

———. 1988. *Von der unsicheren zur sicheren Lebenszeit. Fünf historisch-demographische Studien*. Darmstadt: Wissenschaftliche Buchgesellschaft.

International Labour Organisation. 2013. *Marking progress against child labour*. Geneva: ILO.

Jäckle, Sebastian. 2017. Sequenzanalyse. In *Neue Trends in den Sozialwissenschaften. Innovative Techniken für qualitative und quantitative Forschung*, Hrsg. S. Jäckle, 333–363. Wiesbaden: Springer VS.

Jacob, Marita. 2004. *Mehrfachausbildung in Deutschland: Karriere, Collage, Kompensation?* Wiesbaden: VS.

Jaeger, Hans. 1977. Generationen in der Geschichte. Überlegungen zu einer umstrittenen Konzeption. *Geschichte und Gesellschaft* 3 (4): 429–452.

Jahoda, Marie, Paul Lazarsfeld, und Hans Zeisel. 1933. *Die Arbeitslosen von Marienthal. Ein soziographischer Versuch über die Wirkungen langdauernder Arbeitslosigkeit*. Leipzig: Hirzel.

Joerissen, Peter, und Cornelia Will. 1984. *Die Lebenstreppe Bilder der menschlichen Lebensalter*. Köln: Verlag Rheinland.

Junge, Matthias. 2002. *Individualisierung*. Frankfurt: Campus.

Jungert, Michael, et al., Hrsg. 2010. *Interdisziplinarität. Theorie, Praxis, Probleme*. Darmstadt: Wissenschaftliche Buchgesellschaft.

Jureit, Ulrike. 2006. *Generationenforschung*. Göttingen: Vandenhoeck & Ruprecht.

Kaufmann, Franz-Xaver. 1993. Generationenbeziehungen und Generationenverhältnisse im Wohlfahrtsstaat. In *Generationenbeziehungen in "postmodernen" Gesellschaften*, Hrsg. K. Lüscher und F. Schultheis, 95–108. Konstanz: Universitätsverlag.

———. 2002. *Sozialpolitik und Sozialstaat. Soziologische Analysen*. Opladen: Leske + Budrich.

Keith, Jennie, et al. 1994. *The aging experience. Diversity and commonality across cultures*. Thousand Oaks: Sage.

Kerckhoff, Alan. 2003. From student to worker. In *Handbook of the life course*, ed. J. Mortimer and M. Shanahan, 251–267. New York: Kluwer/Plenum.

Kertzer, David. 1983. Generation as a sociological problem. *Annual Review of Sociology* 9: 125–149.

Kertzer, David, and Jennie Keith, eds. 1984. *Age and anthropological theory*. Ithaka: Cornell University Press.

Keupp, Heiner, und Joachim Hohl, Hrsg. 2006. *Subjektdiskurse im gesellschaftlichen Wandel. Zur Theorie des Subjekts in der Spätmoderne*. Bielefeld: transcript.

Keupp, Heiner, et al. 1999. *Identitätskonstruktionen. Das Patchwork der Identitäten in der Spätmoderne*. Reinbek: Rowohlt.

Klein, Hugh. 1990a. Adolescence, youth, and young adulthood. Rethinking current conceptualizations of life stage. *Youth and Society* 21 (4): 446–471.

Klein, Julie. 1990b. *Interdisciplinarity: History, theory, and practice*. Detroit: Wayne State University Press.

Klein, Thomas, und Wolfgang Lauterbach, Hrsg. 1999. *Nichteheliche Lebensgemeinschaften. Analysen zum Wandel partnerschaftlicher Lebensformen.* Opladen: Leske + Budrich.

Klein, Thomas, Andrea Lengerer, und Michaela Uzelac. 2002. Partnerschaftliche Lebensformen im internationalen Vergleich. *Zeitschrift für Bevölkerungswissenschaft* 27 (3): 359–379.

Kocka, Jürgen, Hrsg. 1987. *Interdisziplinarität. Praxis – Herausforderung – Ideologie.* Frankfurt: Suhrkamp.

Koebner, Thomas, Rolf-Peter Janz, und Frank Trommler, Hrsg. 1985. *"Mit uns zieht die neue Zeit" – der Mythos Jugend.* Frankfurt: Suhrkamp.

Kohli, Martin, Hrsg. 1978a. *Soziologie des Lebenslaufs.* Darmstadt: Luchterhand.

———. 1978b. Erwartungen an eine Soziologie des Lebenslaufs. In *Soziologie des Lebenslaufs*, Hrsg. M. Kohli, 9–31. Darmstadt: Luchterhand.

———. 1980. Lebenslauftheoretische Ansätze in der Sozialisationsforschung. In *Handbuch der Sozialisationsforschung*, Hrsg. K. Hurrelmann und D. Ulich, 299–317. Weinheim: Beltz.

———. 1981. Wie es zur "biographischen Methode" kam und was daraus geworden ist. *Zeitschrift für Soziologie* 10 (3): 273–293.

———. 1983. Thesen zur Geschichte des Lebenslaufs als sozialer Institution. In *Gerontologie und Sozialgeschichte. Wege zu einer historischen Betrachtung des Alters*, Hrsg. C. Conrad und H.-J. von Kondratowitz, 133–147. Berlin: DZA.

———. 1985. Die Institutionalisierung des Lebenslaufs. Historische Befunde und theoretische Argumente. *Kölner Zeitschrift für Soziologie und Sozialpsychologie* 37 (1): 1–29.

———. 1986a. Gesellschaftszeit und Lebenszeit. Der Lebenslauf im Strukturwandel der Moderne. In *Die Moderne – Kontinuitäten und Zäsuren*, Hrsg. J. Berger, 183–208. Göttingen: Schwartz.

———. 1986b. Social organization and subjective construction of the life course. In *Human development and the life course: Multidisciplinary perspectives*, ed. A. Sørensen, F. Weinert, and L. Sherrod, 271–292. Hillsdale: Erlbaum.

———. 1986c. The world we forgot. A historical review of the life course. In *Later life. The social psychology of aging*, ed. V. Marshall, 271–303. Beverly Hills: Sage.

———. 1988. Normalbiographie und Individualität. Zur institutionellen Dynamik des gegenwärtigen Lebenslaufregimes. In *Vom Ende des Individuums zur Individualität ohne Ende*, Hrsg. H.-G. Brose und B. Hildenbrand, 33–53. Opladen: Leske + Budrich.

———. 2007. The institutionalization of the life course: Looking back to look ahead. *Research in Human Development* 4 (3–4): 253–271.

Kohli, Martin, und Marc Szydlik, Hrsg. 2000. *Generationen in Familie und Gesellschaft.* Opladen: Leske + Budrich.

Kohlrausch, Bettina. 2012. Das Übergangssystem – Übergänge mit System? In *Handbuch Bildungs- und Erziehungssoziologie*, Hrsg. U. Bauer, U. Bittlingmayer, und A. Scherr, 595–609. Wiesbaden: Springer VS.

Konietzka, Dirk. 1999. *Ausbildung und Beruf. Die Geburtsjahrgänge 1919–1961 auf dem Weg von der Schule in das Erwerbsleben.* Opladen: Westdeutscher Verlag.

———. 2002. Die soziale Differenzierung der Übergangsmuster in den Beruf. Die "zweite Schwelle" im Vergleich der Berufseinstiegskohorten 1976–1995. *Kölner Zeitschrift für Soziologie und Sozialpsychologie* 54 (4): 674–693.

———. 2010. *Zeiten des Übergangs. Sozialer Wandel des Übergangs in das Erwachsenenalter.* Wiesbaden: VS.

———. 2011. Die Verkopplung und Ordnung von Statusübergängen. Der Übergang in das Erwachsenenalter in kohortenvergleichender Perspektive. *BIOS* 24 (1): 3–28.

———. 2016. Berufliche Ausbildung und der Übergang in den Arbeitsmarkt. In *Bildung als Privileg. Erklärungen und Befunde zu den Ursachen der Bildungsungleichheit*, 5. Aufl., Hrsg. R. Becker und W. Lauterbach, 315–344. Wiesbaden: Springer VS.

Konietzka, Dirk, und Johannes Huinink. 2003. Die De-Standardisierung einer Statuspassage? Zum Wandel des Auszugs aus dem Elternhaus und des Übergangs in das Erwachsenenalter in Westdeutschland. *Soziale Welt* 54 (3): 285–312.

Konietzka, Dirk, und Michaela Kreyenfeld, Hrsg. 2007. *Ein Leben ohne Kinder. Kinderlosigkeit in Deutschland.* Wiesbaden: VS.

Koselleck, Reinhart. 1979. "Erfahrungsraum" und "Erwartungshorizont" – zwei historische Kategorien. In *Vergangene Zukunft. Zur Semantik geschichtlicher Zeiten*, Hrsg. R. Koselleck, 349–375. Frankfurt: Suhrkamp.

Krätschmer-Hahn, Rabea. 2012. *Kinderlosigkeit in Deutschland. Zum Verhältnis von Fertilität und Sozialstruktur.* Wiesbaden: VS.

Kress, Ulrike. 1998. Vom Normalarbeitsverhältnis zur Flexibilisierung – Ein Literaturbericht. *Mitteilungen aus der Arbeitsmarkt- und Berufsforschung* 31 (3): 488–505.

Kron, Thomas, Hrsg. 2000. *Individualisierung und soziologische Theorie.* Opladen: Leske+Budrich.

Kronauer, Martin, und Gudrun Linne, Hrsg. 2005. *Flexicurity – Die Suche nach Sicherheit in der Flexibilität.* Berlin: Edition Sigma.

Krüger, Helga. 1995. Prozessuale Ungleichheit. Geschlecht und Institutionenverknüpfungen im Lebenslauf. In *Sozialstruktur und Lebenslauf*, Hrsg. P. Berger und P. Sopp. 133–153. Opladen: Leske + Budrich.

———. 1996. Die andere Bildungssegmentation. Berufssysteme und soziale Ungleichheit zwischen den Geschlechtern. In *Die Wiederentdeckung der Ungleichheit. Aktuelle Tendenzen in Bildung und Arbeit*, Hrsg. A. Bolder et al., 252–274. Opladen: Leske + Budrich.

———. 2001. Geschlecht, Territorien, Institutionen. Beitrag zu einer Soziologie der Lebenslauf-Relationalität. In *Individualisierung und Verflechtung. Geschlecht und Generation im deutschen Lebenslaufregime*, Hrsg. C. Born und H. Krüger, 257–299. Weinheim: Juventa.

———. 2003. The life-course regime. Ambiguities between interrelatedness and individualization. In *Social dynamics of the life course. Transitions, institutions, and interrelations*, ed. W. Heinz und V. Marshall, 33–56. New York: Aldine de Gruyter.

Krüger, Helga, und René Levy. 2000. Masterstatus, Familie und Geschlecht. Vergessene Verknüpfungslogiken zwischen Institutionen des Lebenslaufs. *Berliner Journal für Soziologie* 10 (3): 379–401.

Kudera, Werner, und Gerd Voß, Hrsg. 2000. *Lebensführung und Gesellschaft. Beiträge zu Konzept und Empirie alltäglicher Lebensführung.* Opladen: Leske + Budrich.

Künemund, Harald, und Marc Szydlik, Hrsg. 2009. *Generationen Multidisziplinäre Perspektiven.* Wiesbaden: VS.

Lange, Andreas, und Frank Lettke, Hrsg. 2006. *Generationen und Familien. Analysen – Konzepte – gesellschaftliche Spannungsfelder.* Frankfurt: Suhrkamp.

Lauterbach, Wolfgang. 1994. *Berufsverläufe von Frauen. Erwerbstätigkeit, Unterbrechung und Wiedereintritt*. Frankfurt: Campus.
Leggewie, Claus. 1995. *Die 89er. Portrait einer Generation*. Hamburg: Hoffmann und Campe.
Leisering, Lutz. 2000. Wohlfahrtsstaatliche Generationen. In *Generationen in Familie und Gesellschaft*, Hrsg. M. Kohli und M. Szydlik, 59–76. Opladen: Leske + Budrich.
———. 2002. Ein moderner Lebenslauf in der Volksrepublik China? Zur Generalisierbarkeit eines Forschungsprogramms. In *Lebenszeiten. Erkundungen zur Soziologie der Generationen*, Hrsg. J. Wolf und G. Burkhart, 25–40. Opladen: Leske + Budrich.
———. 2003. Government and the life course. In *Handbook of the life course*, ed. J. Mortimer and M. Shanahan, 205–225. New York: Kluwer/Plenum.
Leisering, Lutz, and Karl Schumann. 2003. How institutions shape the German life course. In *Social dynamics of the life course. Transitions, institutions, and interrelations*, ed. W. Heinz and V. Marshall, 193–209. New York: Aldine de Gruyter.
Lengerer, Andrea. 2011. *Partnerlosigkeit in Deutschland. Entwicklung und soziale Unterschiede*. Wiesbaden: VS.
Leuze, Kathrin. 2010. *Smooth path or long and winding road? How institutions shape the transition from higher education to work*. Opladen: Budrich UniPress.
Levy, Jonah. 2010. Welfare retrenchment. In *The Oxford handbook of the welfare state*, ed. F. Castles et al., 552–568. Oxford: Oxford University Press.
Levy, René, und Eric Widmer, Hrsg. 2013. *Gendered life courses between standardization and individualisation. A European approach applied to Switzerland*. Zürich: Lit.
Lex, Tilly, und Boris Geier. 2010. Übergangssystem in der beruflichen Bildung. Wahrnehmung einer zweiten Chance oder Risiken des Ausstiegs? In *Das Berufsbildungssystem in Deutschland. Aktuelle Entwicklungen und Standpunkte*, Hrsg. G. Bosch, S. Krone, und D. Langer, 165–187. Wiesbaden: VS.
Liebau, Eckart, Hrsg. 1999. *Das Generationenverhältnis. Über das Zusammenleben in Familie und Gesellschaft*. Weinheim: Juventa.
Lindenberg, Siegwart. 1985. An assessment of the new political economy. Its potential for the social sciences and for sociology in particular. *Social Theory* 3 (1): 99–114.
Linton, Ralph. 1940. A neglected aspect of social organization. *American Journal of Sociology* 45 (6): 870–886.
———. 1942. Age and sex categories. *American Sociological Review* 7 (5): 589–603.
Longitudinal and Life Course Studies (2009ff).
Lucas, Samuel. 1999. *Tracking inequality. Stratification and mobility in American high schools*. New York: Teachers College Press.
———. 2001. Effectively maintained inequality. Education transitions, track mobility, and background effects. *American Journal of Sociology* 106 (6): 1642–1690.
Luhmann, Niklas. 1989. Individuum, Individualität, Individualismus. In *Gesellschaftsstruktur und Semantik Studien zur Wissenssoziologie der modernen Gesellschaft*, 3. Aufl., Hrsg. N. Luhmann, 149–258. Frankfurt: Suhrkamp.
Luhmann, Niklas, und Karl-Eberhard Schorr. 1979. *Reflexionsprobleme im Erziehungssystem*. Stuttgart: Klett-Cotta.
Lüscher, Kurt, und Ludwig Liegle. 2003. *Generationenbeziehungen in Familie und Gesellschaft*. Konstanz: UVK.

Lüscher, Kurt, und Franz Schultheis, Hrsg. 1993. *Generationenbeziehungen in "postmodernen" Gesellschaften.* Konstanz: Universitätsverlag.

Lutz, Burkart. 1984. *Der kurze Traum immerwährender Prosperität. Eine Neuinterpretation der industriell-kapitalistischen Entwicklung im Europa des 20 Jahrhunderts.* Frankfurt: Campus.

Maase, Kaspar. 2005. Farbige Bescheidenheit. Anmerkungen zum postheroischen Generationsverständnis. In *Generationen. Zur Relevanz eines wissenschaftlichen Grundbegriffs,* Hrsg. U. Jureit und M. Wildt, 220–242. Hamburg: Hamburger Edition.

Maatz, Kai, Jürgen Baumert, und Ulrich Trautwein. 2009. Genese sozialer Ungleichheit im institutionellen Kontext der Schule. Wo entsteht und vergrößert sich soziale Ungleichheit? In *Bildungsentscheidungen,* Hrsg. J. Baumert, K. Maatz, und U. Trautwein, 11–46. Wiesbaden: VS.

Macmillan, Ross, ed. 2005. *The structure of the life course: Standardized? Individualized? Differentiated?* Amsterdam: Elsevier.

Macmillan, Ross, and Scott Eliason. 2003. Characterizing the life course as role configurations and pathways. A latent structure approach. In *Handbook of the life course,* ed. J. Mortimer and M. Shanahan, 529–554. New York: Kluwer/Plenum.

Macunovich, Diane. 2002. *Birth quake. The baby boom and its aftershocks.* Chicago: University of Chicago Press.

Mannheim, Karl. 1964. Das Problem der Generationen. In *Wissenssoziologie. Auswahl aus dem Werk,* Hrsg. K. Mannheim, 509–565. Neuwied: Luchterhand (Orig.: 1928).

Marini, Margaret. 1984. Age and sequencing norms in the transition to adulthood. *Social Forces* 93 (1): 229–244.

Marshall, Victor. 2005. Agency, events, and structure at the end of the life course. In *Towards an interdisciplinary perspective on the life course,* ed. R. Levy et al., 57–91. Amsterdam: Elsevier.

Marshall, Victor, and Margaret Mueller. 2003. Theoretical roots of the life-course perspective. In *Social dynamics of the life course. Transitions, institutions, and interrelations,* ed. W. Heinz and V. Marshall, 3–32. New York: Aldine de Gruyter.

Mason, Karen, et al. 1973. Some methodological issues in cohort analysis of archival data. *American Sociological Review* 38 (2): 242–258.

Matthes, Joachim. 1985. Karl Mannheims "Das Problem der Generationen", neu gelesen. Generationen-"Gruppen" oder "gesellschaftliche Regelung von Zeitlichkeit"? *Zeitschrift für Soziologie* 14 (5): 363–372.

Matthes, Britta, Maike Reimer, und Ralf Künster. 2007. Techniken und Werkzeuge zur Unterstützung der Erinnerungsarbeit bei der computergestützten Erhebung retrospektiver Längsschnittdaten. *Methoden – Daten – Analysen* 1 (1): 69–92.

Mayer, Karl Ulrich. 1986. Structural constraints on the life course. *Human Development* 29 (3): 163–170.

———. 1987. Lebenslaufforschung. In *Methoden der Biographie- und Lebenslaufforschung,* Hrsg. W. Voges, 51–73. Opladen: Leske + Budrich.

———. 1988. German survivors of World War II. The impact on the life course of the collective experience of birth cohorts. In *Social structures and human lifes,* ed. M. Riley, 229–246. Newbury Park: Sage.

———. 1990. Lebensverläufe und sozialer Wandel. Anmerkungen zu einem Forschungsprogramm. In *Lebensverläufe und sozialer Wandel*, Hrsg. K.U. Mayer, 7–21. Opladen: Westdeutscher Verlag (KZfSS-Sonderheft 31).

Mayer, Christine. 1992. "… und dass die staatsbürgerliche Erziehung des Mädchens mit der Erziehung zum Weibe zusammenfällt" – Kerschensteiners Konzept einer Mädchenerziehung. *Zeitschrift für Pädagogik* 38 (5): 771–791.

Mayer, Karl Ulrich. 1996. Lebensverläufe und gesellschaftlicher Wandel. Eine Theoriekritik und eine Analyse zum Zusammenhang von Bildungs- und Geburtenentwicklung. In *Kritische Übergänge. Statuspassagen und sozialpolitische Institutionalisierung*, Hrsg. J. Behrend und W. Voges, 43–72. Frankfurt: Campus.

———. 1997. Notes on a comparative political economy of life courses. *Comparative Social Research* 16: 203–226.

———. 1998. Lebensverlauf. In *Handwörterbuch zur Gesellschaft Deutschlands*, Hrsg. B. Schäfers und W. Zapf, 438–451. Opladen: Leske + Budrich.

———. 2001. The paradox of global social change and national path dependencies. Life course patterns in advanced societies. In *Inclusions and exclusions in European societies*, ed. A. Woodward and M. Kohli, 89–110. London: Routledge.

———. 2002. Zur Biographie der Lebensverlaufsforschung. Ein Rückblick auf die letzten zwei Jahrzehnte. In *Lebenszeiten. Erkundungen zur Soziologie der Generationen*, Hrsg. J. Wolf und G. Burkhart, 41–61. Opladen: Leske + Budrich.

———. 2003. The sociology of the life course and lifespan psychology: Diverging or converging pathways? In *Understanding human development. Dialogues with lifespan psychology*, ed. U. Staudinger and U. Lindenberger, 463–481. Boston: Kluwer.

———. 2004. Whose lives? How history, societies, and institutions define and shape life courses. *Research in Human Development* 1 (3): 161–187.

———. 2005. Life courses and life chances in a comparative perspective. In *Analyzing inequality. Life chances and social mobility in comparative perspective*, ed. S. Svallfors, 17–55. Stanford: Stanford University Press.

———. 2009. New directions in life course research. *Annual Review of Sociology* 35: 413–433.

———. 2015. The German life history study – An introduction. *European Sociological Review* 31 (2): 137–143.

———. 2019. On heuristics, theoretical foundations, accounting schemes and theories. *Advances in Life Course Research* 41: 10027. https://doi.org/10.1016/j.alcr.2019.04.007.

Mayer, Karl Ulrich, und Hans-Peter Blossfeld. 1990. Die gesellschaftliche Konstruktion sozialer Ungleichheiten im Lebensverlauf. In *Lebenslagen, Lebensläufe, Lebensstile*, Hrsg. P. Berger und S. Hradil, 297–318. Göttingen: Schwartz (Soziale Welt-Sonderband 7).

Mayer, Karl Ulrich, und Martin Diewald. 2007. Die Institutionalisierung von Lebensverläufen. In *Entwicklungspsychologie der Lebensspanne. Ein Lehrbuch*, Hrsg. J. Brandtstädter und U. Lindenberger, 510–539. Stuttgart: Kohlhammer.

Mayer, Karl Ulrich, und Johannes Huinink. 1990. Alters-, Perioden- und Koherteneffekte in der Analyse von Lebensverläufen oder: Lexis ade? In *Lebensverläufe und sozialer Wandel*, Hrsg. K.U. Mayer, 442–459. Opladen: Westdeutscher Verlag.

———. 1994. Lebensverläufe und gesellschaftlicher Wandel: Von der Kohortenanalyse zur Lebensverlaufsanalyse. In *Mikroanalytische Grundlagen der Gesellschaftspolitik*, Bd. 1, Hrsg. R. Hauser, U. Hochmuth, und J. Schwarze, 92–111. Berlin: Akademie.

Mayer, Karl Ulrich, and Walter Müller. 1986. The state and the structure of the life course. In *Human development and the life course: Multidisciplinary perspectives*, ed. A. Sørensen, F. Weinert, and L. Sherrod, 217–245. Hillsdale: Erlbaum.

———. 1989. Lebensverläufe im Wohlfahrtsstaat. In *Handlungsspielräume. Untersuchungen zur Individualisierung und Institutionalisierung von Lebensläufen in der Moderne*, Hrsg. A. Weymann, 41–60. Stuttgart: Enke.

Mayer, Karl Ulrich, and Urs Schoepflin. 1989. The state and the life course. *Annual Review of Sociology* 15: 187–209.

Mayer, Karl Ulrich, und Eva Schulze. 2009. *Die Wendegeneration. Lebensverläufe des Jahrgangs 1971*. Frankfurt: Campus.

Mayer, Karl Ulrich, Daniela Grunow, und Natalie Nitsche. 2010. Mythos Flexibilisierung? Wie instabil sind Berufsbiografien wirklich und als wie instabil werden sie wahrgenommen? *Kölner Zeitschrift für Soziologie und Sozialpsychologie* 62 (3): 369–402.

Mayntz, Renate. 1992. Modernisierung und die Logik von interorganisatorischen Netzwerken. *Journal für Sozialforschung* 32 (1): 19–32.

McAdams, Dan. 2005. Studying lives in time. A narrative approach. In *Towards an interdisciplinary perspective on the life course*, ed. R. Levy et al., 237–258. Amsterdam: Elsevier.

McAdams, Dan, and Bradley Olson. 2010. Personality development: Continuity and change over the life course. *Annual Review of Psychology* 61: 517–542.

McMunn, Anne, et al. 2015. De-standardization and gender convergence in work-family life courses in Great Britain. A multi-channel sequence analysis. *Advances in Life Course Research* 26: 60–75.

Mead, George Herbert. 1932. *The philosophy of the present*. Chicago: Chicago University Press.

Meulemann, Heiner. 1995. *Die Geschichte einer Jugend. Lebenserfolg und Erfolgsdeutung ehemaliger Gymnasiasten zwischen dem 15. und 30. Lebensjahr*. Opladen: Westdeutscher Verlag.

Meulemann, Heiner, und Klaus Birkelbach. 2012. Herausforderungen und Konsolidierungen. Biographische Selbstreflexionen über Jugend und Lebensmitte in einer Kohorte ehemaliger Gymnasiasten. *BIOS* 25 (1): 3–24.

Meulemann, Heiner, Klaus Birkelbach, und Jörg Hellwig, Hrsg. 2001. *Ankunft im Erwachsenenleben. Lebenserfolg und Erfolgsdeutung in einer Kohorte ehemaliger Gymnasiasten zwischen 16 und 43*. Opladen: Leske + Budrich.

Meyer, John. 1986. The self and the life course: Institutionalization and ist effects. In *Human development and the life course: Multidisciplinary perspectives*, ed. A. Sørensen, F. Weinert, and L. Sherrod, 199–216. Hillsdale: Erlbaum.

———. 1992. The life course as a professionalized cultural construction. In *Institutions and gatekeeping in the life course*, ed. W. Heinz, 83–95. Weinheim: Deutscher Studien-Verlag.

Meyer, John, and Ronald Jepperson. 2000. The "actors" of modern society: The cultural construction of social agency. *Sociological Theory* 18 (1): 100–120.

Mills, Charles Wright. 1959. *The sociological imagination*. New York: Oxford University Press.

Mills, Melinda. 2011. *Introducing survival and event history analysis*. Los Angeles: Sage.

Mitterauer, Michael. 1986. *Sozialgeschichte der Jugend*. Frankfurt: Suhrkamp.

Modell, John. 1989. *Into one's own. From youth to adulthood in the United States, 1920–1975*. Berkeley: University of California Press.

Moen, Phyllis, and Shin-Kap Han. 2001. Reframiing careers: Work, family, and gender. In *Restructuring work and the life course*, ed. V. Marshall et al., 424–445. Toronto: University of Toronto Press.

Möhring, Katja. 2016. Life course regimes in Europe. Individual employment histories in comparative and historical perspective. *Journal of European Social Policy* 26 (2): 124–139.

Mortimer, Jeylan, and Phyllis Moen. 2016. The changing social construction of age and the life course. Precarious identity and enactment of "early" and "encore" stages of adulthood. In *Handbook of the life course*, ed. M. Shanahan, J. Mortimer, and M. Johnson, vol. II, 111–129. Cham: Springer.

Mortimer, Jeylan, and Michael Shanahan. 2003. Preface. In *Handbook of the life course*, ed. J. Mortimer and M. Shanahan, XI–XVI. New York: Kluwer/Plenum.

Mortimer, Jeylan, Sabrina Oesterle, and Helga Krüger. 2005. Age norms, institutional structures, and the timing of markers of transition to adulthood. In *The structure of the life course: Standardized? Individualized? Differentiated?* ed. R. Macmillan, 175–203. Amsterdam: Elsevier.

Motakef, Mona. 2015. *Prekarisierung*. Bielefeld: transcript.

Mückenberger, Ulrich. 1985. Die Krise des Normalarbeitsverhältnisses (Teil 1 und 2). *Zeitschrift für Sozialreform 31(7 und 8)*, 415–435 und 457–475.

———. 1989. Der Wandel des Normalarbeitsverhältnisses unter Bedingungen einer "Krise der Normalität". *Gewerkschaftliche Monatshefte* 40 (4): 211–223.

Müller, Walter, and Markus Gangl, eds. 2003. *Transitions from education to work in Europe. The integration of youth into EU labour markets*. Oxford: Oxford University Press.

Müller, Walter, und Reinhard Pollak. 2016. Warum gibt es so wenige Arbeiterkinder in Deutschlands Universitäten? In *Bildung als Privileg. Erklärungen und Befunde zu den Ursachen der Bildungsungleichheit*, Hrsg. R. Becker und W. Lauterbach, 345–386. Wiesbaden: Springer VS.

Mutz, Gerd. 1997. Arbeitslosigkeit und gesellschaftliche Individualisierung. In *Individualisierung und Integration. Neue Konfliktlinien und neuer Integrationsmodus?* Hrsg. U. Beck und P. Sopp. 161–179. Opladen: Leske + Budrich.

Myles, John. 1992. Is there a post-fordist life course? In *Institutions and gatekeeping in the life course*, ed. W. Heinz, 171–185. Weinheim: Deutscher Studien-Verlag.

Neilson, Brett, and Ned Rossiter. 2008. Precarity as a political concept, or, Fordism as exception. *Theory, Culture & Society* 25 (7–8): 51–72.

Neugarten, Bernice. 1985. Interpretive social science and research on aging. In *Gender and the life course*, ed. A. Rossi, 291–300. Chicago: Aldine Publishing.

Neugarten, Bernice, Joan Moore, and John Lowe. 1965. Age norms, age constraints, and adult socialization. *American Journal of Sociology* 70 (6): 710–717.

Niggl, Günter. 1977. *Geschichte der deutschen Autobiographie im 18. Jahrhundert: Theoretische Grundlegung und literarische Entfaltung*. Stuttgart: Metzler.

Nydegger, Corinne. 1986. Timetables and implicit theory. *American Behavioral Scientist* 29 (6): 710–729.

O'Brien, Robert, Kenneth Hudson, and Jean Stockard. 2008. A mixed model estimation of age, period, and cohort effects. *Sociological Methods & Research* 36 (3): 402–428.

O'Rand, Angela. 2009. Cumulative processes in the life course. In *The craft of life course research*, ed. J. Giele and G. Elder, 121–140. New York: Guilford Press.
O'Rand, Angela, and Margaret Krecker. 1990. Concepts of the life cycle: Their history, meanings, and uses in the social sciences. *Annual Review of Sociology* 16: 241–262.
OECD. 1981. *The welfare state in crisis*. Paris: OECD.
Offerhaus, Judith, Janine Leschke, und Klaus Schömann. 2016. Soziale Ungleichheit im Zugang zu beruflicher Weiterbildung. In *Bildung als Privileg. Erklärungen und Befunde zu den Ursachen der Bildungsungleichheit*, Hrsg. R. Becker und W. Lauterbach, 387–420. Wiesbaden: Springer VS.
Osterland, Martin. 1990. "Normalbiographie" und "Normalarbeitsverhältnis". In *Lebenslagen, Lebensläufe, Lebensstile*, Hrsg. P. Berger und S. Hradil, 351–362. Göttingen: Schwartz.
Pampel, Fred, and H. Elizabeth Peters. 1995. The Easterlin effect. *Annual Review of Sociology* 21: 163–194.
Parsons, Talcott. 1942. Age and sex in the social structure of the United States. *American Sociological Review* 7 (5): 604–616.
———. 1951. *The social system*. Glencoe: Free Press.
Pearlin, Leonard, et al. 2007. The life-course origins of mastery among older people. *Journal of Health and Social Behavior* 48 (2): 146–179.
Pettit, Beckie, and Bruce Western. 2004. Mass imprisonment and the life course. Race and class inequality in U. S. incarceration. *American Sociological Review* 69 (2): 151–169.
Pfeffer, Fabian. 2008. Persistent inequality in educational attainment and its institutional context. *European Sociological Review* 24 (5): 543–565.
Phelps, Edmund. 1972. The statistical theory of racism and sexism. *American Economic Review* 62 (4): 659–661.
Piccarreta, Raffaella, and Matthias Studer. 2019. Holistic analysis of the life course methodological challenges and new perspectives. *Advances in Life Course Research* 41: 100251. https://doi.org/10.1016/j.alcr.2018.10.004.
Pillemer, Karl, und Kurt Lüscher, Hrsg. 2004. *Intergenerational ambivalences. New perspectives on parent-child relations in later life*. Amsterdam: Elsevier.
Pinder, Wilhelm. 1926. *Das Problem der Generation in der Kunstgeschichte Europas*. Berlin: Frankfurter Verlags-Anstalt.
Prins, Adriaan. 1953. *East African age-class systems*. Groningen: Wolters.
Raithelhuber, Eberhard. 2011. *Übergänge und Agency. Eine sozialtheoretische Reflexion des Lebenslaufkonzepts*. Opladen: Budrich UniPress.
Reimer, Maike. 2003. Autobiographisches Erinnern und retrospektive Längsschnittdatenerhebung. Was wissen wir, und was würden wir gerne wissen? *BIOS* 16 (1): 27–45.
———. 2005. *Autobiografisches Gedächtnis und retrospektive Datenerhebung. Die Rekonstruktion und Validität von Lebensverläufen*. Berlin: Max-Planck-Institut für Bildungsforschung.
Rendtel, Ulrich. 1995. *Lebenslagen im Wandel: Panelausfälle und Panelrepresentativität*. Frankfurt: Campus.
Renn, Heinz. 1987. Lebenslauf – Lebenszeit – Kohortenanalyse. Möglichkeiten und Grenzen eines Forschungsansatzes. In *Methoden der Biographie- und Lebenslaufforschung*, Hrsg. W. Voges, 261–298. Opladen: Leske + Budrich.

References

Riedel, Manfred. 1969. *Wandel des Generationenproblems in der modernen Gesellschaft*. Düsseldorf: Diederichs.
Riley, Matilda. 1985. Age strata in social systems. In *Handbook of aging and the social sciences*, ed. R. Binstock and E. Shanas, 2nd ed., 369–411. New York: Van Nostrand Reinhold.
———. 1988. On the significance of age in sociology. In *Social structures and human lifes*, ed. M. Riley, 24–45. Newbury Park: Sage.
Riley, Mathilda, und John Riley. 1994. Structural lag: Past and future. In *Age and structural lag. Society's failure to provide meaningful opportunities in work, family, and leisure*, Hrsg. M. Riley, R. Kahn, und A. Foner, 15–36. New York: Wiley.
Riley, Matilda, Marilyn Johnson, and Anne Foner, eds. 1972. *Aging and society. Volume three: A sociology of age stratification*. New York: Sage.
Rindfuss, Ronald, Gray Swicegood, and Rachel Rosenfeld. 1987. Disorder in the life course – How common and does it matter? *American Sociological Review* 52 (6): 785–801.
Roberts, Brian. 2001. *Biographical research*. Buckingham: Open University Press.
Roberts, Brent, and Wendy DelVecchio. 2000. The rank-order consistency of personality traits from childhood to old age. A quantitative review of longitudinal studies. *Psychological Bulletin* 126 (1): 3–25.
Roberts, Brent, Kate Walton, and Wolfgang Viechtbauer. 2006. Patterns of mean-level change in personality traits across the life course. A meta-analysis of longitudinal studies. *Psychological Bulletin* 132 (1): 1–25.
Robette, Nicolas. 2010. The diversity of pathways to adulthood in France. Evidence from a holistic approach. *Advances in Life Course Research* 15 (2–3): 89–96.
Rodgers, Willard. 1982. Estimable functions of age, period, and cohort effects. *American Sociological Review* 47 (6): 774–787.
Roenneberg, Till. 2010. *Wie wir ticken. Die Bedeutung der Chronobiologie für unser Leben*. Köln: DuMont.
Rogge, Benedikt. 2013. *Wie uns Arbeitslosigkeit unter die Haut geht. Identitätsprozess und psychische Gesundheit bei Statuswechseln*. Konstanz: UVK.
Roos, Jeja-Pekka. 2002. Life's turning points and generational consciousness. In *Lebenszeiten. Erkundungen zur Soziologie der Generationen*, ed. J. Wolf and G. Burkhart, 119–134. Opladen: Leske + Budrich.
Rosemann, Mark, ed. 1995. *Generations in conflict. Youth revolt and generation formation in Germany 1770–1968*. Cambridge: Cambridge University Press.
Rosenbaum, Heidi, Hrsg. 1978. *Seminar: Familie und Gesellschaftsstruktur. Materialien zu den sozioökonomischen Bedingungen von Familienformen*. Frankfurt: Suhrkamp.
———. 1982. *Formen der Familie. Untersuchungen zum Zusammenhang von Familienverhältnissen, Sozialstruktur und sozialem Wandel in der deutschen Gesellschaft des 19. Jahrhunderts*. Frankfurt: Suhrkamp.
Rosenmayr, Leopold. 1978. Die menschlichen Lebensalter in Deutungsversuchen der europäischen Kulturgeschichte. In *Die menschlichen Lebensalter. Kontinuität und Krisen*, Hrsg. L. Rosenmayr, 23–79. München: Piper.
Rosenthal, Gabriele. 2000. Historische und familiale Generationenabfolge. In *Generationen in Familie und Gesellschaft*, Hrsg. M. Kohli und M. Szydlik, 162–178. Opladen: Leske + Budrich.
Rosow, Irving. 1978. What is a cohort and why? *Human Development* 21 (2): 65–75.

Rothermund, Klaus, und Dirk Wentura. 2007. Altersnormen und Altersstereotype. In *Entwicklungspsychologie der Lebensspanne. Ein Lehrbuch*, Hrsg. J. Brandtstädter und U. Lindenberger, 540–568. Stuttgart: Kohlhammer.

Rowntree, Benjamin Seebohm. 1901. *Poverty. A study of town life*. London: Macmillan.

Rustin, Michael. 2000. Reflections on the biographical turn in social science. In *The turn to biographical methods in social science. Comparative issues and examples*, ed. P.J. Chamberlayne, J. Bornat, and T. Wengraf, 33–52. London: Routledge.

Rutter, Michael. 1996. Transitions and turning points in developmental psychopathology – As applied to the age span between childhood and mid-adulthood. *International Journal of Behavioral Development* 19 (3): 603–626.

Ryder, Norman. 1965. The cohort as a concept in the study of social change. *American Sociological Review* 30 (6): 843–861.

Saake, Irmhild. 2006. *Die Konstruktion des Alters. Eine gesellschaftstheoretische Einführung in die Alternsforschung*. Wiesbaden: VS.

Sackmann, Reinhold. 1992. Das Deutungsmuster "Generation". In *Analyse sozialer Deutungsmuster. Beiträge zur empirischen Wissenssoziologie*, Hrsg. M. Meuser und R. Sackmann, 199–215. Pfaffenweiler: Centaurus.

———. 2001. Age and labor market chances in international comparison. *European Sociological Review* 17 (4): 373–387.

Sackmann, Reinhold, und Matthias Wingens. 1995. Individuelle und gesellschaftliche Strukturierung beruflicher Diskontinuität. In *Institution und Biographie. Die Ordnung des Lebens*, Hrsg. E. Hoerning und M. Corsten, 113–130. Pfaffenweiler: Centaurus.

———. 1996. Berufsverläufe im Transformationsprozess. In *Zwischenbilanz der Wiedervereinigung. Strukturwandel und Mobilität im Transformationsprozess*, Hrsg. M. Diewald und K. U. Mayer, 11–31. Opladen: Leske + Budrich.

———. 2001. Theoretische Konzepte des Lebenslaufs – Übergang Sequenz und Verlauf. In *Strukturen des Lebenslaufs. Übergang – Sequenz – Verlauf*, Hrsg. R. Sackmann und M. Wingens, 17–48. Weinheim: Juventa.

———. 2003. From transitions to trajetories – Sequence types. In *Social dynamics of the life course. Transitions, institutions, and interrelations*, ed. W. Heinz and V. Marshall, 93–115. New York: Aldine de Gruyter.

Sackmann, Reinhold, Ansgar Weymann, und Matthias Wingens. 2000. *Die Generation der Wende. Berufs- und Lebensverläufe im sozialen Wandel*. Wiesbaden: Westdeutscher Verlag.

Sackmann, Reinhold, Michael Windzio, and Matthias Wingens. 2001. Unemployment and social mobility in East Germany. *International Journal of Sociology and Social Policy* 21 (4/5/6): 92–117.

Sampson, Robert, and John Laub. 1993. *Crime in the making: Pathways and turning points through life*. Cambridge: Harvard University Press.

———. 1996. Socioeconomic achievement in the life course of disadvantaged men. Military service as a turning point, circa 1940–1965. *American Sociological Review* 61 (3): 347–367.

———. 1997. A life-course theory of cumulative disadvantage and the stability of delinquency. In *Developmental theories of crime and delinquency*, ed. T. Thornberry, 133–161. New Brunswick: Transaction Publishers.

Schafer, Markus, Kenneth Ferraro, and Sarah Mustillo. 2011. Children of misfortune. Early adversity and cumulative inequality in perceived life trajectories. *American Journal of Sociology* 116 (4): 1053–1091.

Schelsky, Helmut. 1957. Soziologische Bemerkungen zur Rolle der Schule in unserer Gesellschaftsverfassung. In *Schule und Erziehung in der industriellen Gesellschaft*, Hrsg. H. Schelsky, 9–50. Würzburg: Werkbund-Verlag.

Scherer, Stefani. 2004. Sprungbrett oder Falle? Konsequenzen der Position des Erwerbseintritts auf den Karriereverlauf in Westdeutschland, Großbritannien und Italien. In *Mehr Risiken – mehr Ungleichheit? Abbau von Wohlfahrtsstaat, Flexibilisierung von Arbeit und die Folgen*, Hrsg. W. Müller und S. Scherer, 137–165. Frankfurt: Campus.

———. 2005. Patterns of labor market entry – Long wait or career instability? An empirical comparison of Italy, Great Britain and West Germany. *European Sociological Review* 21 (5): 427–440.

Scherer, Stefani, und Josef Brüderl. 2010. Sequenzdatenanalyse. In *Handbuch der sozialwissenschaftlichen Datenanalyse*, Hrsg. C. Wolf und H. Best, 1031–1051. Wiesbaden: VS.

Scherger, Simone. 2007. *Destandardisierung, Differenzierung, Individualisierung. Westdeutsche Lebensläufe im Wandel*. VS: Wiesbaden.

Scherr, Adalbert. 2012. Soziale Bedingungen von Agency. Soziologische Eingrenzungen einer sozialtheoretisch nicht auflösbaren Paradoxie. In *Agency. Qualitative Rekonstruktionen und gesellschaftstheoretische Bezüge von Handlungsmächtigkeit*, Hrsg. S. Bethmann et al., 99–121. Weinheim: Beltz Juventa.

Schimank, Uwe. 2002. *Das zwiespältige Individuum. Zum Person-Gesellschaft-Arrangement der Moderne*. Opladen: Leske + Budrich.

Schmeiser, Martin. 2006. Von der "äußeren" zur "inneren" Institutionalisierung des Lebenslaufs. *Eine Strukturgeschichte. BIOS* 19 (1): 51–92.

Schmich, Dieter. 2013. *Lebenslauf, Anschreiben, Erfahrungsprofil, Arbeitszeugnisse*. Schwetzingen: Dielus.

Schmidt, Manfred. 1998. *Sozialpolitik in Deutschland. Historische Entwicklung und internationaler Vergleich*. Opladen: Leske + Budrich.

Schneider, Norbert. 2001. Pluralisierung der Lebensformen – Fakt oder Fiktion? *Zeitschrift für Familienforschung* 13 (2): 85–90.

Schröer, Wolfgang, et al., Hrsg. 2013. *Handbuch Übergänge*. Weinheim: Beltz Juventa.

Schulz, Andreas, und Gundula Grebner. 2003. Generation und Geschichte. Zur Renaissance eines umstrittenen Forschungkonzepts. In *Generationswechsel und historischer Wandel*, Hrsg. A. Schulz und G. Grebner, 1–35. München: Oldenbourg.

Schümer, Gundel, Klaus Tillmann, und Manfred Weiß. 2002. Institutionelle und soziale Bedingungen schulischen Lernens. In *PISA 2000. Die Länder der Bundesrepublik im Vergleich*, Hrsg. J. Baumert et al., 203–218. Opladen: Leske + Budrich.

Schupp, Jürgen. 2009. 25 Jahre Sozio-oekonomisches Panel – ein Infrastrukturprojekt der empirischen Sozial- und Wirtschaftsforschung in Deutschland. *Zeitschrift für Soziologie* 38 (5): 350–357.

Schurtz, Heinrich. 1902. *Altersklassen und Männerbünde. Eine Darstellung der Grundformen der Gesellschaft*. Berlin: Reimer.

Schütz, Alfred, und Thomas Luckmann. 1979. *Strukturen der Lebenswelt*, Bd. 1. Frankfurt: Suhrkamp.

Scott, Jacqueline, and Duane Alwin. 1998. Retrospective vs. prospective measurement of life histories in longitudinal research. In *Methods of life course research: Qualitative and quantitative approaches*, ed. J. Giele and G. Elder, 98–127. London: Sage.

Sennett, Richard. 1998. *Der flexible Mensch. Die Kultur des neuen Kapitalismus*. Darmstadt: Wissenschaftliche Buchgesellschaft.

Settersten, Richard. 1999. *Lives in time and place. The problems and promises of developmental science*. Amityville: Baywood.

———. 2003a. Rethinking social policy. Lessons of a life-course perspective. In *Invitation to the life course. Toward new understandings of later life*, ed. R. Settersten, 191–222. Amityville: Baywood.

———. 2003b. Age structuring and the rhythm of the life course. In *Handbook of the life course*, ed. J. Mortimer and M. Shanahan, 81–98. New York: Kluwer/Plenum.

———. 2005. Toward a stronger partnership between life-course sociology and life-span psychology. *Research in Human Development* 2 (1–2): 25–41.

———. 2009. It takes two to tango: The (un)easy dance between life-course sociology and life-span psychology. *Advances in Life Course Research* 14 (1–2): 74–81.

Settersten, Richard, and Lynn Gannon. 2005. Structure, agency, and the space between. On the challenges and contradictions of a blended view of the life course. In *Towards an interdisciplinary perspective on the life course*, ed. R. Levy et al., 35–55. Amsterdam: Elsevier.

Sewell, Willam. 2001. A theory of structure. Duality, agency, and transformation. *American Journal of Sociology* 98 (1): 1–29.

Shanahan, Michael. 2000. Pathways to adulthood in changing societies: Variability and mechanisms in life course perspective. *Annual Review of Sociology* 26: 667–692.

Shanahan, Michael, and Ross Macmillan. 2008. *Biography and the sociological imagination: Contexts and contingencies*. New York: Norton.

Shanahan, M., J. Mortimer, and M. Johnson, eds. 2016a. *Handbook of the life course*. Vol. II. New York: Kluwer/Plenum.

Shanahan, Michael, Jeylan Mortimer, and Monica Johnson. 2016b. Introduction: Life course studies – Trends, challenges, and future directions. In *Handbook of the life course*, ed. M. Shanahan, J. Mortimer, and M. Johnson, vol. II, 1–23. Cham: Springer.

Shavit, Yossi, and Hans-Peter Blossfeld, eds. 1993. *Persistent inequality. Changing educational attainment in thirteen countries*. Boulder: Westview Press.

Shavit, Yossi, and Walter Müller, eds. 1998. *From school to work. A comparative study of educational qualifications and occupational destinations*. Oxford: Clarendon Press.

Shaw, Clifford. 1930. *The jack-roller: A delinquent boy's own story*. Chicago: University of Chicago Press.

———. 1931. *The natural history of a delinquent career*. Chicago: University of Chicago Press.

Sieder, Reinhard. 1987. *Sozialgeschichte der Familie*. Frankfurt: Suhrkamp.

Simonson, Julia, Laura Gordo, and Nadiya Titovy. 2011. Changing employment patterns of women in Germany: How do baby boomers differ from older cohorts? A comparison using sequence analysis. *Advances in Life Course Research* 16 (2): 65–82.

Skinner, Ellen. 1996. A guide to constructs of control. *Journal of Personality and Social Psychology* 71 (3): 549–570.

Solga, Heike. 1995. *Auf dem Weg in eine klassenlose Gesellschaft? Klassenlagen und Mobilität zwischen Generationen in der DDR*. Berlin: Akademie.
———. 2001. Longitudinal surveys and the study of occupational mobility: Panel and retrospective design in comparison. *Quality & Quantity* 35 (3): 291–309.
———. 2005. *Ohne Abschluss in die Bildungsgesellschaft. Die Erwerbschancen gering qualifizierter Personen aus soziologischer und ökonomischer Perspektive*. Opladen: Budrich.
Solga, Heike, und Dirk Konietzka. 2000. Das Berufsprinzip des deutschen Arbeitsmarktes. Ein geschlechtsneutraler Allokationsmechanismus? *Schweizerische Zeitschrift für Soziologie* 26 (1): 111–147.
Specht, Jule, Boris Egloff, and Stefan Schmukle. 2011. Stability and change of personality across the life course. The impact of age and major life events on mean-level and rank-order stability of the big five. *Journal of Personality and Social Psychology* 101 (4): 862–882.
Spéder, Zsolt, Lívia Murinkó, and Richard Settersten. 2013. Are conceptions of adulthood universal and unisex? Ages and social markers in 25 European countries. *Social Forces* 92 (3): 873–898.
Spittler, Gerd. 1990. Lebensalter und Lebenslauf bei den Tuareg. In *Im Lauf der Zeit*, Hrsg. G. Elwert, M. Kohli, und H. Müller, 107–123. Saarbrücken: Breitenbach.
Stambolis, Barbara. 2003. *Mythos Jugend – Leitbild und Krisensymptom. Ein Aspekt der politischen Kultur im 20. Jahrhundert*. Schwalbach: Wochenschau-Verlag.
Stamm, Margit. 2010. Frühkindliche Bildung als Basis von Schulerfolg? Analysen zur Wirksamkeit früher Bildungsförderung. *Die Deutsche Schule – Zeitschrift für Erziehungswissenschaft, Bildungspolitik und pädagogische Praxis* 102 (3): 255–267.
Statistisches Bundesamt, Hrsg. 2016. *Datenreport 2016. Ein Sozialbericht für die Bundesrepublik Deutschland*. Bonn: Bundeszentrale für politische Bildung.
Stauber, Barbara, Axel Pohl, und Andreas Walther, Hrsg. 2007. *Subjektorientierte Übergangsforschung. Rekonstruktion und Unterstützung biographischer Übergänge junger Erwachsener*. Weinheim: Juventa.
Steinmann, Susanne. 2000. *Bildung, Ausbildung und Arbeitsmarktchancen in Deutschland. Eine Studie zum Wandel der Übergänge von der Schule in das Erwerbsleben*. Opladen: Leske + Budrich.
Strauss, Anselm. 1959. *Mirrors and masks: The search for identity*. Glencoe: Free Press.
Szydlik, Marc. 2000. *Lebenslange Solidarität. Generationenbeziehungen zwischen erwachsenen Kindern und Eltern*. Opladen: Leske + Budrich.
———, Hrsg. 2004. *Generation und Ungleichheit*. Wiesbaden: VS.
———, Hrsg. 2008. *Flexibilisierung. Folgen für Arbeit und Familie*. Wiesbaden: VS.
Thomas, William, and Florian Znaniecki. 1918–1920. *The Polish peasant in Europe and America*. Vol. 1–5. Boston: Gorham Press.
Thomas, George, et al. 1987. *Institutional structure. Constituting state, society, and the individual*. Newbury Park: Sage.
Thomson, David. 1989. The welfare state and generation conflict Winners and losers. In *Workers versus pensioners. Intergenerational justice in an ageing world*, ed. P. Johnson, C. Conrad, and D. Thomson, 33–56. Manchester: University Press.
———. 1996. *Selfish generations: How welfare states grow old*. Cambridge: White Horse Press.

Trappe, Heike. 2006. Berufliche Segregartion im Kontext. Über einige Folgen geschlechtstypischer berufsentscheidungen in Ost- und Westdeutschland. *Kölner Zeitschrift für Soziologie und Sozialpsychologie* 58 (1): 50–78.

Tremmel, Jörg. 2012. *Eine Theorie der Generationengerechtigkeit*. Münster: Mentis.

Uggen, Christopher. 2000. Work as a turning point in the life course of criminals. A duration model of age, employment, and recidivism. *American Sociological Review* 65 (4): 529–546.

United Nations Children's Fund. 2014. *Ending child marriage. Progress and prospects*. New York: UNICEF.

van Gennep, Arnold. 1909. *Les rites de passage*. Paris: Nourry (dt.: Übergangsriten. Frankfurt: Campus 1986).

Voß, Gerd. 1991. *Lebensführung als Arbeit. Über die Autonomie der Person im Alltag der Gesellschaft*. Stuttgart: Enke.

Voß, Gerd, und Hans Pongratz. 1998. Der Arbeitskraftunternehmer. Eine neue Grundform der "Ware Arbeitskraft"? *Kölner Zeitschrift für Soziologie und Sozialpsychologie* 50 (1): 131–158.

Wagner, Michael. 1989. *Räumliche Mobilität im Lebensverlauf. Eine empirische Untersuchung sozialer Bedingungen der Migration*. Stuttgart: Enke.

———. 1997. *Scheidung in Ost- und Westdeutschland. Zum Verhältnis von Ehestabilität und Sozialstruktur seit den 30er Jahren*. Frankfurt: Campus.

Wagner, Gert, u.a. 2008. Das Sozio-oekonomische Panel (SOEP): Multidisziplinäres Haushaltspanel und Kohortenstudie für Deutschland. Eine Einführung (für neue Datennutzer) mit einem Ausblick (für erfahrene Anwender). *Wirtschafts- und Sozialstatistisches Archiv* 2 (4): 301–328.

Wagner, Michael. 2008. Entwicklung und Vielfalt der Lebensformen. In *Lehrbuch Moderne Familiensoziologie. Theorien, Methoden, empirische Befunde*, Hrsg. N. Schneider, 99–120. Opladen: Budrich.

Wagner, Michael, und Isabel Valdés Cifuentes. 2014. Die Pluralisierung der Lebensformen – ein fortlaufender Trend? *Comparative Population Studies* 39 (1): 73–98.

Weber, Max. 1980. *Wirtschaft und Gesellschaft. Grundriss der verstehenden Soziologie*, 5. Rev. Aufl. Tübingen: Mohr (Studienausg.; Orig.: 1921/22).

Weigel, Sigrid. 2002. Generation, Genealogie, Geschlecht. Zur Geschichte des Generationskonzepts und seiner wissenschaftlichen Konzeptualisierung seit dem Ende des 18. Jahrhunderts. In *Kulturwissenschaften Forschung – Praxis – Positionen*, Hrsg. L. Musner und G. Wunberg, 161–190. Wien: WUV.

———. 2006. *Genea-Logik: Generation, Tradition und Evolution zwischen Kultur-und Naturwissenschaften*. München: Fink.

Weisbrod, Bernd. 2005. Generation und Generationalität in der Neueren Geschichte. *Aus Politik und Zeitgeschichte* 55 (8): 3–9.

Wenzel, Ulrich. 2008. Fördern und Fordern aus Sicht der Betroffenen. Verstehen und Aneignung sozial- und arbeitsmarktpolitischer Maßnahmen des SGB II. *Zeitschrift für Sozialreform* 54 (1): 57–78.

Wethington, Elaine, Joy Pixley, and Allison Kavey. 2003. Turning points in work careers. In *It's about time. Couples and careers*, ed. P. Moen, 168–182. Ithaca: Cornell University Press.

Weymann, Ansgar. 1989a. Handlungsspielräume im Lebenslauf. Ein Essay zur Einführung. In *Handlungsspielräume. Untersuchungen zur Individualisierung und Institutionalisierung von Lebensläufen in der Moderne*, Hrsg. A. Weymann, 1–39. Stuttgart: Enke.

———, Hrsg. 1989b. *Handlungsspielräume. Untersuchungen zur Individualisierung und Institutionalisierung von Lebensläufen in der Moderne*. Stuttgart: Enke.

———. 1995. Modernisierung, Generationsverhältnisse und die Ökonomie der Lebenszeit. Gesellschaftsformen und Generationen im "Polish Peasant". *Soziale Welt* 46 (4): 369–384.

———. 2003. The life course, institutions, and life-course policy. In *Social dynamics of the life course. Transitions, institutions, and interrelations*, ed. W. Heinz and V. Marshall, 167–191. New York: Aldine de Gruyter.

Wheaton, Blair, and Ian Gotlib. 1997. Trajectories and turning points. Concepts and themes. In *Stress and adversity over the life course. Trajectories and turning points*, ed. I. Gotlib and B. Wheaton, 1–25. Cambridge: Cambridge University Press.

Widmer, Eric, and Gilbert Ritschard. 2009. The de-standardization of the life course. Are men and women equal? *Advances in Life Course Research* 14 (1–2): 28–39.

Willson, Andrea, Kim Shuey, and Glen Elder. 2007. Cumulative advantage processes as mechanisms of inequality in life course health. *American Journal of Sociology* 112 (6): 1886–1924.

Windzio, Michael. 2013. *Regressionsmodelle für Zustände und Ereignisse: Eine Einführung*. Wiesbaden: Springer VS.

Windzio, Michael, und Matthias Wingens. 2000. "Die müssen Marktwirtschaft doch erstmal lernen …". Arbeitsplatzallokationen im ostdeutschen Transformationsprozess. In *Übergänge. Individualisierung, Flexibilisierung und Institutionalisierung des Lebensverlaufs*, Hrsg. W. Heinz, 109–123. Weinheim: Juventa.

Wingens, Matthias. 1999. Der "gelernte DDR-Bürger": Biographischer Modernisierungsrückstand als Transformationsblockade? Planwirtschaftliche Semantik. *Gesellschaftsstruktur und Biographie. Soziale Welt* 50 (3): 255–280.

Wingens, Matthias, and Herwig Reiter. 2011. The life course approach – It's about time! *BIOS* 24 (2): 187–203.

Wingens, Matthias, und Reinhold Sackmann. 2000. Evaluation AFG-finanzierter Weiterbildung. Arbeitslosigkeit und Qualifizierung in Ostdeutschland. *Mitteilungen aus der Arbeitsmarkt- und Berufsforschung* 33 (1): 39–53.

Wingens, Matthias, Reinhold Sackmann, und Michael Grotheer. 2000. Berufliche Qualifizierung für Arbeitslose. Zur Effektivität AFG-finanzierter Weiterbildung im Transformationsprozess. *Kölner Zeitschrift für Soziologie und Sozialpsychologie* 52 (1): 60–80.

Wingens, Matthias, et al. 2011. The sociological life course approach and research on migration and integration. In *A life-course perspective on migration and integration*, ed. M. Wingens et al., 1–26. Dordrecht: Springer.

Wissenschaftlicher Beirat für Familienfragen. 2012. *Generationenbeziehungen: Herausforderungen und Potenziale*. Wiesbaden: VS.

Wohl, Robert. 1979. *The generation of 1914*. Cambridge: Harvard University Press.

Wohlrab-Sahr, Monika. 1992. Institutionalisierung oder Individualisierung des Lebenslaufs? *Anmerkungen zu einer festgefahrenen Debatte. BIOS* 5 (1): 1–19.

———. 1993. *Biographische Unsicherheit. Formen weiblicher Identität in der "reflexiven Moderne": Das Beispiel der Zeitarbeiterinnen*. Opladen: Leske + Budrich.

———. 1997. Individualisierung: Differenzierungsprozess und Zurechnungsmodus. In *Individualisierung und Integration. Neue Konfliktlinien und neuer Integrationsmodus?* Hrsg. U. Beck und P. Sopp. 23–36. Opladen: Leske + Budrich.

Zhou, Xueguang, and Liren Hou. 1999. Children of the Cultural revolution. The state and the life course in the People's Republic of China. *American Sociological Review* 64 (1): 12–36.

Zimmermann, Okka. 2018. *Dimensionen von Destandardisierung. Eine differenzierte sequenzdatenanalytische Betrachtung der Familiengründung.* Wiesbaden: Springer VS.

Zinn, Jens, and Felicitas Eßer. 2003. Die Herstellung biographischer Sicherheit in der reflexiven Moderne. *BIOS* 16 (1): 46–63.

Zinnecker, Jürgen. 2000. Selbstsozialisation – Ein Essay über ein aktuelles Konzept. *Zeitschrift für Soziologie der Erziehung und Sozialisation* 20 (3): 272–290.

———. 2003. "Das Problem der Generationen" – Überlegungen zu Karl Mannheims kanonischem Text. In *Generationalität und Lebensgeschichte im 20. Jahrhundert*, Hrsg. J. Reulecke, 33–58. München: Oldenbourg.

Zorbaugh, Harvey. 1929. *The gold coast and the slum: A sociological study of Chicago's near north side.* Chicago: University of Chicago Press.

Zulley, Jürgen, und Barbara Knab. 2003. *Unsere Innere Uhr.* Freiburg: Herder.

The manufacturer's authorised representative in the EU is Springer Nature Customer Service Centre GmbH, Europaplatz 3, 69115 Heidelberg, Germany. If you have any concerns regarding our products, please contact ProductSafety@springernature.com

Printed and bound by CPI Group (UK) Ltd, Croydon, CR0 4YY

25/03/2026

02078172-0004